PAM GEMS

Plays Eight

PAM GEMS

Plays Eight

THE FATHER

THE DANCE OF DEATH

THREE SISTERS

STANLEY'S WOMEN

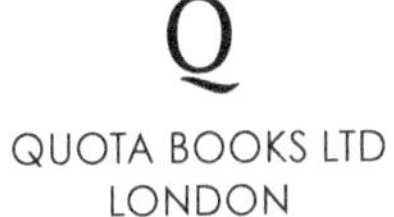

QUOTA BOOKS LTD
LONDON

Published in 2022 by Quota Books Ltd.
197 Hammersmith Grove, London W6 0NP
website: www.quotabooks.com – email: info@quotabooks.com
Twitter: @Quotabooks

Copyright © Pam Gems

Pam Gems is identified as the Author of the Work in accordance with Section 7 of the Copyright, Designs and Patents Act 1988. The author has asserted her moral rights.

All rights whatsoever in these plays are strictly reserved and application for performance etc. should be made before commencement of rehearsals to Rose Cobbe, United Agents, 12–26 Lexington Street, London W1F 0LE, UK. info@unitedagents.co.uk Tel: +44 (0) 20 3214 0800.

No performance may be given unless a licence has been obtained.

This book is sold subject to the condition that it shall not, by way of trade or otherwise, be lent, resold, hired out or otherwise circulated without the publisher's prior consent in any form of binding or cover other than that in which it is published and without a similar condition, including this condition, being imposed on the subsequent publisher.

A CIP record for this book is available from the British Library.

ISBN 978-1-7398894-3-2

Typeset in the UK by M Rules
Printed and bound by Biddles
Picture of Pam Gems courtesy of Jonathan Gems
Cover by TRISTAN

Available from Amazon, Ingram Spark, Quota Books
and all politically correct bookstores.

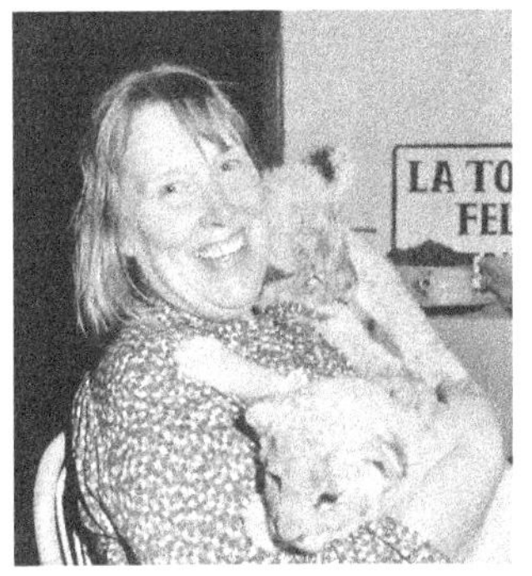

Pam Gems was born in 1925 in Mudeford, near Christchurch, in what was then Dorset, on the south coast of England. Her father, a Welsh ex-coalminer, died when she was six years old, leaving her mother to bring up Pam and her two brothers on her own.

For most of her childhood Pam's family lived in poverty, reliant on charity from the parish church and the Salvation Army. At eleven, she won a scholarship to grammar school, where she flourished, but left at fifteen to go to work.

World War Two broke out and, in 1943 (when she turned eighteen), she joined the Women's Royal Naval Service, and worked with British and Canadian bomber squadrons. She writes about this in FINCHIE's WAR.

After the war, she went to Manchester University, where she studied psychology and met her future husband, Keith.

Always stage-struck, Gems wrote her first play when she was eight, and was an enthusiastic participant in school plays. At university, she joined the dramatic society, wrote skits, produced and directed. After university, she worked in audience research at the BBC – which she loathed – and became part of the 'Ban the Bomb' London beatnik scene, which included Ted Hughes, the poet, Sean Kenny, the designer, and Robert Bolt, the playwright.

After marrying and having her first two children, she and her husband moved to Wandsworth in South London, where she wrote radio plays, beginning an extraordinarily prolific writing career that produced over seventy plays and adaptations. Pam Gems is, without doubt, Britain's greatest woman dramatist, with only Agatha Christie having had more West End productions.

Agatha Christie had ten plays presented in the West End, at a time when the economics of the West End plays weren't as prohibitive as they later became. Pam Gems had six, arguably seven, plays produced in the West End. The first was DUSA FISH STAS and VI, at the Mayfair, presented by Michael Codron, followed by PIAF, at the Piccadilly, presented by the RSC, which also later produced CAMILLE at the Comedy, and THE BLUE ANGEL at the Globe. LOVING WOMEN was presented at the Arts Theatre, and MARLENE had a successful run at the Lyric. STANLEY, which played to full houses at the Olivier Theatre, was offered a West-End transfer by three managements, but the company turned down these offers in favour of a transfer to the Circle in the Square, off-Broadway, in New York, where it ran for six months.

One thing that especially fascinates in Pam Gems' writing is the prophetic element. She perceived, well in advance, the dangers facing the pampered and decadent West, which we now see unfolding. As Victor Hugo said: 'Adversity makes men and prosperity makes monsters.' Her approach is always positive, however. Like the Beatles' song, all you need is love.

Jonathan Gems

ALSO BY THE SAME AUTHOR

Betty's Wonderful Christmas
Go West Young Woman
Queen Christina
Piaf
Camille
Pasionaria
Deborah's Daughter
Marlene
Stanley
The Snow Palace
King Ludwig of Bavaria
Mrs. Pat
Ethel
Not Joan the Musical
The Socialists
Dusa, Fish, Stas, and Vi
Aunt Mary
Garibaldi, Si!

The Incorruptible
The Treat
Franz Into April
Up in Sweden
Next Please
The Synonym
The Whippet
The Russian Princess
The Burning Man
A Builder by Trade
The Nourishing Lie
Mr Watts
In Donegal
Cluster
Down West
The Country House Sale
In The Hothouse
Guin for Guinevere
Marine

The Project
You Should Be Pleased He Likes Me
What Luck
An Ordinary Woman
We Never Do What They Want
Stella Campbell
Finchie's War
The Leg-Up
Maytime
Mabel's Bistro
A Kind of Ecstasy
After Birthday
My Warren
Cedric and Louise
At The Window
Ladybird, Ladybird
Who Is Sylvia?

ADAPTATIONS

Sarah B Divine!
My Name is Rosa Luxemburg
Rivers and Forests
Darling Boy
Uncle Vanya

A Doll's House
The Seagull
Ghosts
Yerma
The Lady from the Sea

The Cherry Orchard
Hedda Gabbler
The Odd Women
The Little Mermaid
Behaving Badly

NOVELS

Mrs Frampton
Bon Voyage, Mrs Frampton

CONTENTS

THE FATHER

by August Strindberg

English version
by Pam Gems

for Frances Barber

THE FATHER

CAST

THE CAPTAIN

LAURA   The Captain's wife

BERTHA   The Captain's daughter

DOCTOR ÖSTERMARK

THE PASTOR (JONAS)   Laura's brother

MARGRET   The Captain's old Nurse

NÖJD (pronounced NOYD)   The Captain's batman

SVÄRD   An orderly

Setting. Swedish army quarters in the 1880s.

THE FATHER

ACT ONE

<u>ACT ONE SCENE ONE</u>

A living room in the Captain's army quarters. A large round table with books and magazines; another table, a leather sofa. A concealed door. A bureau with a clock. On the wall: guns and game-bags. By the door, military greatcoats are hanging. A lamp on the round table.

The CAPTAIN and the PASTOR sit side by side on the sofa.

The CAPTAIN, in his undress uniform, is booted and spurred. The PASTOR is in black, with a white neck cloth but without his clerical collar. He smokes a pipe. The CAPTAIN leans over, and rings a bell.

An ORDERLY – SVÄRD – appears.

>   SVÄRD
> Sir?

>   CAPTAIN
> Where's Nöjd? Is he out there?

>   SVÄRD
> He's in the kitchen, sir.

>   CAPTAIN
> I'll bet he is. What's he doing down there?

>   SVÄRD
> Waiting for orders, sir.

CAPTAIN

Send him up.

SVÄRD

Sir.

He goes.

PASTOR

What is it this time?

CAPTAIN

The same as last time.

PASTOR

The kitchen maid?

CAPTAIN

Again. I've given him a kicking but it doesn't seem to work. Have a go at him – perhaps he'll listen to a parson.

PASTOR

I doubt if the word of God will persuade a cavalryman.

CAPTAIN

Wouldn't cut any ice with me.

PASTOR

Precisely.

CAPTAIN

Worth a try though.

A KNOCK.

CAPTAIN

Come in!

NÖJD enters.

NÖJD

Sir.

CAPTAIN

Stand easy. So, what is it this time?

NÖJD

(All innocence) Sir?

CAPTAIN

What have you been up to?

NÖJD

Nothing, sir.

CAPTAIN

(Roars) Nothing?

NÖJD

Well, not in front of the Pastor, sir.

PASTOR

Don't mind me, lad.

CAPTAIN

Come on! Out with it.

NÖJD

Well sir, it was like this, sir. There was this dance over at Gabriel's. Me and Ludwig goes. Then he says …

CAPTAIN

What's he got to do with it? Stick to the point.

NÖJD

Yessir. So Emma says: 'let's go out to the barn'.

CAPTAIN

Seduced you, did she?

NÖJD

Put it this way, sir: it don't happen if the girl ain't
willing. Sir.

CAPTAIN

Get to the point. Are you the father or not the father?

NÖJD

Don't know, sir.

CAPTAIN

What do you mean, you don't know?

NÖJD

Hard to say, sir.

CAPTAIN

You mean you weren't the only one? That what you're
saying?

NÖJD

That night I was, sir.

CAPTAIN

But you're saying Ludwig was doing her as well?
(*NÖJD shrugs.*) She says you said you'd marry her.

NÖJD

Well you have to say that, sir.

CAPTAIN

(*To the PASTOR*) Bloody hell!

PASTOR

Happens all the time, I'm afraid. (*To NÖJD*) Now look
here, my boy, you must know if you're the father or
not. If you were man enough to go with her . . .

NÖJD

It don't necessarily follow though, does it?

PASTOR

Are you trying to decamp? Leave the girl to have the
child on her own?

NÖJD does not reply.

PASTOR

We can't force you to marry her, but you'll have to
make provision.

NÖJD

Then Ludwig ought to pay his share.

CAPTAIN

I can't be bothered with this. Let the Court decide.
Shove off.

PASTOR

Just a minute. Nöjd, do you really want to leave this
girl penniless, with a baby – your baby – to support.

NÖJD

But is it my baby, sir? If I was sure. (*He fidgets.*) No
man wants to work his arse off for another man's
child all his life, begging your pardon. You do see
that, Pastor?

CAPTAIN

Get out.

NÖJD

Thank you, sir. (*Goes.*)

CAPTAIN

(*Calls*) And stay out of the kitchen! (*To the PASTOR*) I
thought you were going to talk to him!

PASTOR

I did, didn't I?

CAPTAIN

No, you didn't.

PASTOR

To be honest I never know what to say. It's hard luck
on the girl, of course, but what if he isn't the father?
The girl can be sent to the orphanage to suckle the
child then leave it to the parish to support while she
gets a job as a well-paid wet nurse in a decent home.
What about him? If he's thrown out of his regiment
he's finished.

CAPTAIN

I'm not the judge. We do know *she's* guilty.

PASTOR

Do we? Who's to say? What were we discussing before
all this? Ah, Bertha's confirmation.

CAPTAIN

Not just that – her whole future. Every woman in this
household, apparently, wants something different for
my daughter.

PASTOR

Hah … trouble?

CAPTAIN

My mother-in-law fills her with rubbish about
spiritualism; Laura says she must be an artist; her
governess a Methodist; Margret a Baptist, and the
maids plead the virtues of the Salvation Army.

PASTOR

Too many women in charge.

CAPTAIN

I must get her away. It's like a cage of tigers in there.

The PASTOR laughs.

CAPTAIN

You can laugh. I take your sister off your hands and, as a wedding present, you land me with your old stepmother.

PASTOR

As a Pastor, I can hardly share my house with my own stepmother.

CAPTAIN

Why not? I'm allowed to have my mother-in-law under my roof.

PASTOR

We all have our cross to bear.

CAPTAIN

Some more than others. My old nurse still wanders about treating me like a babe in arms.

PASTOR

Keep your women in their place, that's my advice.

CAPTAIN

Yes, but how?

The PASTOR nods in agreement.

PASTOR

Laura's never been the easiest. As her brother, I should know.

CAPTAIN

She's not so bad.

PASTOR

Come on. I grew up with her.

CAPTAIN

She'd be fine if her head wasn't filled with romantic
nonsense. And, well … she is my wife.

PASTOR

So naturally above reproach. Never mind that she
causes more trouble than the rest of the house put
together.

CAPTAIN

We're at an impasse, that's for sure. She won't let the
child go, and I can't let her stay. Not in this madhouse.

PASTOR

When we were children, she would scream for one of
your toys and lie on her back till you gave it to her.
The moment you did, she threw it back at you. Had to
have her own way. All the time.

CAPTAIN

Even then? Sometimes her moods are so violent I
think she's ill.

PASTOR

What do you want for Bertha? Can't you compromise?

CAPTAIN

What I want is not to stand by like a pimp while they
choose the right husband for her. Suppose, in spite of
all their efforts, she doesn't find a man and ends up an
old maid? On the other hand, she can't train for years
like a man and then drop it all for wedding bells.

PASTOR

Then what do you want for her?

CAPTAIN

I'd like her to be a teacher so that if she doesn't marry she can support herself. Better even than a man who has to maintain a wife and family. If she does marry, the teacher training will be useful for the children.

PASTOR

What about her painting? If she's talented shouldn't that be encouraged?

CAPTAIN

(Shakes his head) I took her work to a well-known artist for an appraisal.

PASTOR

No good?

CAPTAIN

No more than schoolgirl standard, he said. Which would have been fine, until some young idiot came here last summer, telling her she was a genius.

PASTOR

In love, I suppose.

CAPTAIN

Apparently.

PASTOR

Doesn't help. So, there's a crisis?

CAPTAIN

They won't give me a fair fight!

PASTOR

(Rising) Oh, I know about that.

The CAPTAIN looks up.

PASTOR

Believe me.

CAPTAIN

But it's all so vindictive. Is that the way to choose
her future? They set themselves up all the time:
"women should have this – we should have that."
It's infuriating. So, you'll stay for supper? The new
doctor's joining us. Have you met him yet?

PASTOR

I overtook him on my way over. He seems a decent sort.

CAPTAIN

Good. Who knows, maybe an ally?

PASTOR

Possibly. If he knows women well enough.

CAPTAIN

So, you'll stay?

PASTOR

Sorry, no. I promised to be home for supper. In fact,
I'd better get going. Don't want to keep my good lady
waiting. She's inclined to get anxious.

CAPTAIN

Annoyed, you mean. Well, if you have to ...

He rises, and helps the PASTOR on with his coat.

PASTOR

Thank you. Cold night.

The CAPTAIN nods goodbye.

PASTOR

Look after yourself. You look a little off-colour.

CAPTAIN

Been on to you, has she? Don't take any notice.
Laura's had me in my grave for the past twenty years.

PASTOR

Take care anyway. Goodbye. Oh, did you want to talk
about Bertha's confirmation?

CAPTAIN

No, that's your department. Leave me out of it. You
know where I stand on religion. My regards to your
wife.

PASTOR

Say goodbye to Laura for me.

The PASTOR goes.

The CAPTAIN sits at his desk, gets out his accounts, and picks up
a pen.

CAPTAIN

Thirty-four. Nine. Forty-three. Sixty-one. Seventy.

LAURA

(Off stage) Are you in there?

CAPTAIN

Eighty-three. Ninety-four. What is it?

LAURA enters.

LAURA

Am I interrupting?

CAPTAIN

No. You want the housekeeping, is that it?

LAURA

Yes.

CAPTAIN

Leave the accounts and I'll go through them.

LAURA

What?

CAPTAIN

The bills.

LAURA

He wants to go through the bills now!

CAPTAIN

Yes, Laura. We're in a bad way. If I don't keep
accounts, I'll be accused of mismanagement.

LAURA

Mismanagement?

CAPTAIN

By the bankruptcy court.

LAURA

Are we bankrupt?

CAPTAIN

If you'll only let me see the bills I can find out.

LAURA

It's not my fault the tenant doesn't pay his rent.

CAPTAIN

Who recommended him? Some lazy pig wants to rent
the farm ...

LAURA

You agreed!

CAPTAIN

Only because I wasn't allowed to eat or sleep until I did. You wanted him so your brother could get rid of him. Your mother wanted him because I didn't. The governess wanted him because he's a Methodist and old Margret because she knew his grandmother's sister at school. I took him on because, if I hadn't, I'd be in the madhouse or my grave by now. Here you are. (*Gives her money.*) The housekeeping. And your allowance. Let me have the bills.

LAURA

(*Curtseys*) Thank you, kind sir. Do you keep an account of what you spend?

CAPTAIN

What I spend has nothing to do with you.

LAURA

Any more than my child's education! Did you and my sainted brother come to a decision tonight?

CAPTAIN

I've already made my decision. Two weeks from now Bertha will leave this house and lodge in town.

LAURA

And who's she going to live with?

CAPTAIN

I've arranged for her to stay with Mr. Särberg, the lawyer.

LAURA

Not that freethinker!

CAPTAIN

Yes, of course. I'm a freethinker too.

LAURA

And a mother has no say in the matter?

CAPTAIN

No, she doesn't. She surrenders those claims when
she accepts her husband's offer to protect and provide
for her and her children.

LAURA

So a woman has no rights over the child of her own
body?

CAPTAIN

That's right. When you make a contract, you can't
keep the goods and ask for your money back.

LAURA

Maybe we can compromise?

CAPTAIN

No. Not in this case. You want Bertha here. I want her
in town. To compromise would mean her living at the
railway station.

LAURA

Then it's war. (*Silence.*) Why was Nöjd here?

CAPTAIN

That's a military matter.

LAURA

That the whole kitchen knows about.

CAPTAIN

So why ask me?

LAURA shrugs.

CAPTAIN

No doubt you've already passed judgement.

LAURA

The law is quite clear about these things.

CAPTAIN

It depends on the paternity.

LAURA

That's usually known.

CAPTAIN

But can one ever be sure?

LAURA

No, you can never be really sure who a child's father is.

CAPTAIN

That's right.

LAURA

But the man still has total rights over the woman's child.

CAPTAIN

Only if he accepts responsibility. Or has it forced upon
him. In marriage, of course, the question doesn't arise.

LAURA

No?

CAPTAIN

Of course not.

LAURA

Never? What if the wife's unfaithful?

CAPTAIN

Not relevant in Nöjd's case. Anything else you want
to know?

LAURA

No.

CAPTAIN

(*Rising.*) Fine. I'll be in my room. Let me know when the Doctor comes. I don't want to keep him waiting.

LAURA

(*Sarcastic.*) Yes, your lordship.

The CAPTAIN exits.

LAURA counts the money he has given her.

MOTHER

(*Off stage*) Laura? Is my tea ready?

LAURA

I'm coming, Mother!

As she turns, the door is opened by SVÄRD.

SVÄRD

Dr. Östermark, ma'am.

DOCTOR

(*Entering*) Mrs. Lassen?

LAURA extends her hand.

LAURA

Ah Doctor, come in. You're very welcome. The Captain's not at home just now, but I'm sure he won't be long.

DOCTOR

(*Gives SVÄRD his coat*) I'm terribly sorry I'm so late. I had to look in on a patient.

SVÄRD hangs up the coat and exits.

LAURA

Oh, don't worry about that. Come and sit down.

DOCTOR

Thank you.

LAURA

We're all hoping you'll settle here. There's a lot of illness about and it's so good to have a doctor who takes a real interest in his patients. We want to see a lot of you.

DOCTOR

Not professionally I trust! *(They chuckle.)* But I hear you're all in excellent health.

LAURA

Well, ye-es. We've been lucky so far – although perhaps not completely.

DOCTOR

Oh?

LAURA

In fact, there's something I'd like to talk to you about.

DOCTOR

Yes? What's that?

He waits for her to speak further.

LAURA

It's difficult. I don't know if I should tell you.

DOCTOR

I'm your doctor.

LAURA

Well, I suppose I can confide in you but . . .

DOCTOR

Perhaps we should postpone this conversation until I've met the Captain?

LAURA

No, it must be before you see him.

DOCTOR

Ah. So it concerns your husband?

LAURA

Yes, sadly, it does.

DOCTOR

I'm sorry to hear that. So, what seems to be the trouble?

LAURA

(*Takes out a handkerchief*) My husband is ... it's so very hard to ... I'm afraid, Doctor, that he may be, well, mentally unbalanced.

DOCTOR

Are you sure? You amaze me, Mrs. Lassen. I've just finished reading the Captain's paper on mineralogy. It's very ... advanced. On the face of it, he appears to have a very rational and orderly mind.

LAURA

I hope we're all wrong. But it's affecting the whole family.

DOCTOR

How does it manifest?

LAURA

Well, different ways. There's his mania for collecting, for example.

DOCTOR

Collecting?

LAURA

Books. Crates and crates of books. Which he never
even reads!

DOCTOR

Scholars do buy books, you know.

LAURA

You don't take me seriously, do you?

DOCTOR

Dear lady, of course I do.

LAURA

Is it rational and orderly when a man says he can see
the planets through a microscope?

DOCTOR

A microscope?

LAURA

Yes.

DOCTOR

He says that?

LAURA

Yes.

DOCTOR

Well, that's ... unusual.

LAURA

You don't believe me, do you? But it's true!

DOCTOR

No, no, I ... I'm honoured that you feel you can talk
to me about it. But you have to appreciate that, as
a medical practitioner, I need to make a thorough
investigation before I come to any diagnosis. Does the
Captain show any signs of depression, irritability?
Sudden changes of mood?

LAURA

In twenty years of marriage I have never, ever,
known him make a single decision without, almost
immediately, changing his mind.

DOCTOR

Hm. Would you say he's a stubborn person?
Obstinate?

LAURA

Yes! Always. But as soon as he gets his way, no matter
what the situation, he loses interest and hands the
reins over to me.

DOCTOR

Does he? That's interesting. You see, Mrs. Lassen, we
often think of the will as the backbone of the mind.
Without a healthy functioning of the will, the mind is
inclined to collapse.

LAURA

If you knew what I've been through over the years!

DOCTOR

You have my sympathies, Mrs. Lassen. And my
promise. I'll see what I can do. In the meantime, I
must ask you not to provoke him. Try to avoid any
topic that might upset him. Thoughts – if there's

an imbalance – can easily develop into obsession, monomania or paranoia. Do you understand that?

LAURA

I mustn't arouse his suspicions.

DOCTOR

Exactly. Best not to. A man who's in danger of losing his wits is highly suggestible.

LAURA

I see. Yes, I understand. That makes sense. Ah! Here's my husband!

The CAPTAIN enters by the concealed door.

CAPTAIN

Ah, Doctor. You're here. Good. I'm delighted to meet you.

They shake hands.

DOCTOR

I'm delighted to meet you too, sir. It's a great honour to meet such a distinguished man of science.

CAPTAIN

Thank you, but my military duties don't leave me much time for science. Although I think I may have stumbled onto something recently.

DOCTOR

Oh really?

CAPTAIN

Are you interested?

DOCTOR

Very much so.

CAPTAIN

I've been subjecting meteorites, which I have on loan from the museum, to spectrum analysis. And what I've found are traces of carbon. Carbon! Evidence of organic life.

DOCTOR

That's amazing. You can see that under a microscope?

CAPTAIN

A microscope? Good God, no. A spectroscope.

DOCTOR

Ah, a spectroscope! I meant a spectroscope of course. You'll be able to tell us what's happening on Jupiter soon.

CAPTAIN

Not what is happening – what has happened in the past. If only the damned bookseller in Paris would send me the books I need! Every bookseller in the world seems to be conspiring against me. I haven't even had my orders acknowledged. If you telegraph they don't reply. It's driving me mad.

DOCTOR

It's probably just incompetence or laziness. I wouldn't let it upset you.

CAPTAIN

Yes, but I can't finish my damn thesis, and there are others working on the same lines in Berlin. Still, we're not here to discuss all that. Tell me, do you want to take an apartment here in the wing, or live in the old doctor's quarters?

DOCTOR

Whatever you wish.

CAPTAIN

It's your decision.

DOCTOR

It's for you to say.

CAPTAIN

Makes no difference to me.

DOCTOR

Surely the decision must be yours.

CAPTAIN

Oh, for God's sake, man, make up your mind!

DOCTOR

All right. I'd be most grateful for an apartment here.

CAPTAIN

Good. Fine. Thank you. Nothing worse than a man
who can't make up his mind.

He rings.

MARGRET, the old family nurse, enters.

CAPTAIN

Margret. Is there an apartment ready for the Doctor?

MARGRET

Oh yes, it's all clean and dusted.

CAPTAIN

Good, then I won't keep you. I daresay you'll be tired.
Goodnight, Doctor. It was nice meeting you. I'll see
you in the morning.

DOCTOR

Good night, Captain.

CAPTAIN

My wife can put you in the picture about our life here.

DOCTOR

She has mentioned one or two things. Good night,
Captain.

The DOCTOR goes.

MARGRET hovers.

CAPTAIN

What is it, Margret?

MARGRET

Listen to me, my love.

CAPTAIN

You're the only one in this house I <u>can</u> listen to
without exploding.

MARGRET

Why can't you go half way with Mrs. Laura? Think
how <u>she</u> feels. She's the child's mother.

CAPTAIN

And I'm her father!

MARGRET

I know, I know. But a man has all sorts of other things
in his life. Women don't.

CAPTAIN

A man has more worries and responsibilities, that's
true. I wouldn't have stayed a soldier all my life if I
didn't have a family to support.

MARGRET

I didn't mean to upset you.

CAPTAIN

I know you didn't. But you're trying to make me give in.

MARGRET

I only want what's best.

CAPTAIN

I know. But you're wrong. It's not enough to give a child life. Her mind, her soul need to be nurtured. You're not on my side, Margret.

MARGRET

(Gasps) How can you say such a thing! You're my baby. I nursed you for the first three years of your life!

CAPTAIN

Oh, I haven't forgotten that. You've been like my mother. You've always stood up for me. Until now. Now, when I need you most, you go over to the enemy.

MARGRET

The enemy!

CAPTAIN

Yes. You know how things are. You should do. you've seen it all from the beginning.

MARGRET

I have. Why in the name of Jesus must two people torment each other day in, day out? Two people who are so good and kind? Mrs. Laura is never like that with me or anyone else.

CAPTAIN

Only with me. And if you desert me now, Margret, you
must answer to God. You know exactly what they're
up to – plotting against me. That Doctor's no friend of
mine either. I can see that already.

MARGRET

You think the worst of everybody. You know why, my
boy? Lack of faith. You don't follow the true path.

CAPTAIN

And you do. You and the Baptists.

MARGRET

There's no need for that. I feel loved and blessed and
so would you if you followed the Lord.

CAPTAIN

Blessed? You should hear your voice when you
mention your Lord. It's like a scythe being sharpened.
Not much love there.

MARGRET

That's pride talking. Never mind all those books you
read, you'll be humbled on the Day of Judgement.

CAPTAIN

Well, if I am, I'll certainly look a fool, won't I?

MARGRET

Shame on you! Come here.

He goes to her obediently. She hugs him.

MARGRET

My big strong boy. I still love him best of all. Don't worry.
Margret won't leave you. She'll be here when it all gets
too much. (*Pats him affectionately.*) My good little boy.

CAPTAIN

I need support, Margret. You're the only one I can count on.

A scream offstage.

CAPTAIN

Who's that? Who's yelling?

BERTHA runs on.

BERTHA

Father, help me. Help me!

CAPTAIN

Bertha! What is it? What's the matter?

BERTHA

She's going to hurt me! She'll hurt me!

CAPTAIN

Who?

BERTHA

Grandmamma! *(She stifles a sob.)* It's my fault. I played a trick on her.

The CAPTAIN disguises a smile.

CAPTAIN

What did you do?

BERTHA

You won't say anything? Promise?

CAPTAIN

All right, but what did you do?

He gestures for MARGRET to leave. She goes.

BERTHA

Well – Grandmamma likes to turn down the lamp and sit me at the table with pen and paper. Then she tells the spirits to write.

CAPTAIN

What? Why haven't you told me this before?

BERTHA

I couldn't! She says the spirits will punish me. The pen does write but I can't tell if it's me that's doing it. Anyway, it won't if I'm tired, and I have to write something. So tonight, I wrote a poem but Grandmamma recognised it and she got really angry. She says I'm a cheat!

CAPTAIN

Do you believe in spirits?

BERTHA

I don't know.

CAPTAIN

They don't exist, Bertha.

BERTHA

Grandmamma says they do. (*Glances at him shyly.*) She says you go to other planets.

CAPTAIN

What else does she say?

BERTHA

She says even if you say you go to other planets, you don't because you can't do magic.

CAPTAIN

I never said I could, Bertha. Do you know what meteorites are? They're rocks that come from outer

space. What I do is look at them under a spectroscope
and try to see what they're composed of.

CAPTAIN

BERTHA

Grandmamma says she can see things you can't.

CAPTAIN

Such as spirits?

Bertha nods

CAPTAIN

You shouldn't believe everything she says,
sweetheart.

BERTHA

Grandmamma doesn't tell lies.

CAPTAIN

How do you know?

BERTHA

'Cause Mama says so.

CAPTAIN

Hmm.

BERTHA

And Mama doesn't tell lies. And if you say she does, I
won't believe you.

CAPTAIN

Bertha, would you be happier away from here? Would
you like to go and live in town and learn something
useful? What do you think?

BERTHA

I'd love it! Anywhere to get away, so long as I can see
you sometimes. A lot! It's so horrible here, except

when you come home. Then it's like taking down the storm windows and the sun coming in!

CAPTAIN

Oh, my darling girl. (*Embraces her.*)

BERTHA

Daddy, be nice to Mama. She cries all the time.

CAPTAIN

Mmm. So, you do want to go and live in town?

BERTHA

Yes please!

CAPTAIN

Suppose she doesn't want that?

BERTHA

Mama? Oh, she will. She must!

CAPTAIN

But what if she doesn't?

BERTHA

She must!

CAPTAIN

You'd better ask her.

BERTHA

She won't listen to me, Daddy. Why don't you ask her? But do it nicely.

CAPTAIN

Hmm. And if you want it, and I want it, and your mother doesn't – what then?

BERTHA

Everything will be horrible again. Daddy, why can't you just get along with her … ?

LAURA enters

LAURA

There you are, Bertha. Now would be an excellent time to hear what you think about your future.

CAPTAIN

Yes, but she can't decide. She's a child. She doesn't have the experience.

LAURA

But since we can't agree, why not give her the casting vote?

CAPTAIN

I'm not giving up any of my rights, or my responsibilities. Bertha, would you leave us, please?

BERTHA goes.

LAURA

You sent her out because she agrees with me!

CAPTAIN

No I didn't. She agrees with me. But I know you're going to put so much pressure on her she'll change her mind.

LAURA

Am I so powerful?

CAPTAIN

Yes, when you want something. Look at Nördling!

LAURA

Nördling?

CAPTAIN

You insulted a perfectly good doctor until he
couldn't stand it any longer and left the district. Hey
presto! What a surprise, you have a suggestion for a
replacement. Surprise again! You make your brother
vote him in.

LAURA

What's wrong with that? So what about Bertha? Is
she going?

CAPTAIN

In two weeks' time.

LAURA

And that's your final decision?

CAPTAIN

Yes.

LAURA

Does she know?

CAPTAIN

Yes.

LAURA

Then I'll have to stop it.

CAPTAIN

You can't.

LAURA

Do you think I'm going to let my daughter go to
a bunch of freethinkers who'll teach her that

everything I've told her is wrong? They'll teach her
to despise me!

CAPTAIN

And do you think I'm prepared to leave my daughter –
my only child – in the hands of a bunch of ignorant
women?

LAURA

You're only her father. It's not so important.

CAPTAIN

What?

LAURA

A mother is closer to her child.

CAPTAIN

Who says?

LAURA

Especially now science has proven that nobody can be
one hundred per cent sure.

CAPTAIN

Sure of what?

LAURA

Who the father is.

CAPTAIN

What's that supposed to mean?

LAURA

Are you sure you're Bertha's father?

CAPTAIN

Of course I'm sure.

LAURA

Science says not.

CAPTAIN

Is this a joke?

LAURA

I'm simply talking science, like you. How do you know
I wasn't unfaithful?

CAPTAIN

You're capable of a lot, but not that. And if it were
true, you wouldn't tell me.

LAURA

I would if I'd do anything not to lose my child.
Suppose it's true? Suppose . . .

CAPTAIN

Stop it.

LAURA

If it's true, you'd have no power over her.

CAPTAIN

Can you prove I'm not the father?

LAURA

It wouldn't be that difficult. Do you want me to?

CAPTAIN

Stop it. Just stop it.

LAURA

I'd have to name her real father, and state the time
and place. For instance, when was Bertha born? We'd
been married for at least three years before . . .

CAPTAIN

Stop it! Stop it or I'll . . .

LAURA

What? Okay, I'll stop. But think very carefully – very
carefully – before you send my daughter away. It
might end up being very embarrassing for you.

CAPTAIN

Oh my God! But what about you? It's going to be
embarrassing for you. Everyone's going to think
you're a whore.

LAURA

Don't worry about me. I'll survive.

CAPTAIN

(*Sighs*). We can't win, can we?

LAURA

No, you can't. So, don't fight us. The day I find a man
who's stronger than me, I'll . . .

CAPTAIN

No. This time you've met your match. Battle orders.

LAURA

(*Smiles.*) I look forward to it.

MARGRET enters.

MARGRET

Dinner. Will you come through?

LAURA

Thank you.

MARGRET goes.

The CAPTAIN slumps down in an armchair.

LAURA

Aren't you coming?

CAPTAIN

(*Shakes his head.*) I'm not hungry.

LAURA

You mean you're in a sulk.

CAPTAIN

I mean I'm not hungry.

LAURA

Come to dinner. They'll think something's wrong. Oh,
I don't care. Do what you want!

LAURA goes.

A pause. MARGRET enters.

MARGRET

Now what's all this? What's going on?

CAPTAIN

Tell me something, Margret. Am I, or am I not, a
grown man?

MARGRET

Of course you are.

CAPTAIN

Then why do you treat me like a child?

MARGRET

I don't know, my dear. Perhaps it's because man is
born of woman.

CAPTAIN

But no woman is born of man, is that it? Well, let me
ask you something. Do you think I'm Bertha's father?

MARGRET

Dear Lord, of course you are! Don't be so silly. Who else is her father? Now come and eat your dinner. Come on.

The CAPTAIN rises.

CAPTAIN

No. Leave me alone. This is a houseful of witches!

He goes to the door and calls.

CAPTAIN

Svärd!

The ORDERLY enters.

SVÄRD

Yessir?

The CAPTAIN crosses for his greatcoat. He turns to MARGRET.

CAPTAIN

Don't expect me back before midnight.

The ORDERLY helps him on with his coat.

CAPTAIN

(*To SVÄRD*) Harness up for me, will you?

They go.

MARGRET

God help us!

Fade to black.

ACT TWO

ACT TWO – SCENE ONE

It is night. The lamp is lit. The DOCTOR and LAURA are talking.

DOCTOR

Well, I haven't formed a diagnosis yet. After talking
to your husband, the exact state of his health is
still not clear. It turns out you were mistaken about
his claims to study planets with a microscope. He
uses a spectroscope, which is an entirely different
instrument.

LAURA

I never said that.

DOCTOR

Mrs. Lassen, forgive me, but I made notes of our
conversation. And you should know it's important
not to make accusations of this kind unless you're
absolutely sure – because they can lead to a man
being committed.

LAURA

Committed?

DOCTOR

Yes. And a person who is committed – that is, certified
insane – loses all his rights.

LAURA

Really? I didn't know that.

DOCTOR

There's another thing I feel uneasy about. The
Captain spoke of his correspondence with booksellers
not being answered. Can I ask you: did you, with the
best intentions, interfere with his letters at all?

LAURA

Yes, I did. I felt it was in the best interests of the
family. I can't allow him destroy us.

DOCTOR

Yes, but I don't think you understand the
consequences of such actions. If your husband
discovers what you've done, what is he going to
think? All his suspicions will be confirmed. It will
increase his paranoia. It's not wise to block his
wishes. You must know how it is to have what you
want obstructed.

LAURA

No one knows that better than me.

DOCTOR

Good. So you can understand how he feels.

LAURA

(*Rises.*) It's midnight and he's still not back. I'm
worried something might have happened.

DOCTOR

Did something upset him after I left?

She acts reluctant to reply.

DOCTOR

Mrs. Lassen? Did something happen? What
happened? Tell me.

LAURA

He started saying bizarre things! Really crazy
things! I didn't know what to think!

DOCTOR

What things?

LAURA

Was he Bertha's father? Was he the father of his
child?

DOCTOR

Whatever gave him that idea?

LAURA

I don't know. Unless it was our maid. One of his men
has got our maid in trouble. She's pregnant. And
when I stood up for her, he lost his temper and said
nothing could be proven. That nobody could say
who the child's father was. I tried to calm him but
he just got worse. By the end, he was raving! He was
completely out of his mind!

She weeps.

DOCTOR

Don't worry, Mrs. Lassen, we'll do something. Don't
upset yourself. We'll find a solution, I promise you.
But we mustn't alarm him. Are you all right?

LAURA

(Drying her tears). Yes ... Thank you.

DOCTOR

Tell me, has the Captain ever expressed ideas like
this before?

LAURA

Yes. Six years ago, the same thing happened. He even wrote to his doctor saying he was scared he was losing his sanity.

DOCTOR

I see. So there's a history here. I don't like to cast aspersions, but it does seem as if this should have been seen to earlier. Do you know where your husband is now? Where he might have gone?

LAURA

I haven't a clue. He has such wild ideas these days.

DOCTOR

Do you want me to wait up for him? I could say I'd looked in to see your mother.

LAURA

That would be very kind, yes. Thank you very much. *(Touches his arm.)* Please don't leave us. I'm really worried.

DOCTOR

I know, but it'll be fine. You'll see. Hm. It might be better if I wait in the other room rather than have him see us here together.

LAURA

Yes, you're right. Yes. Margret can come in here. She always waits up for him, and he trusts her. *(She calls)* Margret! Margret!

MARGRET

(Enters) What is it, madam, is the Master back?

LAURA

Not yet, but why don't you sit here and wait for him?
And when he comes in, would you mind telling him
the Doctor's in the next room? You can say Mother
wasn't feeling well.

MARGRET

All right, fine. Leave it to me.

LAURA opens a door, ushers the DOCTOR through, and follows
him off.

MARGRET sits down, puts on her glasses, and takes out her book.

MARGRET

(*Reads*) 'A vale of misery our life,
Full of sorrow, fear and gloom,
Above the Avenging Angel cry,
"All is vanity, all is doom."'
Ah yes. 'Every creature on this earth
Crushed with sorrow, strife and pain.'
Very true.

BERTHA enters with a coffee pot and her embroidery.

BERTHA

Can I come and sit with you, Margret?

MARGRET

You should be in bed.

BERTHA

I want to finish Daddy's Christmas present.

MARGRET

But it's gone twelve o'clock.

BERTHA

I'm making something for you, too. I can't stay up
there. It's haunted.

MARGRET

Haunted?

BERTHA

I heard something.

MARGRET

What did I say! There's evil in this house. What did
you hear, my love?

BERTHA

Somebody was singing, up in the attic.

MARGRET

Singing? At this time of night?

BERTHA

It was coming from the room where we keep the
cradle.

MARGRET

Oh dear. And what a night! Those chimneypots won't
last long. They'll all come tumbling down, you'll see.
'What is life but pain and woe. Till to the sepulchre we
go'. Well, Happy Christmas, dear.

BERTHA sews.

BERTHA

Is it true Daddy's ill?

MARGRET

Yes, my love, I'm afraid it is.

CAPTAIN
BERTHA

Then how can we have a happy Christmas? And if he's ill, why isn't he in bed?

MARGRET

It's not that sort of illness, dear. Ssh! *(She listens)* Someone's come in. Go on, off you go. Take the coffee pot; your father will be cross if he sees it left about.

BERTHA

(Takes the tray.) Good night, Margret.

MARGRET

Good night. God bless.

BERTHA goes.

Pause. Then the CAPTAIN enters noisily, taking off his greatcoat.

CAPTAIN

What are you doing here?

MARGRET

Waiting for you.

CAPTAIN

Go to bed. *(He lights a candle, and sits at his desk.)*

MARGRET

Captain, sir.

CAPTAIN

What?

MARGRET

The doctor's here. The old lady's not well.

CAPTAIN

What's the matter with her?

MARGRET

A chill I think.

The CAPTAIN rises and detains MARGRET as she turns to go.

CAPTAIN

Margret, who was the father of your child?

MARGRET

(Surprised) You know who. That rogue Johansson.

CAPTAIN

You're sure it was him?

MARGRET

Don't be silly, of course I'm sure. He was the only one.

CAPTAIN

But was *he* sure? He couldn't be, could he? You could be, but he couldn't. You see the difference?

MARGRET

The difference?

He turns the pages of a photograph album on the table.

CAPTAIN

Yes. Do you think she looks like me, Bertha?

MARGRET

Looks like you? You're as alike as two peas.

CAPTAIN

So, did he admit it, Johansson? That he was the father of your child?

MARGRET

Well, he had to.

The DOCTOR comes in.

CAPTAIN

(*As he enters*) Ah, good evening Doctor. How's my mother-in-law?

DOCTOR

Oh, nothing serious. Just a slight sprain of the left ankle.

CAPTAIN

Huh! There seems to be a difference of opinion. Margret says it's a cold. (*To MARGRET*) You'd better get off to bed.

MARGRET

Yes. Goodnight.

MARGRET leaves.

CAPTAIN

Do sit down.DOCTOR (*Sits*) Thank you.

CAPTAIN

Tell me something: if you cross a zebra with a mare, is it true you get striped foals?DOCTOR (*Surprised*) I think so, yes.

CAPTAIN

And that subsequent foals of that mare – even when she's served by an ordinary stallion – they can be striped too?

DOCTOR

I'm not sure.

CAPTAIN

A black stallion can throw a striped foal?

DOCTOR

I've heard that said, but . . .

CAPTAIN

So likeness to the father is meaningless? Paternity
can't be proved.

DOCTOR

Difficult to prove it, yes.

CAPTAIN

You're a widower, aren't you?

DOCTOR

Yes, I am.

CAPTAIN

Any children?

The DOCTOR inclines his head.

CAPTAIN

Didn't you ever feel ridiculous?

DOCTOR

I beg your pardon?

CAPTAIN

Ridiculous. Walking down the street with your
children. "Here they are: 'my children,' when you
should be saying: 'my wife's children!' You've never
had any doubts?

DOCTOR

No. As Goethe said, you 'take it on trust.' I think it
was Goethe

CAPTAIN

On trust? Where a woman's concerned?

DOCTOR

There's more than one kind of woman.

CAPTAIN

Not according to my research. Two examples. When
I was young and – though I say so myself – good-
looking, some friends and I were travelling on a
steamer, when the young waitress sat down with us
and started to cry. She said her fiancé had been lost
at sea. I got her some champagne. After the second
glass, I touched her foot; after the fourth, her knee;
and before morning I'd consoled her completely.

DOCTOR

You took advantage of her. The girl was bereft.

CAPTAIN

Was she? Who's to say she didn't take advantage of
me? The second time was at Lysekil. I met a woman
there, staying with her children. Her husband was in
town. Very religious girl; very high-principled – even
lectured me. Totally virtuous. Or so I thought. I lent
her some books which she returned just before I left.
Three months later I found a calling card in one of
the books – with a declaration of love. What do you
think of that? From a married woman to a complete
stranger! You can't trust women, Doctor. If you do,
you're finished.

DOCTOR

These are just morbid thoughts, Captain.

CAPTAIN

Morbid thoughts? Let me tell you something,
Östermark. All boilers have a bursting point.

The Doctor is discomfited.

CAPTAIN

You're here to keep an eye on me, aren't you?

DOCTOR

Oh, please …

CAPTAIN

If I were a woman, I could complain, put on a big performance, point the finger, assign the blame, and get cart-loads of sympathy. But I'm a man, so it's arms across the chest like a Roman, and silence until death.

DOCTOR

Captain, if you are ill, I need the full story. I need to hear your side.

CAPTAIN

One side's not good enough for you?

DOCTOR

You're teasing me. No. When I saw 'Ghosts' the other night in the theatre and heard Mrs. Alving slander her dead husband. Well it seemed unfair that the man wasn't there to defend himself.

CAPTAIN

Would he have defended himself if he had been there? If a dead man did rise from his grave, would he be believed against the word of a woman?

The Doctor doesn't know what to say.

CAPTAIN

It's late, and I'm ready to turn in. As you see, Doctor, I'm perfectly calm, so you can go to bed.

DOCTOR

Very well. Let's leave it for now. Good night.

CAPTAIN

Are we on opposite sides?

DOCTOR

Not at all. I want to be friends.

He goes.

The CAPTAIN sees him out, then crosses immediately, and opens the other door.

CAPTAIN

You may as well come in, Laura. I know you're there.

LAURA, out of face, walks past him as he holds the door open for her. He sits at his desk.

CAPTAIN

Take a seat. I went to the post office this afternoon for my letters.

LAURA

Yes? So?

CAPTAIN

And I discovered you've been intercepting my mail. You've been deliberately sabotaging my research.

LAURA

You were neglecting your duties. I was trying to protect you.

CAPTAIN

No, you weren't. You were trying to deny me scientific honours. Why? Because, for some absurd reason, you

think that me being honoured would diminish your
importance.

LAURA

That's complete rubbish.

CAPTAIN

You've stolen my letters. Well, now I have some of
yours.

LAURA

(Sarcastic). Oh, how noble of you!

CAPTAIN

And the first thing I see, from what you've written, is:
I'm insane. Friends, staff, servants – you've told them
all I'm mad. But I'm not. There's nothing wrong with
me. I'm perfectly capable of performing my duties
as a soldier and my obligations as a husband and a
father. My emotions are under control, for the most
part. My will power's intact, despite you gnawing at
it constantly. But, don't worry, I'm not going to appeal
to your feelings, seeing as you have none. No, instead,
I'm going to appeal to your self-interest.

LAURA

Go on.

CAPTAIN

If I have a nervous collapse, thanks to your
unrelenting pressure, consider the consequences. I
lose my job. That means: no money for you. If I die,
you'll get my life insurance but, if I kill myself you'll
get nothing because they don't pay out for suicide. See
what I mean?

LAURA

What is this?

CAPTAIN

You can either stick your head in the noose or walk around it.

LAURA

Is this a trick? You wouldn't kill yourself.

CAPTAIN

Yes, I would. Do you think I want to carry on living when there's nothing and no one to live for?

LAURA

Then give up. Surrender. Let Bertha stay here with us.

CAPTAIN

(Pause.) All right. What I propose is an armistice.

LAURA

On what terms?

CAPTAIN

I will let Bertha stay at the house on two conditions. One: that you tell everyone I'm not insane. And there must be no doubts. I want no doubts about that.

LAURA

And the second condition?

CAPTAIN

I want to know who Bertha's father is.

LAURA

You know who he is.

CAPTAIN

Do I?

LAURA

Of course you do.

CAPTAIN

Then why are you putting these ideas in my head?

LAURA

What ideas?

CAPTAIN

(*Roars*) That she's not mine!!

LAURA

I said that?

CAPTAIN

Yes, you said that! And you've been dripping so much
poison into my ear, I've started to believe it. Venom
works! Tell me if it's true. If she's another man's child,
I forgive you. I have already.

LAURA

Why should I plead guilty to something I haven't
done?

CAPTAIN

You have my word no one will know. I'm hardly likely
to broadcast it.

LAURA

If I say it isn't true, will you believe me? If I say it is
true, you'll believe that. So, you'd rather it were true!

CAPTAIN

You're saying that if it isn't true, it can't be proved.
All I have is your word for it, which I can't trust.

LAURA

Do you have any grounds for suspicion?

CAPTAIN

Yes, you! You said you'd been unfaithful.

LAURA

No, I didn't. I know what you're playing at. You want
me to be guilty. If I'm guilty you can turn me out and
keep Bertha for yourself. You won't catch me that
way!

CAPTAIN

Would I want to keep another man's child?

LAURA

No, you wouldn't. (*Scornfully.*) 'Forgive me!' I knew
that was a lie!

CAPTAIN

Laura. If you say the child isn't mine, I have no rights
over her. That's what you want isn't it? Or do you
want power over the child and me?

LAURA

I don't know what you're talking about.

CAPTAIN

Laura, I don't believe in an afterlife. That child is my
only hope of immortality. Take that away and I'm
destroyed.

LAURA

(*After a pause.*) We should have separated. Why didn't
we separate when there was still time?

CAPTAIN

Because of the child. We had the child. And now, after
all these years ... (*He paces.*) It wasn't the fever. I
wasn't delirious. The door was open. I heard you!
When I was ill. You were asking who would inherit. I
had money then. I can hear his voice: "Not you, Mrs.
Lassen, you have no children." And why was that? A
year later we had a daughter – and no more children
after that. Who's the father?

LAURA

You are.

CAPTAIN

No. Not me. There's been a crime and now it's coming
to the surface. Women! Oh, so softhearted! "The
poor must be clothed, the hungry fed. Slaves must be
freed!" Yes, so long as they're black! I have slaved for
you, your child, your family, and sacrificed my life,
my career, undergone every torment and anxiety
known to man to keep you secure. Why? For one
reason only. Because I thought I was the father of our
child!

LAURA

You're mad.

CAPTAIN

I wish I were. (*Sits*) I even sympathised with you –
listening to you crying in your sleep. Only last night
I heard you shouting: "Go away. Go away!" I knocked
on your wall. (*Shakes his head*) All these years ...
Suspicions. Pushing them down. Not allowing myself
to believe that ... When I think of it! Sixteen years!

LAURA

What am I supposed to say? All I can do is swear by Almighty God on the Holy Bible that you are Bertha's father.

CAPTAIN

What use is that? You've already admitted you'd commit any crime to keep your child. Please, I beg of you! Look, forget I'm a man. Take pity on me – as one human being to another.

LAURA approaches, touches him.

LAURA

You're crying.

CAPTAIN

Why shouldn't I? Doesn't a man have a heart the same as a woman? Live under the same stars, the same sun? Why is it unmanly for a man to weep?

He looks up at her and she takes him in her arms.

LAURA

Mama's here. I was your Mama before, remember? When we first came together and I held your big, strong body, and you held on to me like some lost, unwanted child.

CAPTAIN

I was an unwanted child. That's what I was. Not knowing why or how to deal with it. Until you. When you accepted me, I thought: "Now I'm whole – now I'm complete!" I let you take me over – me, a soldier, a commander of men. You were a goddess from another world and I was your child.

LAURA

But you weren't my child. You were my lover and it
felt like incest. Like sleeping with my own son.

CAPTAIN

That's why I was even rougher when you held back. To
prove I was a man.

LAURA

The mother in me was your friend – but the woman,
the lover? No. I couldn't give myself to you. Not fully.
So, I took what I wanted. But you're still the man. You
have the upper hand.

CAPTAIN

No, you have it. You've always had that. You
hypnotized me till I could neither hear, see nor
think. You could make me believe a raw potato was a
peach, your stupid ideas brilliant. I'd have committed
crimes for you. I didn't know you lacked intelligence –
reason; that everything depended on your whim,
your mood. When I woke up, and saw the damage, my
honour had to be restored – by action, by some noble
cause – so I turned to science. Now, when I'm about to
receive recognition for my work, you chop my arm off.
I'm without honour. A man can't live without honour.

LAURA

But a woman ...

CAPTAIN

She has children. He doesn't. We live in illusion.
When women grow old and cease to be women, they
grow beards. What about men? No longer cocks but
capons – useless to the hens sitting in the moonlight

among the ruins. Nothing but fantasy. All a dream
with no awakening.

LAURA

You should have been a poet. I'm tired. You'll have to
save the rest of these fantasies for tomorrow.

CAPTAIN

No. No more fantasies. Do you hate me?

LAURA shrugs

CAPTAIN

We're so different. If we *are* descended from apes it
must be from two different species.

LAURA

What are you saying?

CAPTAIN

What I'm saying is: this is a war. And one of us has to
lose.

LAURA

Which one?

CAPTAIN

The weaker, of course.

LAURA

So the stronger is in the right?

CAPTAIN

He has the power.

LAURA

Might means right?

CAPTAIN

(*Nods.*) In effect.

LAURA

Then I win.

CAPTAIN

So, you have the power do you?

LAURA

Yes. And I'll have the law on my side too tomorrow
when I have you certified.

CAPTAIN

Certified?

LAURA

When you're safely in the asylum, I'll be free to bring
up my child in my own way without any interference
from you!

CAPTAIN

And how will you pay for everything?

LAURA

With your pension.

CAPTAIN

And how, may I ask, are you going to have me
certified?

LAURA

With this letter - a copy of which I've had signed by
witnesses and lodged with the authorities.

CAPTAIN

What letter?

LAURA

(*Moving to the door*) Your letter to the doctor saying
you were insane! (*He stands, transfixed.*) It's over.
You're not needed. Your responsibilities as a father

and breadwinner aren't needed anymore. Since you won't accept that my will and my intelligence are more than equal to yours, you must go!

She leaves.

The CAPTAIN picks up the lamp and throws it after her.

Fade to black.

ACT TWO –SCENE TWO

Lights up on the same scene.

The lamp has been replaced by another, and a chair now barricades the concealed door. The sound of heavy steps above.

LAURA enters with MARGRET.

LAURA

Did he give you the keys?

MARGRET

I took them from his clothes when I left them out for Nöjd to brush.

LAURA

Nöjd's on duty today?

MARGRET

Yes.

LAURA

Give me the keys.

MARGRET

Oh dear. *(She hands over the keys.)* I feel like a thief.
Is that him up there? *(She looks up at the ceiling.)*
Back and forth – back and forth.

LAURA

Is the door locked?

MARGRET

Oh, it's locked all right!

LAURA opens the desk and sits at it.

LAURA

Calm down. If we stay calm, everything will be fine.

A KNOCK. She screams.

LAURA

Who's that?

MARGRET looks outside.

NÖJD

(Head around the door) It's me, ma'am.

LAURA

Let him in.

NÖJD

(Holding out a letter) Dispatch from the Colonel.

LAURA

I'll take it.

She holds out her hand, so he gives it to her. She reads and nods.

LAURA

Yes! Nöjd, have you emptied all the rifles and
cartridge bags?

NÖJD

Like you said, ma'am.

LAURA

Good. Wait outside while I answer the Colonel's letter.

NÖJD goes. LAURA begins to write.

The sound of SAWING.

MARGRET

Oh, my Lord, what's he doing now?

LAURA

Quiet! I'm trying to write.

MARGRET

(To herself) God have mercy on us! How is it going to end?

LAURA

Ssh. Give this to Nöjd and don't say a word to my mother.

MARGRET takes the letter and goes. LAURA rifles the desk, pulling out papers. She looks up as the PASTOR enters.

He takes a chair and sits beside her.

PASTOR

My dear sister, what on earth's wrong? I've been out all day. They've just told me.

LAURA

I've been through the worst twenty-four hours of my life.

PASTOR

You seem well enough.

LAURA

Well, I've survived. When I think what could have happened!

PASTOR

What's going on? I've been hearing all kinds of stories.

LAURA

It began with his deranged idea that he's not Bertha's father. And it ended when he threw a burning lamp in my face!

PASTOR

But that's dreadful!

LAURA

Yes. The doctor has sent to the asylum for a straitjacket. I've written to the Colonel. Now I'm trying to sort out all this. *(She indicates the papers.)* You've never seen such a mess!

PASTOR

I've always been afraid of this. Fire and water – they don't mix.

LAURA opens a drawer.

PASTOR

What's in there?

LAURA

Look at all this crap!

PASTOR

That's your doll. Your favourite doll. I remember that! Good heavens! Your christening cap. Bertha's rattle. What are these? Your letters – tied up in purple ribbon. *(He blows his nose.)* He must have loved you Laura, to keep these things.

LAURA

I daresay he loved me once. But times change.

PASTOR

(He picks up a large paper.) The receipt for a funeral plot! Well, better that than the asylum. What's your part in all this?

LAURA

What do you mean?

PASTOR

(Looks her straight in the face) What have you done?

LAURA

(She stares back) It's not my fault he's mad.

He continues to stare into her face, then he suddenly turns away.

PASTOR

(Defeated). Oh well, blood is thicker than water I suppose.

LAURA

What do you mean by that?

PASTOR

Just that you're going to be free to do what you want.

LAURA

I don't understand.

PASTOR

Leaving me to be guardian to your afflicted, freethinking spouse, no doubt.

LAURA

Would you please not insult my husband?

PASTOR

Oh you're good, Laura. Very good. Too good for me!
You'd chew off your own leg in a trap. No accomplices
for you! Oh no, not your brother, not even your own
conscience.

He pushes her to the mirror.

PASTOR

Look at yourself. Go on! Take a look!

LAURA

I never look at myself.

PASTOR

I'm not surprised.

He takes her hand and scrutinizes it.

LAURA

What?

PASTOR

Not one speck. (*He sniffs her hand*) Not even a whiff
of blood. An invisible murder – beyond the arm of the
law. Brilliant – absolutely brilliant. But you'd better
watch out. If he ever gets loose, he'll break you in
pieces.

LAURA

You talk a lot, don't you? Bad conscience, is it? If
you've got any proof, let's see it.

PASTOR

I don't.

LAURA

No, you don't. So why not go and look after your flock?
Including my husband. I've got more important
things to do.

The DOCTOR enters.

LAURA

Oh, doctor! Thank you for coming. You'll help won't
you? Not that there's much we can do. Listen!

They listen to the KNOCKING.

LAURA

D'you hear it?

DOCTOR

Yes. I gather there's been some violence here.

PASTOR

(*Ironic*) I'm afraid so.

LAURA

(*Irritated*). Ohh!

DOCTOR

What needs to be decided is whether it was the
product of anger or psychosis. Mrs. Lassen, it's up to
you. Do you want your husband imprisoned, or fined,
for assault? Or do you want him sent to the asylum?

LAURA hesitates.

DOCTOR

You have no strong feelings either way? Pastor?

PASTOR

There'll be a scandal whatever we choose.

LAURA

If he's just ordered to pay a fine he'll do it again!

DOCTOR

And if he's sent to prison he'll be out in no time. So, do we agree that it's best to have him certified? Where's the Nurse?

LAURA

Why?

DOCTOR

She must put on the straitjacket. But not until I give the order. One moment.

He goes out, and immediately returns with a bundle under his arm.

DOCTOR

Please ask the Nurse to come in.

LAURA rings.

PASTOR

This is awful!

MARGRET enters. The DOCTOR produces the straitjacket.

DOCTOR

When I give you the sign, I want you to put this on the Captain. Approach him from behind to avoid any struggle. Fasten the sleeves behind his back, put the straps through these buckles, and harness him to the chair. Can you do that?

MARGRET

No I couldn't, Doctor. I couldn't!

LAURA

Why don't you do it yourself?

DOCTOR

He doesn't trust me. Normally you'd be the one to
do it, but he doesn't trust you either. How about you,
Pastor?

PASTOR

Me? No way!

LAURA rings. NÖJD enters.

LAURA

Did you deliver the letter?

NÖJD

Yes, ma'am.

DOCTOR

Ah, Nöjd. As you know, the Captain's been taken ill.
His mind's given way. We need you to help us look
after him.

NÖJD

If it's for the Captain sir, nothing's too much to ask.
He knows that.

DOCTOR

We need you to put this jacket on him.

MARGRET

No! He can't. He'll be too rough! I'll do it. Tell him to
wait outside in case I need him.

There is LOUD KNOCKING on the concealed door.

DOCTOR

It's him! Hide the jacket under that shawl.

Margret hides it.

DOCTOR

Good, now outside everyone please. Pastor, you stay.

MARGRET

(*Going*) Lord in Heaven help us.

LAURA closes the desk.

She and NÖJD leave.

The door bursts open, the chair overturned, and the CAPTAIN appears. His arms are full of books. He topples them onto the table, picking them out in turn as he speaks.

CAPTAIN

You see, it's all here! I'm not mad. It's all here! (*Picks up a book, and waves the marker.*) The Odyssey. Book 1, line 215. (*Looks at cover*) Uppsala translation. Telemachus to Athene: "My mother claims that the man known as Odysseus is my father. Can I be sure? Can any man know for certain by whom he is sired?" And he says this of the virtuous Penelope. And here – look. (*He picks up a Bible; throws away the marker.*) The prophet Ezekiel "The fool saith: 'Lo, here is my father!' but who can say truly from whose loins he is sprung?" Well, that's clear enough! And what do we have here? Merslekon's 'History of Russian Literature.' (*He furrows for the place.*) Ah. "Aleksander Pushkin, Russia's greatest poet, died more from the agony of suspecting his wife of infidelity than from the bullet he took in the fatal duel. On his deathbed, he asserted her innocence. Idiot! Fool! Jonas – you here? And the Doctor of course. Have I told you what I said to the Englishwoman when she complained that the Irish

throw burning lamps at their wives? "Well, when a
woman goads a man ... "

DOCTOR

Captain ...

CAPTAIN

Shut up, I'm not talking to you. You're the enemy.
(To the Pastor:) Tell me, Jonas, you're the father of
your children, aren't you? Are you? Are you sure?
Remember that tutor you had? The young, good
looking one? The one they all gossiped about?

PASTOR

Be careful what you say.

CAPTAIN

Put your hand here. *(Touches his own head.)* Can you
feel two bumps?

The PASTOR does so, uncertainly.

CAPTAIN

Oh! You've gone pale! I wonder why? We're laughing
stocks. All of us. Every married man on earth. Isn't
that so, Doctor? How was your marriage? Wasn't
there a young subaltern billeted with you? Let me
see, wasn't he called ... *(He leans and whispers in
the Doctor's ear. The Doctor stiffens.)* Now he's as
white as a sheet! I knew him, by the way. Major in the
Dragoons ...

DOCTOR

(Upset) Captain, could we please change the subject?

CAPTAIN

You see? He wants to change the subject!

PASTOR

Calm down. You're acting like a madman.

CAPTAIN

And so would you – both of you! Cuckolds! *(He picks up the photograph album.)* Dear God, there she is. My daughter. Mine? Who knows? There's only one way to be sure. Get married to placate society, divorce, live together in sin and adopt your own children. At least then if you're the father and she's your adopted child, well, that's something you can be sure of. But that's no good to me now – now you've stolen it from me.

PASTOR

Stolen what?

CAPTAIN

My immortality. What's the good of science, philosophy – life itself – without honour? I grafted my right arm, half my brain, half my spine onto another stem to make a more perfect tree. A woman with a knife sliced through the graft leaving half a man. She grows and thrives using the best of me, given to her in love. What's left withers and dies! Do what you want. I don't care. I don't exist anymore.

The DOCTOR whispers to the PASTOR.

The PASTOR nods in agreement and they exit.

The CAPTAIN sits, slumped in his chair.

BERTHA runs in.

BERTHA

Daddy?

He looks up as she approaches and stands before him, gazing down at him.

BERTHA

Are you ill? (*He gazes up at her.*) You know what you did? You threw a lamp at Mama!

CAPTAIN

I did?

BERTHA

Yes! You could have hurt her.

CAPTAIN

What if I had?

BERTHA

You're not my father when you speak like that.

CAPTAIN

What did you say? I'm not your father? Who _is_ your father?

BERTHA

Not you, anyway.

CAPTAIN

Who then? You seem to know. Still at it, are they? I never thought to hear my own child tell me to my face she wasn't my daughter. If I'm not your father, what does that make your mother?

BERTHA

Stop it.

CAPTAIN

A slut.

BERTHA

You are not to say such things about Mama.

CAPTAIN

Yes, stick together, like always.

BERTHA

Daddy!

CAPTAIN

Don't use that word.

BERTHA

Daddy, Daddy!

CAPTAIN

(*Draws her close*) Bertha! Oh, my love, of course you're mine. Let me look at you. Look at me. Let me see my own soul in your eyes. But she's there too! Two souls – with mine you love me, with hers – no! You must love only me. Be mine, the offshoot of me, my thoughts, my being ...

BERTHA

No Daddy, I want to be myself.

CAPTAIN

I won't let you. I'm a cannibal. I want to eat you. She wants to eat me but she can't. I'm Saturn who ate his children. Eat or be eaten! If I don't eat you, you will eat me. And you've already shown me your teeth! Don't be afraid, darling, I'm not going to hurt you. He goes to the guns on the wall and takes down a revolver.

BERTHA

(*Trying to evade him*) Mama! Help me! He's going to shoot me!

MARGRET

(*Enters*) What is it? What are you doing?

BERTHA slips out.

CAPTAIN

(*Inspecting the revolver*) Have you taken the
cartridges?

MARGRET

I tidied them away. Now sit down and I'll get them for
you.

She takes him by the arm and persuades him over to the chair. He
sits, his energy gone.

She goes behind him and brings out the straitjacket.

MARGRET

Now dear, remember when you were a little boy and
I used to tuck you up at night and we'd say prayers?
Remember how I'd get up in the night and fetch you
a drink? How I'd light a candle and tell you fairy
stories when you had a bad dream and couldn't sleep?
Do you remember that?

CAPTAIN

(*Relaxing*) Yes. Go on.

MARGRET

All right, but you must sit quiet and listen. Do you
remember when you took the big carving knife to
make a boat and I had to coax it back by telling you a
story so's you wouldn't hurt yourself. "Give me that
snake," I said, "before it bites!" And you let go. And
the times you wouldn't get dressed, so I'd say you'd be
a prince in a golden coat and I'd take your little jacket
and I'd say: "In we go – both arms!" and then I'd say

"Sit still now. Be a good boy while I do you up." *(She has the straitjacket on him.)* And then I'd say: "Stand up and we'll see how you look." And then: "Bedtime!"

CAPTAIN

Bedtime? What are you talking about? Damnation! What have you done to me? *(He tries to free himself)* Goddammit, woman! You as well? Out-manoeuvred! I can't even kill myself!

MARGRET

Oh my dear, forgive me. I couldn't let you hurt the child.

CAPTAIN

Why not? Life is Hell! Children belong in Heaven!

MARGRET

What do you know about Heaven?

CAPTAIN

It can't be less than I know about life.

MARGRET

You must humble your heart and pray for mercy. It's not too late. It wasn't too late for the thief on the Cross. Didn't Jesus say: "Today shalt thou be with me in Paradise?"

CAPTAIN

Croaking over my corpse already are you, you old crow?

MARGRET affronted, takes out her prayer book.

CAPTAIN

(Calls) Nöjd? Nöjd, are you there?

NÖJD enters.

CAPTAIN

Throw her out! Trying to shove her prayer book
down my throat. Shove her out the window – up the
chimney – anywhere!

NÖJD

(*Looks towards MARGRET*) Captain, I can't do that.
Tell me to take on half a dozen Cossacks, I'll do it. But
a woman? I'm sorry. (*He shakes his head*).

CAPTAIN

Can't get the better of her, eh?

NÖJD

Of course I could, sir. But I can't raise my hand to a
woman.

CAPTAIN

They've been raising their hands to me, Goddammit!

NÖJD

Just can't do it, sir. It goes against the blood.

LAURA enters, gestures for NÖJD to go. He exits quickly.

CAPTAIN

Who was that queen who owned Hercules as a slave?
Omphale! Omphale, the queen of Lydia! Here she is,
Omphale, bearing the club while Hercules winds the
wool.

LAURA

Oh my gosh! Look at you. Ohh! You don't really think
I'm your enemy, do you?

CAPTAIN

You're all my enemies. My mother who starved me in
the womb; my vicious bully of a sister; my first love

who destroyed my confidence, my nurse, my turncoat
daughter and – most of all – you.

LAURA

Me?

CAPTAIN

For bleeding me white and throwing away the bones.

LAURA

I never planned this. It never entered my head. If
it did, I wasn't aware of it. It's true I've wanted to
be free. But, if I've hurt you, I'm sorry. It wasn't on
purpose.

CAPTAIN

What use is that to me, even if it's true? Whose fault
is it? Yours? Mine? Marriage? In the old days, a
man married a wife. Now he enters a partnership
with a businesswoman and seduces other women on
the side. What happened to 'love you till death do us
part'? And what of the issue of this limited company?
Who pays when the crash comes? Who honours the
cheques? Who's the father of our child?

LAURA

You are.

CAPTAIN

I can't believe you. That's what's so terrible! Nothing's
real. Nothing's definite. Nothing to fight but shadows.
If I <u>knew</u> it to be true, I could fight. It's <u>not</u> knowing!
My brain races on and on till it bursts into flame! I'm
cold.

LAURA spreads her shawl over him.

MARGRET goes off to fetch a pillow.

LAURA

Give me your hand, dear.

CAPTAIN

My hand? You've tied it behind my back! Omphale –
Omphale. Oh, I can feel your shawl on my mouth. It's
soft and warm and smells of vanilla like your hair
when you were young and we used to walk in the
birch woods. So lovely, with the primroses and the
thrushes. Did you want it to come to this? I didn't.
Somebody did. Who?

LAURA

God.

MARGRET enters with a pillow.

CAPTAIN

The god of war then – or goddess of war. Take this cat
off me ...

MARGRET removes the shawl, and puts a pillow behind his neck.

CAPTAIN

Get my tunic, put that over me.

MARGRET takes down his tunic and lays it over him.

CAPTAIN

Omphale! That's better. My skin that you'd have off
me. Cunning, nefarious women, preaching peace and
disarmament. Wake up, Hercules! They'll trick us out
of our armour! They'll tell us it's tinsel! Away goes
the armourer. Now it's the seamstress. Force gives
way to weakness. Damn you! I could curse the lot of
you! What's this pillow, Margret, it's hard. Let me put
my head on your lap.

MARGRET lets him put his head on her lap.

CAPTAIN

Ah, that's better. Lean over so that I can feel your breast. Oh, it's warm! So good to sleep on a woman's breast. The mother or the mistress. The mother most of all.

LAURA

Do you want to see her, your child?

CAPTAIN

A man doesn't have children. Women have children. We die childless. The future's theirs, not ours. Dear Lord, thou who lovest the meek . . .

MARGRET

(*Whispers*) He's praying!

CAPTAIN

No, I just, want to go to sleep. Put me to sleep. I'm tired . . . So tired. Good night, Margret, blessed among women . . .

He raises himself up, but falls back with a cry into her lap.

LAURA runs to the door.

LAURA

Doctor!

The DOCTOR runs on, followed by the PASTOR.

LAURA

Help me – is it too late? He's not breathing.

DOCTOR

(*Feeling a pulse.*) He's had a stroke.

PASTOR

Is he dead?

Everyone is in shock.

DOCTOR

No, not dead. And he may recover consciousness – but what level of consciousness we don't know. We'll have to wait and see.

MARGRET

Pastor, in his last moment he was praying!

PASTOR

(To LAURA) Is that true?

LAURA

Yes.

DOCTOR

(Examines the CAPTAIN) I can't do anymore. I leave him to you, Pastor.

BERTHA

(Runs in to her MOTHER, weeping.) Mama! Oh Mama!

LAURA

(Embracing her). Ah my darling. My own sweet, darling girl!

Fade to black.

The End

THE DANCE OF DEATH

by August Strindberg

English version
by Pam Gems

For Antonia Bird

THE DANCE OF DEATH

CHARACTERS

EDGAR	A Captain in the Artillery
ALICE	His wife, formerly an actress
KURT	Alice's cousin
JENNY	The maid
OLD WOMAN	
SENTRY	

THE DANCE OF DEATH

ACT ONE

ACT ONE – SCENE ONE

The interior of a circular grey fortress tower.

Upstage, glass doors with shoreline emplacements and the sea in sight. A piano, sewing table, easy chairs. A writing table with a telegraph apparatus, a whatnot with photographs, a chaise longue and a sideboard. On the wall a large theatrical portrait of a woman flanked by beribboned laurel wreaths. By the door is a stand for swords and coats. A desk, a barometer, and, in the corner, a tall porcelain stove.

An autumn evening. Outside, the SENTRY can be seen, his sabre glittering in the evening sun. The sea dark and still.

The CAPTAIN sits by the sewing table, fingering his cigar, which is not alight. He wears shabby undress uniform, is booted and spurred. He looks bored and tired.

ALICE sits in an armchair. She, too, looks tired, but her manner is more expectant.

CAPTAIN

(*Gestures at the piano*) You're not going to play?

ALICE

(*Indifferent*) What do you want?

He shrugs.

ALICE

You don't like my repertoire?

CAPTAIN

You don't like mine.

ALICE

(After a pause) Do you want the doors open?

He doesn't respond

ALICE

Leave them then. *(Pause)* Why aren‹t you smoking?

CAPTAIN

I've gone off it.

ALICE

(Almost friendly) I thought it was your only
enjoyment.

CAPTAIN

Enjoyment? What's that?

ALICE

Don't ask me. *(Pause)* Isn't it time for your whisky?

CAPTAIN

I'll have it later. What's for supper?

ALICE

How should I know? Ask Kristin.

CAPTAIN

The mackerel will be running. *(No response.)* It is
autumn.

ALICE

(Sarcastic) Yes. It's autumn.

CAPTAIN

Indoors and out. (*Slight pause*) Never mind the chill, there are worse things than a grilled mackerel with a slice of lemon and a glass of Burgundy – white Burgundy. Any left in the cellar?

ALICE

We haven't <u>had</u> a cellar for the last five years, as far as I know.

CAPTAIN

It's your department. (*Slight pause*) You'll need to lay some in.

ALICE

What for? Why?

CAPTAIN

The celebrations.

ALICE

What celebrations?

CAPTAIN

For the silver wedding.

ALICE

(*Mystified*) Silver wedding? Whose?

CAPTAIN

Ours!

ALICE

Ours? Our silver wedding? You want to celebrate our silver wedding?

CAPTAIN

Why not?

ALICE

Celebrate twenty-five long years of misery? Are you
serious?

CAPTAIN

Why not?

ALICE

We'd do better to keep our heads down.

CAPTAIN

(*Slight pause*) We might as well try and enjoy what's
left.

ALICE

The sooner it's over the better as far as I'm concerned.
What's left!

CAPTAIN

What's left, in the end, is a barrow-load of muck for
the garden.

ALICE

So the only point of all this misery is to end up as
manure!

CAPTAIN

Don't blame me.

ALICE

(*After a pause*) Is the post in?

CAPTAIN

Yes.

ALICE

The butcher's bill?

CAPTAIN

I think so.

He fishes in his pocket, takes out a piece of paper, and searches for his glasses. ALICE waits irritably. He puts on his glasses, taking his time, and looks at the paper with heavy concentration.

ALICE

Well?

CAPTAIN

(*Thrusts the paper at her*) You read it.

ALICE

What's the matter, can't you see?

CAPTAIN

You'd need a magnifying glass to read that.

ALICE

Your eyes are going!

CAPTAIN

Nothing wrong with my eyes.

ALICE

It's old age!

CAPTAIN

Old age – me? Rubbish.

ALICE

At least I haven't reached that stage yet.

CAPTAIN

(*Takes off his glasses.*) Hmph!

ALICE

(*Snatching the bill and opening her mouth at the size of the debt*) Can we pay this?

CAPTAIN

It'll keep.

ALICE

Until next year I suppose. When they've kicked you out on a miserable pension, and you're ill again.

CAPTAIN

I'm never ill. Off colour, yes – not ill. I'll live another twenty years.

ALICE

The Doctor doesn't think so.

CAPTAIN

Doctor!

ALICE

He should know.

CAPTAIN

There's nothing wrong with me. There never was. There never will be. I'll die like a soldier, with my spurs on.

ALICE

(*After a pause.*) He's giving a party tonight.

CAPTAIN

We're not invited because we don't choose to mix! And we don't choose to mix because they are scum, the lot of them.

ALICE

(*Drily*) Every man and woman on this Island.

CAPTAIN

Yes.

ALICE

Except you.

CAPTAIN

Precisely.

ALICE

What sets you apart? Why should you be exempt?

CAPTAIN

Because, whatever they throw at me I behave with honour. Like a gentleman. Not scum.

ALICE

(*After a pause.*) Cards?

CAPTAIN

If you say so.

ALICE

(*Takes out cards from the sewing table and begins to shuffle*) You know he's got the Regimental Band. The Regimental Band, playing for a private party. How has he managed that?

CAPTAIN

By licking the Colonel's arse! By creeping off to town with him. I wonder what for. If that's what you choose to do ...

ALICE

(*Dealing*) I <u>was</u> friends with Gerda. Till I caught her cheating.

CAPTAIN

They're all cheats. What's trumps?

ALICE

Put your glasses on – spades!

CAPTAIN

(*Not pleased*) Oh.

ALICE

(*Plays a card*) Now all the <u>new</u> wives have turned
against us.

CAPTAIN

What does that matter? We're not inviting them here,
so what's the difference? I'll manage on my own,
thank you … always have, always will.

ALICE

I worry that it's bad for the children. Growing up
without friends.

CAPTAIN

Friends? What do they want friends for? If they want
friends, they can find them in town – my trick! Have
you got any trumps left?

ALICE

Yes – that was mine!

CAPTAIN

Six and eight. That's fifteen.

ALICE

Fourteen. Fourteen!

CAPTAIN

Six and eight, that's fourteen points – plus two,
sixteen. (*Yawns*) Your deal.

ALICE

Are you tired?

CAPTAIN

No.

ALICE lifts her head, listens.

> ALICE

Listen!

He tilts his head to listen.

> ALICE

Can you hear the music?

He ignores this. They play.

> ALICE

I wonder if they invited Kurt?

> CAPTAIN

Kurt?

> ALICE

He'll have had time to settle in.

> CAPTAIN

Time enough to unpack a dress shirt, I daresay. Not enough to see us.

They play.

> ALICE

Such a surprise. What is he here for?

> CAPTAIN

Quarantine.

> ALICE

(Alarmed) Quarantine?

He takes the trick.

> CAPTAIN

New post. Quarantine Master.

ALICE

Quarantine ... ?

CAPTAIN

General orders. Precaution against disease.

ALICE

It'll be wonderful to have him here. *(No response.)* He
is my cousin. We shared the same name once.

CAPTAIN

Where's the honour in that?

ALICE

You leave my family alone, I'll do the same for yours.
(Takes the trick.)

CAPTAIN

All right, don't start on that one.

ALICE

(As they pore over their cards) I don't understand.
Shouldn't a Quarantine Master be a doctor?

CAPTAIN

No, just a pen-pusher. Suit Kurt down to the ground.
Well, he's never amounted to anything.

ALICE

Poor Kurt. He's had such a hard life.

CAPTAIN

Cost me money, you mean. A man who abandons his
wife and children deserves a hard life.

ALICE

Edgar, there's no need for that.

CAPTAIN

Off he goes to America. What's he been doing there?
Well, he hasn't been missed here.

ALICE

Do be quiet.

CAPTAIN

Nice enough lad. At least there was someone to talk
to. I enjoyed our discussions.

ALICE

Only because he always agreed with you.

CAPTAIN

At least you could talk to him. Nobody here
understands a word I say – imbeciles, the lot of them.
(*Throws down his cards.*)

ALICE

(*Packing up the cards*) Odd though. Well, a
coincidence.

CAPTAIN

Coincidence?

ALICE

Kurt arriving here in time for our silver wedding ...

CAPTAIN

Why?

ALICE

... whether we celebrate it or not.

CAPTAIN

Oh, you mean because he brought us together – got
you married off.

ALICE

Thank you.

CAPTAIN

For better or for worse. He fixed that up all right.

ALICE

Of course he didn't.

CAPTAIN

Yes, he did.

ALICE

Kurt was in a silly mood, that's all.

CAPTAIN

Which we've had to pay for.

ALICE

Yes.

CAPTAIN

For twenty-five years.

ALICE

I've often wondered. If I'd stayed in the theatre ...
I don't know of one friend of mine who isn't famous
now.

CAPTAIN

(*Rising*) Here we go again. Whisky!

He crosses to the sideboard and pours himself a large whisky and
soda. He stands, drinking.

CAPTAIN

If there was a rail here to put your foot on we could be
in the American Bar.

ALICE

Ah ... Copenhagen!

CAPTAIN

We'll have one built, to remind us.

ALICE

We enjoyed Copenhagen.

CAPTAIN

(*Drinking*) Remember the navarin au pommes at
Nimb's Restaurant? Mmm!

ALICE

What I remember most are the concerts in the Tivoli
Gardens.

CAPTAIN

Refined as ever.

ALICE

You should be glad of it.

CAPTAIN

I am.

ALICE

Only when you need to show me off.

The CAPTAIN freshens his drink, becomes mellower with the
whisky.

CAPTAIN

Hullo, I can hear music!

ALICE

They must be dancing.

CAPTAIN

Oompapah – oompapah!

ALICE

(*Listening*) A waltz, they're playing a waltz – oh it's
so long since I went to a dance.

CAPTAIN

Still capable, are you?

ALICE

Me?

CAPTAIN

Come on, face it. Your dancing days are over.

ALICE

I'm ten years younger than you!

CAPTAIN

I never met a woman who wasn't.

ALICE

Don't be so stupid. You may be an old man. I'm still in
my prime.

CAPTAIN

Oh, you can lay on the charm. To other people. When
it suits you.

ALICE

Could we have the lamp lit?

CAPTAIN

We could.

ALICE

Then ring!

The CAPTAIN, taking his time, walks to the desk and rings the bell.

JENNY enters.

CAPTAIN

Ah, Jenny. Good evening. Would you be very nice and light the lamps for me please. Can you manage?

ALICE

(*Sharply, to JENNY*) Light the lamp.

JENNY

(*Impudent*) Yes, my lady. At once my lady.

She lights the ceiling lamp, watched by the CAPTAIN.

ALICE

Did you wipe the glass?

JENNY

It'll do.

ALICE

What sort of answer is that?

CAPTAIN

Alice ...

ALICE

(*To JENNY*) Get out, I'll do it myself.

JENNY

(*Going*) Go on, then.

ALICE

Get out!

JENNY

You'll be sorry if I do go.

JENNY exits.

ALICE

(*Uneasy*) Do you think she will?

CAPTAIN

What?

ALICE

Go.

CAPTAIN

Wouldn't surprise me.

ALICE

Oh!

CAPTAIN

We'll be stuck if she does.

ALICE

Wretched girls.

CAPTAIN

They're polite enough to me.

ALICE

Because you creep round them. Different matter
with the officers, isn't it? You're like all bullies, sweet
enough when you've got the upper hand.

He doesn't reply.

ALICE

(*ALICE fidgets.*) You don't think she'll leave, do you?

CAPTAIN

You'd better go down and talk to her.

ALICE

Me? Why me?

CAPTAIN

If I go I'll be accused of flirting.

ALICE

But what if she does leave? I'll be left to do it myself.
Ruin my hands like last time.

CAPTAIN

I'll tell you something else. If Jenny goes, Kristin will
go too.

ALICE

Oh, stop it.

CAPTAIN

We won't get another girl to come out here.

ALICE

Why not?

CAPTAIN

The ferry pilot warns them off. If he doesn't, my
sentries do.

ALICE

What? You mean they … ? As well as eating us out
of house and home because you're too scared to keep
them out of the kitchen!

CAPTAIN

If I did that, they'd all put in for transfers. We'd be left
without a garrison.

ALICE

(*Mutters*) Then we'd be ruined.

CAPTAIN

Look, the mess committee is applying to His Majesty
for a subsistence grant.

ALICE

For us?

CAPTAIN

For the sentries.

ALICE burst out laughing.

CAPTAIN

What?

ALICE

For the sentries!

CAPTAIN

At least you find it funny … you even laughed.

ALICE

I've almost forgotten how to.

CAPTAIN

(*Lighting his cigar*) I shouldn't do that. Life's boring
enough as it is.

ALICE

(*She picks up the cards.*) Do you want to play again?

CAPTAIN

No. I'm tired.

ALICE

(*After a pause.*) My own cousin. Goes off to a party
with strangers before he comes to see us. How could
he do that?

CAPTAIN

Forget it.

ALICE

Did you see the piece in the paper? About the new
arrivals? After his name, they put 'independent.'
That means of independent means! Kurt!

CAPTAIN

He must have come into some money. So, he'll be throwing his weight about. Two can play at that game.

The TELEGRAPH apparatus begins to click.

ALICE

Who could that be?

CAPTAIN

Sssh.

ALICE

What's it saying?

CAPTAIN

Be quiet, I can't hear. (*He listens.*) It's from the children.

He crosses to the apparatus and taps out a reply.

The apparatus responds. The CAPTAIN answers.

ALICE

Well?

CAPTAIN

Wait a minute! (*He clicks a final signal.*) It's the children. They're down at headquarters. Judith's not well, she's off school.

ALICE

Again? She's working too hard! What an earth is the hurry? She can wait another year, take her exams then.

CAPTAIN

You tell her.

ALICE

Why not you?

CAPTAIN

I have told her, over and over again. They don't listen,
you know that.

ALICE

Not in your house, they don't.

The CAPTAIN yawns loudly.

ALICE

Must you do that?

CAPTAIN

What am I supposed to do? Every day the same
"not in your house" and then I say: "it's not only my
house." I've said it five hundred times. Why not a
yawn instead? Meaning 'I can't be bothered' or 'suit
yourself' or 'let's leave it, my angel.'

ALICE

You're being very charming tonight.

CAPTAIN

Surely it's time to eat.

ALICE

I hear they ordered supper from the mainland. The
Grand Hotel, no less.

CAPTAIN

The Grand? That means grouse. Finest eating bird
in the world, so long as they don't cook it in lard.
Criminal that.

ALICE

Must you talk about food?

CAPTAIN

I wonder what they're drinking. Some rubbish I
daresay.

ALICE

Do you want me to play for you?

CAPTAIN

(*Sits at his desk*) The last resort! (*He hums the
Funeral March.*) Dum dum da dum. 'Oh, I'm so
miserable. Oh, it's unbearable! Why doesn't he die?'
(*Sings cheerfully*) Diddlepom, diddlepom, diddle
pom pom pom! Speaking of which, let's have our own
party. Isn't there a bottle of champagne in the cellar?

ALICE

That's mine. It was a present.

CAPTAIN

Trust her to be mean.

ALICE

Not as mean as some – at least to their wives.

CAPTAIN

Right. No champagne. (*He hums, searching for ideas.
Holds out his arms.*) Dance?

ALICE

You?

CAPTAIN

Perhaps we should import some company.

ALICE

We tried that.

CAPTAIN

It changed the atmosphere.

ALICE

And then what happened?

Silence. A KNOCK at the door.

ALICE

Who's that at this hour? Well – go and open the door!

He goes.

ALICE

And don't bawl 'Come in!' as though you're in
barracks.

The CAPTAIN goes out, then sticks his head in the door.

CAPTAIN

It's Kristin.

He goes out.

CAPTAIN

Where's Jenny?

Inaudible reply.

The CAPTAIN reappears in the doorway with a visiting card in
his hand.

CAPTAIN

Jenny's left.

ALICE

Oh no! What's that card? Jenny wouldn't leave a card,
who's it from?

He squints, trying to read the small print. She snatches the card
from him, reads.

ALICE

Kurt! It's Kurt! Let him in! Kurt!

The CAPTAIN exits.

CAPTAIN

(Off) Kurt?

ALICE tidies herself swiftly, and comes alive.

The CAPTAIN enters with KURT.

CAPTAIN

Here he is! The renegade returns. Welcome, my dear boy. It's very good to see you.

ALICE

Kurt! *(She embraces him fondly, then stands back to inspect him.)* Welcome home!

KURT

Thank you. It's been a long time.

CAPTAIN

What is it? Fifteen years? We're all older ...

ALICE

Kurt hasn't changed a bit. He looks splendid.

CAPTAIN

Sit down, sit down! Wait – are you engaged for tonight? What are your plans for dinner?

KURT

I've been invited to the Doctor's, but I haven't confirmed.

ALICE

Surely you'd rather eat here, with your relations?

KURT

I'd much prefer to, naturally, but it might be awkward.

CAPTAIN

Awkward? Why?

KURT

He is my new superior.

CAPTAIN

Rubbish! Never be frightened of those in authority. I
never have.

ALICE pulls a face.

KURT

I've only just arrived. I don't want to cause offence on
my first day.

CAPTAIN

Listen to me, my boy. On this island, there is one man
in charge – me. You stick with me, they won't lay a
finger on you.

ALICE

Edgar, that's enough! *(She takes KURT'S hand.)*
Never mind who's in charge. People will think it only
natural if you dine with us.

KURT

Thank you. For the invitation, and for the welcome.

CAPTAIN

Why shouldn't we welcome you?

KURT looks at him warily.

CAPTAIN

All right, we all remember the time when you ...
ah ... when you behaved thoughtlessly. All behind us.
I don't hold grudges. I never have, and I never will.
Not my way.

ALICE turns away at this. They all sit by the sewing table.

CAPTAIN ALICE
So, you've been out in the great, wide world!

KURT
After a fashion. Anyway, here I am, happy to be back with the two of you.

CAPTAIN
Yes, the two of us. The two you married off, twenty-five years ago.

KURT
Is it so long? Surely not. Never mind, it's splendid to see you both, still together after twenty-five years.

CAPTAIN
Oh, ups and downs, ups and downs, but – as you say – still together. She has no cause for complaint, wants for nothing, money pouring in. I'm a well-known writer now, did you know that? Military textbooks.

KURT
I remember! When we last me you'd just published an instruction manual. Is it still in use? It was doing well at the time, I believe.

CAPTAIN
Still in print and still the best!

ALICE
They replaced it.

KURT
Ah.

CAPTAIN
Some inferior rubbish. Quite worthless.

A painful silence.

KURT

Have you been abroad at all?

ALICE

Oh yes! We've been to Copenhagen!

CAPTAIN

Five times. You see, when I captured Alice from the
theatre ...

ALICE

Captured?

CAPTAIN

Yes, captured – as a woman should be!

ALICE

Very heroic.

CAPTAIN

Since she's shoved it down my throat ever since.
'You ruined my career!' I've had to concede trips to
Copenhagen. Five times! (*Counting them out on the
fingers of his left hand.*) Five visits, promised and
fulfilled like a soldier. Ever been to Copenhagen?

KURT

Ah – no.

ALICE

But you've travelled?

KURT

Oh yes.

She looks up at him expectantly.

KURT

Mostly in America.

CAPTAIN

America? Rough sort of place I hear. Full of
savages ...

KURT

It's certainly not Copenhagen.

ALICE

(*After a pause.*) Have you heard anything? Have you
been in touch with your children?

KURT

No.

ALICE

Forgive me, Kurt dear. I shouldn't have brought it up.

KURT

Not at all.

ALICE

It's just – well, it's still painful to remember your
leaving them.

KURT

I didn't leave them. The court awarded custody to
their mother.

CAPTAIN

Never mind about all that mess, you were well out of
it.

KURT

(*After a pause*) How are your children?

ALICE

Very well, thank you. They're at school on the
mainland. Growing up now.

CAPTAIN

Yes. Both clever. The boy has a brilliant mind. He's
bound for the General Staff.

ALICE

If they take him.

CAPTAIN

If! He'll be Minister of Defence!

KURT

Changing the subject – we're setting up the
Quarantine Station here to check incoming ships for
infection. I'll be working directly under the Doctor.
What sort of man is he?

CAPTAIN

He's not a man, he's an ignorant rogue.

KURT

(*To ALICE*) My bad luck, it seems.

ALICE

Not a man you'd warm to. Though not as bad as Edgar
says.

CAPTAIN

He's a rogue. They all are. The Customs' Officer, the
Postmaster, the pilot, the – what does he call himself?
Alderman. Scoundrels the lot!

KURT

All of them?

CAPTAIN

Every man jack. Which is why I keep to myself.
There's not a bullying little bureaucrat in Sweden
who doesn't end up here.

ALICE

(*Ironic*) True.

CAPTAIN

(*Jovial*) Not a reference to me I hope! If there's one
thing I've never been it's a bully, and certainly not
in my own house. My old lady here has nothing to
complain about. Best wife in the world!

ALICE

Kurt, would you like a drink?

KURT

Ah . . . no thank you.

ALICE

You haven't become a . . .

KURT

No, no, no. I've just cut down.

CAPTAIN

American temperance, eh?

KURT

Very like.

CAPTAIN

I've no time for it. A man must be able to hold his
drink.

KURT

I was wondering . . . about the people here. I'm going
to have to work with them, become involved whether
I like it or not.

The wind begins to rise, softly at first.

ALICE

Of course, but there's no need to mix. You'll have us.

KURT

Isn't it lonely? Seeing no-one? Surrounded by people
you dislike?

ALICE

It lacks delight, I can tell you.

CAPTAIN

Not at all! I've had enemies all my life. Believe me,
they're a help, not a hindrance. I've had to fight for
everything I've earned. When they sound that bugle
over me I shall owe nothing. Not to a single soul.

ALICE

As you may gather, Edgar's life has not been strewn
with roses.

CAPTAIN

More like stones and flints. Same for you?

KURT

(Simply) No. I learned the inadequacy of retreat a
long time ago.

CAPTAIN

Retreat?

KURT

Withdrawal then. From society. I take life as it is.

CAPTAIN

Then you're a poor sort of man.

ALICE

Edgar!

CAPTAIN

I mean it. If that's his outlook, he doesn't trust his
own strength to see him through. We may all end up
as a barrow-load of shit. But, as long as you're alive,
it's kick – hit out – survive. That's my philosophy.

KURT

(*Laughs*) It's one way to look at things.

CAPTAIN

But you don't agree.

KURT

No.

CAPTAIN

It's true, all the same!

The wind slams the upstage door. The CAPTAIN rises, and taps
the barometer.

CAPTAIN

I knew it! There's going to be a storm.

ALICE

(*To KURT*) You will stay for supper.

KURT

Thank you, I'd like to.

CAPTAIN

I felt it coming. The barometer's right down.

ALICE

(*Whispers to KURT*) It's his nerves.

CAPTAIN

Time to eat!

ALICE

I'll see to it. You two stay here and philosophize. (*Aside to KURT.*) Don't contradict him, he'll lose his temper. (*Dodges back again.*) And don't ask him why he never became a major.

ALICE goes.

KURT crosses and sits. The CAPTAIN sits down beside him.

CAPTAIN

(*Calls*) And cook us something decent, woman!

ALICE

(*Offstage*) Give me the money and I will!

CAPTAIN

Money, money. That woman treats me like a walking wallet. D'you know the feeling?

KURT

Walking cheque book in my case.

CAPTAIN

(*Laughs*) That's for sure! Women! (*He laughs again.*) You certainly drew the short straw.

KURT

(*Patiently*) Oh, that's all in the past.

CAPTAIN

A real jewel you picked. No, mine's a good woman, for all her faults.

KURT

(*Laughs*) "For all her faults?"

CAPTAIN

What are you laughing at?

KURT

For all her faults.

CAPTAIN

Absolutely. Stand by it. Faithful wife, fine mother. (*He glances off*) She's got a devil of a temper, mind. I've cursed you more than once for saddling me with her.

KURT

(*Mildly*) But I didn't.

CAPTAIN

(*Loudly*) Come on, old chap! Don't talk rubbish! You've forgotten what you don't want to remember!

KURT flinches.

CAPTAIN

Don't take it amiss. I'm used to shouting at people. Giving orders. I hope you're not offended?

KURT

Not in the least. But I must correct you. I didn't bring you two together, quite the opposite.

CAPTAIN

(*Not listening to him*) No. A strange thing, life – don't you think?

KURT

That's certainly true.

CAPTAIN

Take growing old. You wouldn't call that pleasant.
Interesting, perhaps. I'm no age, of course, but ... you
begin to ... you start to ... People you know, you read
of their deaths. All of a sudden, you're alone.

KURT

But you're a lucky man. You have a wife to share your
old age.

CAPTAIN

Lucky?! Yes, I suppose I am. Your children grow up,
leave home. You abandoned yours, of course.

KURT

No! I didn't. They were taken from me.

CAPTAIN

I'm sorry. I shouldn't have brought it up. Didn't mean
to upset you.

KURT

It wasn't like that.

CAPTAIN

Well, whatever happened, best forgotten. All in the
past. Left you on your own though, hasn't it?

KURT

I'm used to it.

CAPTAIN

Can you? Get used to it? Being alone?

KURT

As you can see, I've survived.

CAPTAIN

Ye-es. I was going to ask you. What have you been
doing with yourself for the past fifteen years?

KURT

My dear Edgar! Where to begin?

CAPTAIN

I hear you've come into money.

KURT

Oh, I wouldn't say that.

CAPTAIN

Don't worry, I'm not after a loan.

KURT

You'd be very welcome.

CAPTAIN

Thank you, but I am not without funds. Which is just
as well. If I were, she'd be out of that door.

KURT

No, no …

CAPTAIN

Never lets it pass when funds are low. Likes to rub it
in. I'm not providing for her in the style demanded.

KURT

But surely. You have a good income, didn't you say?

CAPTAIN

Certainly, I do.

KURT

(Smiles) Not big enough?

CAPTAIN

You could say so. Funny thing, life.

KURT

Yes.

CAPTAIN

And people.

The TELEGRAPH begins to click.

KURT

Ah, a telegraph machine! Don't you have a telephone?

CAPTAIN

It's in the kitchen. We don't use it. The telephonists
listen in all the time.

KURT

I see. (*Slight pause.*) It must be a very grim life for
you, marooned out here.

CAPTAIN

Bloody. Absolutely bloody. Tell me, do you believe in
an after-life? Some sort of relief from all this?

KURT

Who knows? Maybe storms and battles there too.

CAPTAIN

If there is a 'there.' My view is – better annihilation.
(*Snaps his fingers*) That's the way I intend to go. Over
in a flash.

KURT

You seem very sure.

CAPTAIN

I am. In a flash. And the day I drop dead, I shall be a happy man.

KURT

Is there something wrong?

CAPTAIN

What?

KURT

You seem distressed. Is there something going on?

CAPTAIN

What?

KURT

It's the atmosphere. You feel it as you come through the door. *(He shudders)* So much … I don't know. If I hadn't told Alice I'd stay for supper, I'd be off.

The CAPTAIN slumps in his chair. His gaze becomes vacant.

KURT, on his feet, turns and looks at him.

KURT

Edgar! What's the matter? *(He shakes the CAPTAIN's shoulders)* Edgar?

CAPTAIN

(Coming to.) Did you say something? *(Looks round)* Oh, it's you, I thought it was Alice. *(He slumps into vacancy again.)*

KURT

My God! *(He goes to the door and calls)* Alice! Alice!

ALICE enters, wearing an apron.

ALICE

What is it?

KURT

I don't know. Look at him!

ALICE

(*Unmoved*) Oh, he goes like that sometimes. I'll play some music. That'll wake him up.

KURT

No, don't do that. Don't! Let me look at him. Can he hear? Can he see?

ALICE

Not when he's like this.

KURT

Alice! Doesn't it worry you? What's going on?

ALICE

Ask that thing there.

KURT

That thing?! He's your husband!

ALICE

He's a stranger to me. As much as he was twenty- five years ago. I know nothing about this man, except . . .

KURT

Sssh! He'll hear you!

ALICE

I've told you. He can't hear a thing.

A BUGLE sounds outside. The CAPTAIN jumps to his feet, and picks up his sabre and cap.

CAPTAIN

I must inspect the sentry posts.

The CAPTAIN marches out.

KURT

Is he ill? Is he out of his mind?

ALICE

How should I know?

KURT

Is he drinking?

ALICE

Not as much as he brags about.

KURT

Sit down. Alice, I want to know.

ALICE

(Sits) What do you want me to say? That I've been a prisoner in this tower for a lifetime? Confined by a man I've always hated? Whom I now detest with such violence that the day he dies, I shall weep with joy?

KURT

But ... why are you together? Why didn't you separate?

ALICE

Good question! Twice we broke off the engagement. Since then, not a day has gone by that we haven't tried to part. But we're welded together. We can't break free! Once, we lived completely separate lives in this house – for five years. Now, what is there to do? Wait for death to set us free.

KURT

But why are you both so alone here? Why do you cut
yourselves off from people?

ALICE

It's him! First, he ejected all my relations from the
house. That's the word he used – 'ejected.' Then my
women friends, neighbours ...

KURT

What about <u>his</u> relations?

ALICE

I turned them out, they were killing me. First my
reputation as an actress, then my good name. Do you
know how I stay in touch with the world now? With
that! (*She points to the telegraph machine.*) I've had
to learn how to use that. Don't tell him, he'd kill me if
he knew.

KURT

But this is horrible. And why does he blame me for
your marriage? You remember how it was. Edgar and
I were friends. He fell in love the first time he saw
you and I warned him off. Forgive me, but I knew how
vile you can be in a temper. Forgive me. It was only
because he pestered me so much that I suggested
he use your brother as a go-between. I was totally
against it.

ALICE

I believe you. But he's been fooling himself for so long,
you'll never get him to change his mind now.

KURT

Oh, let him blame me if it makes him feel better.

ALICE

Hardly fair to you.

KURT

I'm used to that. What hurts is when he says I
abandoned my children.

ALICE

You will come and see us? He seems to like you.
Please don't desert me. We're the most miserable
people on God's earth. *(She weeps.)*

KURT

I've seen one marriage at close quarters. That was
frightening enough – but this is worse. *(Slight pause.)*
Perhaps you should accept things as they are.

ALICE

I can't. *(She gets up.)* It's hopeless.

KURT

I'm so sorry.

ALICE

Do you know what he hates most of all? The thought
that he'll die before me and I'll be free to marry again.

KURT

So he does love you?

ALICE

Possibly. Probably. It doesn't stop him from hating me.

KURT

I know that hell. *(Pause)* Tell me, where are the
children?

ALICE

You know we lost two?

KURT

No, I didn't know. So, you've been through that?

ALICE

Children don't survive here.

KURT

What about the other two?

ALICE

I sent them away!

KURT

For their health?

ALICE

He was turning them against me. They had to
go! What should have been a blessing became a
nightmare. How could they stay in this horrible
house? *(She shudders)* Ohh! Sometimes I think
there's a curse on all of us. *(She lowers her head onto
clasped hands.)* Oh -hah! *(She laughs)* I can't even
feed you.

KURT

I'm sorry?

ALICE

There's nothing to eat! He'll be here in a minute, then
you'll see. You'll see how he is!

KURT

(Rises) I'll go out and find some food for us.

ALICE

(Waves him down) There's nothing to be had. Not
here on the Island at this time of night.

KURT

We must think of something. Make a joke of it. I'll
suggest a drink, and you can play for him. Put him in
a good humour.

ALICE

Look at my hands, I have to lay the fire, clean the
pots, polish the brass!

KURT

But you've got two servants.

ALICE

They all leave. They won't stay here. Oh, if the whole
place would only burn down!

KURT

Alice!

ALICE

I wish the sea would rise and swallow us up.

KURT

Stop it.

ALICE

What will he say? Don't go, Kurt, don't leave me!

KURT

I won't.

ALICE

But when you've gone ...

KURT

Does he beat you?

ALICE

Beat me? No, I'd leave him if he ever did that. I do have some pride.

Outside, shouts of 'Who goes there?' and 'Friend.'

KURT

(*Rises*) Is that him?

ALICE

(*Frightened*) Yes.

KURT

What on earth are we to do?

ALICE

I don't know!

CAPTAIN

(*Enters cheerfully*) There! Now I'm free. Been pouring her heart out, has she? About the terrible life she has here? Out with the violins!

KURT

What's the weather like?

CAPTAIN

Stormy! (*Opens the door slightly, joking*) Bluebeard's Castle and the Maiden in the Tower! Ah, the sentry! Her brothers try to rescue her in vain. There he goes, clip clop, clip clop. Let's have a sword dance. Kurt should see that!

KURT

I'd rather have a good military march.

CAPTAIN

Alice! Alice in your apron. Play! Come on, come on!

ALICE reluctantly sits at the piano. The CAPTAIN bends over her, and pinches her arm.

> CAPTAIN

Been telling lies about me, have you?

> ALICE

No.

He turns away.

ALICE plays 'The Entry of the Boyars.'

The CAPTAIN dances, performing a Hungarian dance, his spurs jangling. He reels and falls behind the desk, unnoticed by the others.

> ALICE

(Calls to him) Do you want it again?

Silence. She turns, and sees the CAPTAIN, hidden from the audience, lying on the floor behind the desk.

> ALICE

Sweet Jesus.

She stands, arms crossed on her chest and sighs deeply, as with relief. KURT turns.

> KURT

What is it? What's happened?

He sees the CAPTAIN, hurries over to him.

> ALICE

Is he dead?

> KURT

I don't know. Help me!

ALICE

(*Motionless*) I can't touch him. Is he dead?

KURT

No. He's alive.

ALICE sighs deeply.

The CAPTAIN staggers to his feet. KURT helps him to a chair.

CAPTAIN

What happened? (*Silence*) What happened?

KURT

You fell. On the floor. Is there something wrong?

CAPTAIN

With me? Nothing. Not that I'm aware of. What are
you looking at me like that for?

KURT

Edgar, you're ill.

CAPTAIN

Rubbish. Play on, Alice – ahh! (*He clutches his head.*)

ALICE

You see? You are ill!

CAPTAIN

Don't start. I'm dizzy, that's all.

KURT

We must get a doctor. I'll go and telephone.

CAPTAIN

I don't want any doctor!

KURT

You must. For our sakes if not your own. They'll hold
us responsible.

CAPTAIN

If he comes in here I'll put a bullet through him.
Ahhh! *(He clutches his head.)*

KURT

I'll telephone.

KURT goes.

CAPTAIN

Get me a glass of water.

ALICE shrugs, takes off her apron, folds it, crosses, taking her time, pours a drink and brings it to him.

CAPTAIN

(Taking it) Very loving.

ALICE

(Standing over him) Are you ill?

CAPTAIN

I do beg your pardon.

ALICE

Well if you are, I hope you can look after yourself.

CAPTAIN

Meaning that you won't?

ALICE

What do you think!

CAPTAIN

The moment you've been waiting for!

ALICE

Which you said would never happen.

CAPTAIN

Why are you in a temper then? Smile!

KURT enters.

KURT

It's monstrous.

ALICE

What did he say?

KURT

He hung up. Just like that!

ALICE

(To CAPTAIN) That's what you get for your
arrogance.

CAPTAIN

It's getting worse. Get a doctor from the mainland.

ALICE

(Crosses to telegraph) I'll need to telegraph.

CAPTAIN

(Half rises, astonished) You know how to work that
thing?

ALICE

(Sending a message) Of course.

CAPTAIN

You deceitful, lying bitch! Go on, do it – quick! *(He
holds out his hand for KURT to sit with him.)* Hold my
hand, I feel as if I'm falling. So strange – ahh …

KURT

Have you had these attacks before?

CAPTAIN

Never.

KURT

While we're waiting for a reply, I'll go across to the
Doctor. Has he treated you before?

CAPTAIN

No.

ALICE

Yes.

KURT

Then he'll know your history. (*Going.*)

ALICE

(*By the telegraph*) Thank you, Kurt. We'll get a reply
soon. You'll come back, won't you?

KURT

I'll be as quick as I can.

KURT exits.

CAPTAIN

He's a good fellow.

ALICE

He always was. Too good to be involved in all this.

CAPTAIN

Funny the way he doesn't want to talk about himself.

ALICE

We haven't asked him.

CAPTAIN

He's seen enough trouble.

ALICE

And kept it to himself. Unlike us. Have we ever known
anybody happy? A happy marriage – family?

They think.

CAPTAIN

(*At last*) The Kraffts?

ALICE

The cousin turned out to be an embezzler, and they couldn't show their faces.

CAPTAIN

That other family?

ALICE

Cancer.

CAPTAIN

(*After a pause.*) I can't think what's wrong.

ALICE

With you?

CAPTAIN

(*He moves, restless.*) It's as if I want to fly out of myself, and dissolve in a cloud of smoke.

ALICE

What do you want?

CAPTAIN

Something to eat. What have you got?

ALICE

(*Rises, nervous*) I'll ask Jenny.

CAPTAIN

She's not here. She left, remember? Ring for Kristin, I need some more water.

ALICE

(*Rings. And again . . .*) That's odd. No answer.

CAPTAIN

Go and see. So long as she hasn't left!

ALICE crosses, opens the door and looks out.

ALICE

What on earth is that? (*Goes and returns*) It's
Kristin's trunk, in the hall.

CAPTAIN

Then she's gone too.

ALICE collapses, weeping.

ALICE

This is hell!

CAPTAIN

And of course, Kurt has to come just now, to see our
humiliation!

ALICE

Do you know what I think? He's gone too. He won't be
back.

CAPTAIN

The same as he always was.

ALICE

There's a curse on us. We're damned. They all ignore
us. It's as if we don't exist.

CAPTAIN

Who gives a damn?

The TELEGRAPH starts to click.

CAPTAIN

Quiet, let me listen. (*He listens. The telegraph stops.*)

ALICE

Well?

CAPTAIN

No-one available. Scum!

ALICE

That's what you get for abusing your doctors. And not paying them.

CAPTAIN

Untrue.

ALICE

Even when you could, you didn't because you said they were crap – as my work was crap, and everybody else's. Now they won't come. And they're cutting off the telephone tomorrow. The only things left working are your rifles and cannons.

CAPTAIN

Don't talk rubbish.

ALICE

You'll see. We owe Kristin six months' wages. Did you know that?

CAPTAIN

Not as much as she's stolen from us.

ALICE

And I've had to borrow from her.

CAPTAIN

That doesn't surprise me.

ALICE

It was for the children! You know that.

CAPTAIN

Kurt timed it well. A rogue like the rest of them. And a coward. He'll be eating his head off at the Doctor's. Saw he wasn't going to get anything here, so off! He hasn't changed.

KURT hurries in.

KURT

Look … my dear Edgar, this is how it is. (*He gets his breath back.*) The Doctor knows all about your heart.

CAPTAIN

Heart?

KURT

He says you've had a bad heart for some time … a hardening …

CAPTAIN

A hardening of the heart?

KURT

He says.

CAPTAIN

Is it dangerous?

KURT

Yes, that's to say …

CAPTAIN

Serious.

KURT

Yes.

CAPTAIN

Death?

KURT

You must take great care. First, no more cigars.

The CAPTAIN throws away his cigar.

KURT

No more whisky. And straight into bed.

CAPTAIN

(*Frightened*) No. That's the end. You never get up again. I'll sleep here, on the sofa. What else did he say?

KURT

He was very friendly. He says he'll come at once. You've only to ask.

CAPTAIN

Friendly? The bloody hypocrite. What else can I eat?

KURT

Not tonight. And for the next few days, nothing but milk.

CAPTAIN

Milk? I can't drink milk. I can't stand the stuff!

KURT

You'll have to learn.

CAPTAIN

I'm too old for that. (*He clutches his head.*) Ohh! (*He suddenly becomes rigid in his chair, staring vacantly into space.*)

ALICE

What did the Doctor say?

KURT

He could die.

ALICE

Thank God!

KURT

Alice, for God's sake! Go and get a pillow and a blanket. We'll put him to bed on the sofa. I'll sit up with him.

ALICE

What about me?

KURT

You seem to make him worse. I should go to bed.

ALICE

Very well. I know you want what's best.

KURT

For both of you. I'm not taking sides in this.

ALICE goes.

KURT picks up the carafe and goes out.

The wind rises and the upstage door blows open. An OLD WOMAN, unpleasant and shabby looking, peers in.

The CAPTAIN wakes up, rises, and looks round.

CAPTAIN

Left me on my own, the devils! (*He sees the OLD WOMAN and jumps, frightened.*) Who's there? What do you want?

OLD WOMAN

I'm just shutting the door, sir.

CAPTAIN

Why? What for?

OLD WOMAN

It blew open. I was just going by.

CAPTAIN

You were going to steal, you old witch!

OLD WOMAN

Oh, no sir. Kristin says there's nothing left worth taking.

CAPTAIN

(*Grinding his teeth*) Kristin!

OLD WOMAN

Good night sir. Sleep well.

She goes, closing the door with emphasis.

ALICE enters with pillows and a blanket.

CAPTAIN

Who was that at the door? Was somebody there?

ALICE

Old Maria, from the poorhouse. She was just passing. You weren't frightened, were you?

CAPTAIN

Me – frightened? Of course not.

ALICE

Since you won't go to bed, you might as well come and lie down.

The CAPTAIN crosses and lies on the sofa.

CAPTAIN

This will do.

He tries to take ALICE'S hand but she draws it away.

KURT enters with the carafe.

> CAPTAIN

Kurt, don't leave me!

> KURT

I'm staying all night. Alice is going to bed.

> CAPTAIN

(*Looks up at ALICE*) Goodnight then.

> ALICE

(*To KURT*) Goodnight, Kurt.

> KURT

Goodnight.

She goes.

KURT takes a chair and sits by the CAPTAIN.

> KURT

Don't you want to take off your boots?

> CAPTAIN

No! A soldier must always be ready for action.

> KURT

You're expecting a battle, then?

> CAPTAIN

Perhaps. (*He sits up.*) Kurt, you're the only person
I've ever confided in. Listen, if I die tonight look after
my children.

> KURT

I will.

CAPTAIN

Thank you. I trust you.

KURT

Why is that?

CAPTAIN

We've never been friends. I don't believe in friendship.
Our families have always been at loggerheads . . .

KURT

And yet you trust me?

CAPTAIN

I don't know why that should be.

Silence.

CAPTAIN

Am I going to die?

KURT

We all are.

CAPTAIN

Doesn't that make you bitter?

KURT

Yes. What about you? Are you afraid of being spread
over the garden from a wheelbarrow?

CAPTAIN

Suppose it isn't the end?

KURT

Many think it isn't.

CAPTAIN

What then?

KURT

Some surprises, perhaps.

CAPTAIN

No-one knows for sure.

KURT

We should be ready for anything.

CAPTAIN

You're not such a fool as to believe in hell?

KURT

I might, if I were in the middle of it, like you.

CAPTAIN

I was speaking metaphorically.

KURT

I hardly think so. What you were saying about your life was hardly metaphorical, poetic, or anything but real and now.

Silence.

CAPTAIN

If you knew the agonies I've suffered. For what? (*A slight pause, then he raises himself on the sofa.*) I don't want to die!

KURT

Just now you were longing for annihilation.

CAPTAIN

Well, why not? So long as it's painless.

KURT

Who can guarantee that – a good death?

CAPTAIN

Am I dying?

KURT

Possibly.

CAPTAIN

(*Turns away from him*) Goodnight.

KURT

Goodnight.

Fade to black.

End of Act One

ACT TWO

The same setting.

An overcast morning and a rolling sea outside. The SENTRY as before. The CAPTAIN lies asleep. KURT sits beside him, hollow-eyed from lack of sleep.

ALICE enters.

ALICE

Is he asleep?

KURT

Yes, since day-break.

ALICE

What sort of night did you have?

KURT

He dozed off now and then. Most of the time he was talking.

ALICE

What about?

KURT

Religion mostly. Like a schoolboy after the secrets of the universe. Towards dawn he discovered the immortality of the soul.

ALICE

Edgar decides he has a soul?

KURT

He really is the most arrogant man I've ever met. I am, therefore God exists.

ALICE

Now you know. He'd have trampled the earth flat in
those boots given the chance – the way he's trampled
over his men and everyone else, including me. Now
it's his turn to feel the knife.

KURT

He'd be comic if he weren't tragic. There's a kind
of grandeur about all the pettiness. Can't you find
anything to say in his favour?

ALICE

(*Sits*) Oh yes. But not in his hearing. One word of
of encouragement, and his arrogance becomes
unbearable.

KURT

He can't hear anything. I've given him morphine.

ALICE

Perhaps it's his poor background. His useless father –
having to support all those brothers and sisters. I
remember the first time I saw him. I was a little girl. It
was winter and they were all in warm coats. Except him.
It was admirable. But he was ugly. He frightened me.

KURT

I know what you mean. He can look hideous,
especially in a bad mood. It used to make me
shudder – after picking a quarrel, his image would
stay with you. (*He shudders.*)

ALICE

Imagine what it's been for me! I know it was a
struggle for him at first but he's had help. Not that he
ever admits it. He takes anything he gets as his right.

KURT

I suppose we shouldn't speak ill of him.

ALICE

After he's dead, I'll say no more. He can be kind. No, he's a monster.

KURT

Why did he never make Major?

ALICE

Are you surprised? Give him seniority when he'd proved to be a tyrant as a subordinate? Don't say a word about this – he maintains that he never wanted promotion. Did he mention the children?

KURT

Yes, he said he wanted to see Judith.

ALICE

Of course! His alter ego! My own daughter, trained in his image to spite and despise me. Do you know that girl has raised her arm against me!

KURT

Judith?

ALICE

Ssh! He's moving! What if he heard us?

KURT

No, he's just stirring.

ALICE

He's very cunning. He looks like Satan himself.

The CAPTAIN stirs, rises, looks around.

CAPTAIN

It's morning – at last!

KURT

How are you feeling?

CAPTAIN

Bad.

KURT

Do you want a doctor?

CAPTAIN

No, I want to see Judith. I want to see my daughter.

KURT

Edgar, wouldn't it be wise to put your affairs in order
before … in case anything happens …

CAPTAIN

In case what happens? I'm not going to die. Apologies,
Alice. You'll have to save the celebrations for a few
years.

KURT

You should, at least, make a will. See that your wife
has a roof over her head.

CAPTAIN

Hand it over while I'm still alive. Is that what she's
after?

KURT

No, but if anything should happen, you wouldn't want
her to be out on the street without a stick of furniture.
She's cleaned and polished all this for twenty-five
years. Surely she has some rights? Would you like me
to send for a lawyer?

CAPTAIN

No!

KURT

Then you're a crueller man than I thought.

The CAPTAIN groans suddenly, and falls back unconscious.

ALICE

(*Looks away.*) I think I hear someone in the kitchen.

KURT

Yes, go and see to it. There's nothing you can do here.

The CAPTAIN regains consciousness, sits up, and glares balefully
at KURT.

CAPTAIN

Thought out your tactics, have you?

KURT

(*Startled*) Sorry?

CAPTAIN

A quarantine station on this island? How are you
going to manage that?

KURT

I don't know yet. I'll manage.

CAPTAIN

Will you? I'm in command here, don't forget. You'll
have to deal through me.

KURT

I hope we can work together. Have you seen a
quarantine in action?

CAPTAIN

Are you stupid, man, of course I have. Before you
were born. I'll give you one piece of advice for
nothing. Don't put your disinfecting ovens onshore,
close to the sea.

KURT

But I was told they needed to be near water.

CAPTAIN

Haha! Shows how much you know about your job.
Water is just the element for germs, they thrive in it.

KURT

Surely salt water cleanses impurities.

CAPTAIN

Don't be an idiot. (*A pause.*) First thing is to find you
a place to live. Get you settled in. You can bring your
children over.

KURT

If they'll come.

CAPTAIN

Of course they'll come, if you say so. If you're any sort
of a man. It'll make a good impression.

KURT

I'm sorry?

CAPTAIN

If people here see you fulfilling your responsibilities.

KURT

I have always fulfilled ...

CAPTAIN

(*Loud*) A man who abandons his own children ...

KURT

Oh, leave it!

CAPTAIN

As your kinsman and senior member of the family, it
is my duty to tell you the truth, however unpalatable.
So there is no need to take offence.

Silence.

KURT

Are you hungry?

CAPTAIN

Yes I am.

KURT

I'll get you something light.

CAPTAIN

No! I missed dinner. I want a decent five-course meal.

KURT

I am reliably informed that such a thing could finish
you.

CAPTAIN

Bad enough being ill without being starved as well!

KURT

I'm sorry but it's what the ...

CAPTAIN

No drinking, no smoking. What is there left to live for?

KURT

Edgar. Look. Death doesn't play games. It's either do
as you're told or – kkk! (*He draws a finger across his
throat.*)

ALICE enters with FLOWERS and MESSAGES.

CENTER ALICE

These are for you.

The CAPTAIN lifts his arms for them, his face alive with joy.

ALICE

They're only from the sergeant's mess.

She throws the lot in his lap.

CAPTAIN

Oh, jealous! *(Smelling the flowers)* Flowers! For me ...

ALICE

Hardly accolades. Are they fresh?

CAPTAIN

And a telegram from the Colonel. Read it for me, Kurt, would you? Very decent of him – even if he is a fool. This is from ... it's from Judith! Telegraph her right away to come by the next boat. This one ... *(reads.)* Well! I'm not without friends after all! It's gratifying to be remembered. People respect an honest soldier. A man deserving beyond his rank.

ALICE

I don't understand. Are they congratulating you on being ill?

CAPTAIN

She can't bear it, can she?

KURT

What?

CAPTAIN

The limelight on me!

ALICE

We had a doctor once who was so hated that the whole
Island gave a banquet when he left.

CAPTAIN

(To KURT.) Put the flowers in water for me. I'm not
easily fooled. People, in the main, are fools, rogues
and scum. But to be given simple homage like this,
straight from the heart ... genuine affection ...

ALICE

You idiot!

KURT

(Reading) This telegram's from Judith.

CAPTAIN

(Eager) And?

KURT

The steamer's been delayed by the storm.

CAPTAIN

And? Is that all? What else does she say?

KURT

(Awkwardly) She ... ah ... She says not to drink so
much.

CAPTAIN

Bloody impertinence. Sharper than a viper's tongue.
That's children for you. Can you believe it? Judith,
my pride and joy.

ALICE

Your spitting image, you mean.

CAPTAIN

Oh, to hell with it. Have you asked Kurt to breakfast?

ALICE

No.

CAPTAIN

Then fry us two really good steaks. On the double.

ALICE

Two? What about me?

CAPTAIN

All right, three.

ALICE

There's nothing in the kitchen! You ask him to supper
when there isn't a crust in the house. He's had to sit
up all night with you on an empty stomach. Not even
a cup of coffee!

CAPTAIN

Then get some!

ALICE

How can I when our credit's run out?! They won't
deliver!

Humiliated, she throws herself down weeping.

CAPTAIN

(*To KURT*) Oh dear, now she's upset. (*Bawls at her*)
Sorry I didn't manage to die last night! What a pity!

ALICE

A pity you didn't die twenty-five years ago. I wish
you'd died before I was born!

CAPTAIN

You hear that, Kurt? So much for your match-
making, my friend. This is one you certainly didn't
make in heaven.

KURT looks at ALICE, who shrugs helplessly. To their surprise the CAPTAIN gets up, and goes to the door.

CAPTAIN

However, time for duty!

He puts on his crested helmet, his sabre and military cape.

ALICE

What are you doing? Where do you think you're going?

CAPTAIN

If anyone wants me, I'm down at the battery.

They try to stop him from leaving.

CAPTAIN

Out of my way!

The CAPTAIN goes.

ALICE

Yes, go! Retreat, walk away! Whenever there's trouble, he's off. He disappears. And I'm here without a penny. *(She calls off.)* That's right! Run off – you drunken, lying bastard!

KURT

(Shocked.) Alice! My God, is there no end to all this?

ALICE

You haven't seen the half of it.

KURT

There's worse?

ALICE

Kurt, I couldn't bear to tell you.

KURT

Where is he going? Where does he find the strength?

ALICE

You may well ask. He'll go down to the men to thank them for their flowers. Then he'll drink with them and slander their officers. He's been threatened with dismissal again and again for it. The only reason they let him stay is the girls and me. When the officers' wives do put in a good word for us, he slanders them too. He hates them.

KURT

And to think I came here to find peace and quiet by the sea.

ALICE

Poor Kurt. You must be ravenous. How will you get something to eat?

KURT

The Doctor will feed me. What about you? Would you like me to bring you something?

ALICE

Please, could you? So long as he doesn't find out. He'd kill me.

KURT turns, then crosses and looks outside.

KURT

Good God, he's out there on the rampart. In this weather!

ALICE

(*Joins him, gazes out.*) You could almost feel sorry for him.

KURT

I feel for you both. Can't anything be done?

ALICE

There are bills he hasn't even seen. Or chooses not to.
Look! He wants to die!

KURT

I don't think so.

ALICE

But he's opened his cape to the storm. He's trying to
kill himself.

KURT

I think it's defiance. Last night, when he was feeling
weak, he began to fasten on to my life, as though he
wanted to take it. To be me.

ALICE

Yes, because he's a vampire! His own life is so empty
that he sucks the life out of anyone who has the
misfortune to cross his path. He battens on. Never
let him near your family – most of all your children.
He'll take them over. Make them his own. Oh, he's
hellishly good at disaffection. It's relentless – every
waking hour. Whatever your wishes, your needs,
your desires, they must all be thwarted, impeded,
destroyed.

Silence.

KURT

He did it, didn't he?

ALICE

(After a pause) Yes.

KURT

He took them from me. I always suspected it, but I
wasn't sure.

ALICE

When you sent Edgar to your wife as a peacemaker,
he started a flirtation with her. And then he told her
how to get custody of the children. How it could be
done.

KURT

My God. God in Heaven.

ALICE

Now you know.

KURT

(*After a pause*) Shall I tell you something? Last night,
when he thought he was dying, he asked me to look
after his children.

ALICE

Well now you can pay him back. Refuse to do it.

KURT

You don't honestly think I'd do that – abandon your
children? You know what the best revenge is? Behave
impeccably despite his intentions.

ALICE

That would really be cruel. If there is one thing he
fears and despises, more than anything else in the
world, it's generosity.

KURT

Hah. So I'll get my revenge by not taking revenge.

ALICE

Isn't it glorious, when vengeance and justice are one?
Not that I wouldn't be a hypocrite if I said I could
forgive my enemy.

KURT

Sometimes it's better to let go. Why did you marry
him?

ALICE

He seduced me! I don't know. I wanted to go up in the
world.

KURT

Leave the theatre?

ALICE

People look down on actresses. He cheated me. I was
promised a good life. A beautiful home. All I got was
debts! The only gold I ever saw was on his uniform,
and that wasn't real.

KURT

Oh, hang on. When a young man falls in love, he's
full of dreams. I was myself. The hopes aren't always
realised, but it's too harsh to call us cheats. What are
you looking at?

ALICE

I'm looking to see if he's fallen off the rampart.

KURT

And?

ALICE

No such luck. He's still there. Still cheating me.

KURT

I must go and see the Doctor.

ALICE

(*Sits by the window*) Yes, you go, dear. I'll sit here and
wait. I'm used to waiting.

Fade to black.

ACT TWO – SCENE TWO

Lights up on the same setting. Daylight.

The SENTRY on duty outside the window as before. ALICE sits in
the armchair. Her hair is now grey.

KURT knocks and enters.

KURT

Good morning, Alice.

ALICE

Kurt! Good morning. Sit down.

KURT

(*Sitting*) The steamer's in.

ALICE

And I know what to expect, if he's on it.

KURT

He is. I saw the glint of his helmet. What was he doing
in town?

ALICE

I can guess. He took his dress uniform and his suede
gloves, so he was seeing the Colonel and gadding about.

KURT

Did you notice? He was very quiet yesterday. Since he stopped drinking he's been a different man.

ALICE

Just as well he did drink all those years.

KURT

Why?

ALICE

Can you imagine him sober? He'd have been a real menace instead of a ludicrous idiot.

KURT

The genie in the bottle kept him tamed? He's certainly altered. There's a sort of dignity, almost nobility about him. He's thinking of immortality perhaps.

ALICE

Don't deceive yourself. He's up to something. Whatever you do, don't believe a word he says. He's a genius at lying and scheming. What is it?

KURT

Alice! Your hair! You've gone grey overnight!

ALICE

No. I've been grey for a long time. Now that he's about to leave us, I've stopped using the hair dye. There'll be no-one to shame with the sight of my wasted youth and beauty. Twenty-five years in this fortress! You know it was a prison once?

KURT

You can feel it in the walls. It's hard to imagine children playing in a place like this.

ALICE

They didn't. Two died. Lack of light!

KURT

Oh, my dear.

Silence.

KURT

What do you think he's planning?

ALICE

An attack – against both of us! I saw the hate in his
eyes when you read Judith's telegram.

KURT

Against me?

ALICE

Of course you. He can't hate his beloved doppelganger,
Judith. Anyway, she's out of reach. You're not.

KURT

I'm in the line of fire?

ALICE

Exactly.

KURT

But what can he do to me?

ALICE

I don't know, but he has a genius for ferreting out
secrets. Did you notice? All day yesterday? Your job –
your children. Questions, questions – devouring you
alive. It's as though he's already dead.

KURT

Yes! Did you notice? His face has a kind of
phosphorescence, as if he's rotting already.

ALICE

And his eyes!

KURT

God yes, his eyes, flaming like marsh gas over the
swamp. Ssh! Here he comes. I wonder . . . do you think
he could possibly be jealous?

ALICE

Of you? Never. He's much too conceited for that. (She
imitates his voice) "Show me the man I need to envy!"

KURT

(Laughs) At least his faults have some advantages.
Shall I go and greet him?

ALICE

No, he'll think you're up to something. Whatever he
says, pretend to believe him. I know how to get at the
truth. And Kurt, whatever you do, don't lose control.
In all the years, my one advantage has been staying
sober and keeping my wits about me. Something
terrible's going to happen. I can feel it.

The CAPTAIN enters in dress uniform, helmet, cloak and gloves.
He looks dignified, but pale. He stumbles and sits, at a distance
from them, his sabre between his knees.

CAPTAIN

Good morning. Forgive my sitting down. The journey.

ALICE & KURT

Good morning.

ALICE

How are you?

CAPTAIN

Fine. A little travel-weary.

ALICE

Any news from town?

CAPTAIN

This and that. Oh, I saw a doctor. Nothing wrong.
Gives me another twenty years if I look after myself.

ALICE

(To KURT) He's lying. *(To the CAPTAIN)* Well, that
was good news, my dear.

CAPTAIN

Wasn't it!

A silence. He looks at them, waiting for them to speak.

ALICE

(To KURT) Don't say a word. Let him show his hand.

CAPTAIN

Did you say something?

ALICE

No.

CAPTAIN

(Slowly) Kurt, old man . . .

ALICE

(To KURT) Here it comes.

CAPTAIN

I . . . ah . . . I was in town, as you are aware.

KURT nods.

CAPTAIN

I ... er ... I met a few people, amongst them. Ah, a young cadet.

KURT stirs, uneasy.

CAPTAIN

Since ... ah ... since we're short of staff on the island, I arranged with the Colonel for him to be transferred here. I'm sure you'll be delighted when I tell you that ... it's your son!

ALICE

(To KURT) You see? A vampire!

KURT

(A pause) Normally that would be good news. As you must know, however, I am bound to find the prospect painful.

CAPTAIN

I fail to understand. Why? *(Silence.)*

KURT

Surely it's enough that I'd rather he didn't come here.

CAPTAIN

Is that so? Then you must know that the young man has been posted to the Island, under my command.

KURT

He'll have to apply for another regiment.

CAPTAIN

Who says so?

KURT

I do.

CAPTAIN

You have no jurisdiction over him.

KURT

He's my son.

CAPTAIN

Any rights over your son were awarded to his mother.

KURT

Then I'll write to his mother.

CAPTAIN

No need. I have already done so.

KURT starts to rise, but sits heavily.

KURT

(*To ALICE*) He *is* a vampire.

ALICE

He ... must ... die.

CAPTAIN

So much for that. Did either of you say something?

ALICE

No. Are you going deaf?

CAPTAIN

A little, perhaps. I'm a gunnery man. Come here. I've something to tell you. In confidence.

ALICE

Oh? (*She remains where she is.*) Perhaps we should have a witness.

CAPTAIN

Quite right. Always good to have a witness. But first, is my will ready?

ALICE rises, crosses, picks up a document, and hands it to him.

ALICE

Drawn up by the judge himself.

CAPTAIN

In your favour. Good!

He reads through the document carefully, turning the pages and taking his time. He then tears it slowly into small pieces, which he throws on the floor.

CAPTAIN

So much for that! Yes?

ALICE

(To KURT) Have you ever met a man like that?

KURT

No. He's not human.

CAPTAIN

Oh, and Alice. I've something else to tell you.

ALICE

Yes?

CAPTAIN

(Calmly) In view of your long-expressed wish to bring
the misery of your unhappy marriage to an end,
and given the total lack of affection shown to your
husband and children, plus the negligence with which
you have managed our domestic economy, I decided,
during my visit to the mainland, to file a petition for
divorce.

ALICE

Oh? *(A pause)* On what grounds?

CAPTAIN

(*Still calm*) In addition to those already stated,
there are further, personal reasons. Now it's been
established that I may live another twenty years, I
have decided to exchange my present unhappy state
of matrimony for something more suited to myself
and my position. I intend to unite myself with a lady
capable of bringing into my home affection, respect,
youth and – dare I say it – a little beauty.

ALICE takes off her ring and throws it at him.

ALICE

Go ahead! There you are!

The CAPTAIN picks up the ring and puts it in his pocket.

CAPTAIN

She throws away her wedding ring. Will the witness
be good enough to note that?

ALICE

(*Rises, indignant*) You intend to chuck me out and
bring another woman into my house?

CAPTAIN

Yes.

ALICE

I see. In that case, cousin Kurt, you do know that this
man tried to kill me?

KURT

Alice …

ALICE

He tried to drown me. I was thrown into the sea.

CAPTAIN

(*Chants*) No witnesses.

ALICE

You're lying, Judith was there!

CAPTAIN

What's that got to do with it?

ALICE

She can testify.

CAPTAIN

No, she can't. She says she didn't see anything.

ALICE

Because you taught her to lie!

CAPTAIN

I didn't need to. You'd done that already.

ALICE

(*A pause*) Did you go and see her?

CAPTAIN

Of course.

ALICE

Oh God. Oh God.

CAPTAIN

Right. Capitulation. The fortress surrenders! (*Bark of laughter.*) The enemy is granted ten minutes to withdraw under safe conduct. (*Places his watch on the table.*) Ten minutes, by my watch!

He suddenly clutches his chest. ALICE grasps his arm.

ALICE

What is it?

CAPTAIN

(*Gasping*) I don't know.

ALICE

Do you want something, do you want a drink?

CAPTAIN

Whisky ... Alice, I don't want to die. (*He reels, staggers, and recovers himself.*) Don't touch me, what are you doing? Ten minutes. Ten minutes, or you'll be cut down. (*He draws his sabre.*) Ten minutes!

He goes out.

KURT

Who <u>is</u> this man?

ALICE

He's not a man, he's a demon.

KURT

What does he want with my son?

ALICE

To control you! He wants him as a hostage. Then he'll cut you off from every source of support and assistance, except himself. You know what they call this island? Mini Hell.

KURT

They're right. Alice, I always felt ... well, for years now, I felt that women deserved most of what they got. But not this. You don't deserve this.

ALICE

You will stay, won't you? If you go, he'll knock me down. He's been doing it for twenty-five years. Even in front of the children.

KURT

He really tried to drown you?

ALICE

Oh yes.

KURT

Right, that's it. I came here without malice. I was prepared to forget that he used to humiliate me – how he blackened my name. Because he was sick and dying, I even forgave him when you told me he'd manipulated my wife and had my children taken from me. But not this. Not my son. I'm not having that.

ALICE

What will you do?

KURT

Kill him. Or he'll kill me.

ALICE

Good. No surrender. We'll blow him and his fortress to smithereens – even if we go up with it. I'll supply the dynamite.

KURT

I had no animosity when I came here. When yours began to infect me, I thought: 'I'll leave.' Not now. Not any longer. He's evil. What can we do?

ALICE

Leave it to me. I've learned strategy – from him. First, round up his enemies and look for allies.

KURT

To track down my wife! Those two should have met
twenty-five years ago. That would have been a pairing
to make the earth tremble.

ALICE

They're working together now. We must stop it. I
know his weak spot. I know where we can catch him.
I've known it for years.

KURT

Who is his worst enemy here?

ALICE

The Ordnance Officer.

KURT

Can we trust him?

ALICE

Oh yes. And he knows what I know. He knows what
the Sergeant-Major and my husband have been up to
together.

KURT

Up to? What do you mean?

ALICE

Embezzlement.

KURT

But that's atrocious! No. Look, I want nothing to do
with this …

ALICE

What sort of man are you? Can't you fight?

KURT

(*Shakes his head.*) I could once. Not anymore.

ALICE

Why not?

KURT

Because I've learned that, in the end, justice will be
done.

ALICE

So you'll wait? Till he suborns your son? Alienates
him forever, as he has Judith? Look at this. *(She lets
down her hair.)* Grey. But still thick, glossy – feel! *(He
steps back, startled.)* He wants to remarry? Good! I'm
free! I can do the same. In ten minutes, he'll be down
there under arrest. *(Stamps on the floor.)* Down in
the cells. And I'll be dancing on his head. *(She turns,
dancing and laughing, then leaps to the piano, and
crashes out chords)* We'll give him something to listen
to! *(Laughs, and points at the SENTRY outside.)* No
more guarding the gates. The sentry's for him now.
Him, him, him! Ta titta, ta titta, ti titta dum! Him!

KURT watches her, stunned.

KURT

Alice! Are you a demon as well?

ALICE

(Jumps up and takes down the laurel wreaths) The
laurels of triumph! I'll wear them as I walk through
the gates. Look, they're still green. I'm still young,
Kurt!

KURT

(Enmeshed) You are a demon.

ALICE

Of course. This is Mini Hell and I live in it. Give
me two minutes to dress. Two minutes to see the
Ordnance Officer and then watch the fortress blow
sky-high!

KURT

You are a demon!

ALICE

You called me that when we were children,
remember? We got engaged. Do you remember that?
(*Laughs*) You were so shy ...

KURT

(*Seriously*) Alice ...

ALICE

It suited you. There are strong women who love shy
men. And shy men who love strong women. You liked
me a little then, didn't you?

KURT

I don't know where I am.

ALICE

You're with an actress, who goes her own way, never
mind convention. I'm a woman and I'm free, free,
free! Turn round while I change my dress.

She starts to unbutton her dress.

KURT rushes towards her, lifts her high in his arms, and then bites
her on the throat, making her scream loudly.

He throws her down on the chaise longue and runs out.

Fade to black.

ACT TWO – SCENE THREE

Lights up on the same scene. Evening.

The SENTRY is still visible outside. The laurel wreaths are looped over the back of a chair. The ceiling lamp is lit. SOFT MUSIC.

The CAPTAIN, pale and hollow-eyed in his shabby undress uniform, with riding boots, is playing patience. He wears glasses and bends over the cards but looks up now and then, and listens.

The game does not come out. He sweeps the cards together, and throws them out of the window, which remains open, rattling on its hinges.

He goes to the cupboard, then turns, alarmed, at the noise of the rattling window. He takes out three dark, square-sided whisky bottles, looks at them intently, and throws them through the window. He takes out boxes of cigars, lifts the lid of the top box and sniffs, and throws the boxes out of the window.

He then takes off his glasses, cleans them, puts them back on to test how well he can see through them. He throws them out of the window, then stumbles over the furniture and lights a six-branched candelabrum.

He sees the laurel wreaths on the chair, picks them up and takes them to the window, but turns, takes the piano cloth, wipes the wreaths carefully and wraps them in the cloth, pinning the corners with pins from the desk. He places the bundle on a chair. He goes to the piano, strikes the keys, making loud discords, closes the piano, locks it, and throws the key out of the window.

He lights the candles on the piano, crosses to the whatnot, takes down his wife's photograph, looks at it, then tears it into small pieces, scattering the pieces on the floor.

The window rattles on its hinges, alarming him again.

He calms himself, takes down the photographs of his son and daughter, kisses them briefly, and puts them into his breast pocket.

The other photographs he sweeps off with his elbow and kicks into a heap on the floor.

Tired, he sits at the desk and feels his heart. He lights the candle on the table and groans – staring as if at visions.

He gets up, opens the secretaire, takes out a bundle of letters tied with blue ribbon, and throws them in the stove.

The TELEGRAPH clicks and is silent. It makes him jump, and he holds his heart. He waits, but the machine is silent. He listens at the door. Opens it, goes out, and returns with a CAT in his arms, stroking it. Then he goes out. The MUSIC stops.

Pause.

ALICE enters, dressed for walking, with hat and gloves, her hair now coloured black. She looks round, surprised at the candles.

KURT enters left. He is nervous.

> ALICE

It looks like Christmas Eve in here.

> KURT

Well . . .

> ALICE

(*Extends her hand for him to kiss it.*) Thank me.

KURT kisses her hand reluctantly.

> ALICE

Six witnesses. Four of them reliable and unshakeable.
Charges filed – to be confirmed by telegraph. Here, in
the heart of the fortress!

KURT

I see.

ALICE

Say 'thank you!' Not 'I see.'

KURT

Why has he lit so many candles?

ALICE

He's afraid of the dark! Look at the telegraph. Doesn't it look like a coffee mill? I grind and the beans crunch like teeth being pulled …

KURT

What has he been doing in here?

ALICE

Obviously clearing out. Planning to go. Down to the cells. That's where you're going!

KURT

Alice, don't. He was good to me when I was young. I feel sorry for him.

ALICE

More than for me? I sacrificed my career for that monster.

KURT

Was it so brilliant, your career?

ALICE

(*Furious*) What the hell do you mean by that? Don't you know who I am? Who I was?

KURT

All right, all right.

ALICE

Are you starting too ... already?

KURT

Already?

She throws her arms around his neck and kisses him.

He pins her arms and bites her neck. She screams.

ALICE

You're biting me!

KURT

(*Out of control*) Yes, I want to bite, and suck your blood. I thought I was sane. Reasonable. I'm worse than either you or Edgar. I want to strangle you! (*He embraces her.*)

ALICE

(*Shows him her wrist*) Look at that. See those marks? He did that. Now I'm free.

KURT

(*Holding her arms*) No you're not.

ALICE

Aren't I? I think I am.

KURT

What?

ALICE

I think you're all talk and virtue, Kurt.

KURT

Wait until we get into town. Then you'll see.

ALICE

We'll go to the theatre after. Show ourselves. Shame him.

KURT

Sending him to prison not enough for you?

ALICE

No! I want him humiliated. Publicly.

KURT

You commit adultery, but he's blamed. God, it's as if these walls were soaked in the evil of every prisoner who's been here. And all you can think about is going to the theatre.

ALICE

Why not? What are <u>you</u> thinking about?

KURT

My son.

ALICE

(*Hits him on the mouth with her glove*) Pompous prig.

He raises his hand to strike her.

ALICE

That's enough!

KURT

I'm sorry.

ALICE

On your knees.

KURT kneels.

ALICE

On your face!

He presses his face to the floor.

ALICE

Now kiss my foot.

He kisses her foot.

ALICE

Don't do that again. Get up.

KURT

(*Rises*) Where am I? Where have I come to?

ALICE

You know very well where you are.

KURT

In hell?

The CAPTAIN enters, looking grey, and leaning on a stick.

CAPTAIN

I would like to speak to Kurt. Alone.

ALICE

About our safe-conduct, is it?

CAPTAIN

(*Sits*) Kurt, would you sit with me? Alice, could you give us a moment's peace?

ALICE

What's all this? A change of tune! All right. (*to KURT*) Sit down, listen to the voice of age and wisdom. Call me if the telegram arrives.

ALICE goes out. A long pause.

CAPTAIN

Tell me something. Can you see any point at all in a life like mine?

KURT

No more than in my own.

CAPTAIN

Then tell me what in God in Heaven's name does any
of it mean?

KURT

Is there anyone who can answer that?

CAPTAIN

What is it all for?

KURT

Who knows? We submit nonetheless. What choice do
we have?

CAPTAIN

With no fixed point? No meaning?

KURT

Ah, meaning. Meaning, I suppose, is there to be
sought.

CAPTAIN

How?

KURT

You're the mathematician.

CAPTAIN

You seem resigned. Where did you learn submission?

KURT

Don't overestimate me.

CAPTAIN

As you may have noticed, my way of survival is to
blot out the past. Cross out and carry on! Early on

in life, I shoved all the defeats, all the humiliations, in a sack and kicked them in the sea. I don't believe any man on earth has been humiliated as often, and as severely, as I have. But blot them out. Where are they? They don't exist.

KURT

I've noticed that you invent a life for yourself and for those around you.

CAPTAIN

How else do I survive? (*He clutches at his heart.*)

KURT

Are you all right?

CAPTAIN

No. Bad. (*Pause*) When you can't invent any more, the view becomes ... unpleasant. (*His voice breaks, he sounds old and tearful.*) You see, my dear friend. (*Controls himself and speaks normally.*) I'm sorry. When I was in town, I saw a doctor. (*Tearfully again.*) He says I'm done for. (*Normal voice.*) Very little time left.

KURT

He said that?

CAPTAIN

(*Broken*) Yes.

KURT

Then it wasn't true – the rest of what you said?

The CAPTAIN shakes his head.

KURT

Is my son coming here, as a cadet?

CAPTAIN

First I've heard of it.

KURT

And you haven't petitioned for a divorce against your wife?

CAPTAIN

(*Puzzled*) Divorce?

KURT

So it was all lies. Now conveniently forgotten.

CAPTAIN

That's perhaps a touch harsh. We all need a little leeway.

KURT

You've found that out?

CAPTAIN

(*Firm, clear voice*) I have. Forgive me, Kurt. Will you forgive me, for everything?

KURT

There's nothing to forgive. I'm not the man you seem to think I am – least of all now. The last man you should confess to.

CAPTAIN

(*Clear voice*) Life is so cruel. It's never been anything else for me. It makes you cruel yourself.

KURT crosses and looks uneasily at the telegraph.

CAPTAIN

What are you looking at?

KURT

Can this be shut off?

CAPTAIN

No, not easily.

KURT

(*Rising unease*) Who is Sergeant-Major Östberg?

CAPTAIN

Not a bad sort. Bit of a dealer on the side, of course.

KURT

What about the Ordnance Officer?

CAPTAIN

No friend of mine. Not a bad sort.

KURT looks out of the window, where a lantern can be seen moving.

KURT

What are they doing with that lantern, down by the
guns?

CAPTAIN

Lantern?

KURT

Yes. There are people moving about.

CAPTAIN

Probably a special detail.

KURT

What's that?

CAPTAIN

A platoon with a corporal. Some poor devil is about to
be arrested.

KURT

Oh.

CAPTAIN

(*After a pause.*) Well, now you know Alice better, what
do you think of her?

KURT

I can't say. The fact is I don't understand her any
more than I understand you. Or myself. I'm getting
to the age when you admit you understand nothing.
Why did you push her into the sea?

CAPTAIN

I don't know. She was standing there on the jetty and
it seemed the proper thing to do.

KURT

You've never regretted it?

CAPTAIN

No.

KURT

Strange.

CAPTAIN

Yes. So strange I can't believe I did something so . . .
trivial.

KURT

It never occurred to you that she'd get her revenge?

CAPTAIN

Oh, she's done that all right.

KURT

You sound resigned.

CAPTAIN

I'm facing death. If you had to choose, who would you
say was in the right? Alice or me?

KURT

Neither! I'm acutely sorry, for both of you. Perhaps
you the more.

CAPTAIN

Give me your hand.

KURT extends his hand.

CAPTAIN

Kurt ...

KURT

(*His other hand on the CAPTAIN'S shoulder.*) My dear
friend.

ALICE enters, carrying a parasol.

ALICE

Did I hear the word 'friend?' How affecting. Has the
telegram arrived?

KURT

(*Cold*) No.

ALICE

I'm getting impatient. When I get impatient, I
hurry things up. Here we go, Kurt ... the coup de
grace. Load – see, I know the drill from the famous
manual that didn't sell five, let alone five thousand
copies – take aim, fire! (*She aims the parasol at
the CAPTAIN.*) How is your new wife? The young,
beautiful – unknown – girl. You see? He doesn't know.
But I know how my love is.

She puts her arms around KURT'S neck and kisses him.

He pushes her away.

> ALICE
>
> He's wonderful! Still a little shy. *(To the CAPTAIN.)*
> You pitiful thing, do you think I could ever love you?
> He's so conceited he's never dreamt he could be led by
> the nose.

The CAPTAIN draws his sabre and slashes at her, but only hits the furniture.

> ALICE
>
> Help! Help me!

KURT stands, motionless.

> CAPTAIN
>
> *(Falling, sabre in hand.)* Judith. Judith …

> ALICE
>
> Hurray – he's dead.

KURT moves to the door.

> CAPTAIN
>
> *(Rises)* Not yet! *(He sheathes his sabre, and sits.)*
> Judith.

> ALICE
>
> *(Crosses to KURT)* Time for you to take me away.

> KURT
>
> *(Pushes her so hard that she falls on her knees)* No!
> *(Going.)* Get back to the hell you came from.

> CAPTAIN
>
> Don't leave me, Kurt, she'll kill me!

ALICE

Kurt, don't leave me! Please. Don't leave us!

KURT

Goodbye.

KURT goes.

ALICE

What a wretch! There's a friend for you.

CAPTAIN

(Gently) Forgive me, Alice. Come here.

ALICE

The most contemptible hypocrite I've ever met in my life. At least you're a man.

CAPTAIN

Alice. Listen to me. I'm on the way out.

ALICE

What?

CAPTAIN

I'm dying. I saw a doctor in town.

ALICE

What?! Then you were lying!

CAPTAIN

Yes.

ALICE

All that – that – oh my God, what have I done?

CAPTAIN

It can be put right.

ALICE

Not this.

CAPTAIN

Nothing's irreparable, if we put it behind us.

ALICE

But the telegram. The telegram!

CAPTAIN

What telegram?

ALICE

(*On her knees beside him.*) It'll destroy us. I've destroyed us both. Why did you have to lie? Why did he have to come here, under my nose? We're finished. You could have forgiven me …

CAPTAIN

When haven't I?

ALICE

I know. Not this time.

CAPTAIN

What have you done?

ALICE

What will become of the children? Their name dishonoured.

CAPTAIN

You've dishonoured our name?

ALICE

They'll have to leave school. And when they go out in the world, they'll be as horrible and lonely as we are. You didn't see her? Judith? In town?

CAPTAIN

No.

The TELEGRAPH taps. ALICE jumps up.

ALICE

(*Shrieks*) We're done for. Don't listen to it!

CAPTAIN

(*Calm*) Very well. (*Covers his ears.*)

ALICE cranes to look out of the window.

ALICE

Don't listen!

CAPTAIN

(*Holding his ears*) Lissy ... !

ALICE

Oh, God help us, they're coming. They're coming to
arrest you. It's the detail ... (*Weeps.*) God in Heaven!

She moves her lips in silent prayer. The TELEGRAPH clicks, then,
at last, is silent.

ALICE rises, tears off the strip, and reads it. She raises her eyes to
heaven, crosses, and kisses the CAPTAIN on the forehead.

ALICE

(*Breathless*) It's all right. It was nothing.

She sits across from him and sobs into her handkerchief.

CAPTAIN

What secret have you got there?

ALICE

Nothing! It's over now.

CAPTAIN

As you wish, my dear.

ALICE

You wouldn't have spoken like that three days ago.
Why now?

CAPTAIN

When I collapsed, I . . . I crossed over. Something . . . I
can't tell you. I don't remember. Just an impression.

ALICE

Of what?

CAPTAIN

Something better. I've never felt the least attachment
to our life. It's been more like a death. As though we
were doomed to . . .

ALICE

Torment each other?

CAPTAIN

(After a silence.) Time for a refit?

ALICE

Is that possible?

CAPTAIN

Redeployment? Not in a day. *(Pause.)* So, you didn't
escape, and you didn't get me put away. *(She looks at
him, astonished.)* You tried to send me to prison. Well,
you've done worse. *(Pause)* I didn't embezzle.

ALICE

I suppose I'm to be your nurse now.

CAPTAIN

Think it'll suit you?

ALICE

What choice do I have? What else can I do?

CAPTAIN

I've no idea.

ALICE sits, in despair.

ALICE

So, it's to be Mini Hell forever.

CAPTAIN

I wonder if, in death, life begins again.

ALICE

I wish I could believe that.

CAPTAIN

(*Pause*) So Kurt, after all, is just another evil rogue?

ALICE

You know he is.

CAPTAIN

Happens to them all in this orbit, unless they escape. He's too weak for evil. God, the pettiness of it all! In the old days you could fight! Now you pull faces, shake a fist. (*Pause.*) Hah! (*He laughs.*) You know what we'll be doing in three months' time? Celebrating our silver wedding. With Kurt as Master of Ceremonies, toasts and speeches from the Doctor, the Ordnance Officer – even the Colonel will invite himself.

ALICE laughs briefly.

CAPTAIN

You may well laugh. Remember Östermann's silver wedding? The bride had to wear the ring on her right finger. The gallant cavalryman had cut off the left one with a bill-hook in a moment of tenderness.

ALICE puts her handkerchief in her mouth, stifling a laugh.

CAPTAIN

What's the matter, are you crying? You're laughing!
Did I tell you about the man who married and
divorced seven times, and ended up with the first
one? Is it all serious or a hoax? Comedy or tragedy?
Treat it as a joke, you get nightmares. Take it
seriously, you end up under the waves. Do you want to
celebrate it? The silver wedding? They'll laugh at us
either way. Silver wedding. Hah!

She looks across at him.

CAPTAIN

Well ... bivouac over. Pick up the weaponry. Forced
march, here we go.

She crosses and stands over him.

Fade to black.

The End.

THREE SISTERS

By Anton Chekhov

Version by Pam Gems

For John Caird

FOREWORD

One of the problems facing actors when they audition, or are considered for a role, is that their previous roles accompany them. If you have just played a pawky Scots lass in a successful comedy series, you may not be cast as Hedda Gabler next time round and, unfair as you know that to be, there is some sense in it. An audience will have a harder job suspending disbelief.

It is the same with the classics. We bring to a production of a play the sum of our previous experiences of it (and the sum of our lives.)

Like many people, I came to Chekhov first on the page. When I saw the plays in the fifties, productions were languorous, with rounded English vowels from gentlemen actors in tweeds, with slightly funny hats. There were three sorts of women: fat servants who didn't count; chilly though, sometimes, sprightly ladies of uncertain age, who wore the paler dresses to denote the lead; and lumpy girls (sometimes they were pretty but wore their hair back and no eye makeup) who stayed out of the main acting area. Everything was very mournful and, quite often, leaves fell down from the flies, to the pluck of an uncertain guitar. There was a good deal of upstaging. I remember an Astrov who firmly detached his map of Africa from down left and rehung it upcentre before commenting on the climate. I thought it was all lovely.

Then came a sea-change. Chekhov, amazingly, was funny. How did that happen? Hard to say. Sometimes, the perception of one director will do it – as when William Gaskill made people real and verminous in *The Recruiting Officer*, and took the 'La Sir' out of Restoration. At all events, attention was drawn to the fact that Chekhov called both

The Seagull and *The Cherry Orchard* comedies, and had hoped for laughs in *Three Sisters*. Drooping was out, briskness and irony, and jokes, were in – and so was pace.

The most recent fashion has been for revolutionary Chekhov. Bigger names as the servants, throwing the leads slightly off-centre, and heraldic emphasis on Chekhov's frequent references to the future. Presage, like universality, being the well-known child of genius, giving Chekhov his card.

All of which means, I suppose, that we are children of fashion. We change. Garbo as Anna Karenina is still, ineluctably, a divine of the thirties, never mind the costume budget. Thus, a new version of a classic is merely a link in the chain. But why the chain? Why re-present the thought?

In order to connect.

Theatre is ephemeral, live and now. It must constantly be reborn. And I should like, with special pleading, to speak for playwrights being given the job. Apart from being paid (modestly) for the close examination of a master's work, playwrights may be able to contribute something of their craft to an acting version of a foreign classic. The loss in too many scholarly translations is, to a playwright, woeful.

I find it fascinating, for example, that Chekhov was a choirboy as a child. He had a musical education. His ear was trained. Creating rhythms for the stage is complicated work. There *are* playwrights with cloth ears who manage to blurt out their meaning nonetheless; but it is like a man with no arms trying to drink soup.

And there is the matter of the nature of the communication that goes on in a theatre. Dramatic line proffers not information, not explication, but clue. Not only the emotion, but the cognition too, is supplied, not by the actor, supported by production for the benefit of a paying public, but by the public itself. The audience is a member of the cast, playing its role every night – and not always knowing its lines.

The play, on the page, is a diagram, a blueprint; and a pretty odd blueprint at that, since most of it is not there at all but in the spaces between the lines. Just about all of which, come to think of it, was invented by Anton Chekhov.

More than any other playwright, he saw that drama lies in the particular, and not in the general statement, which belongs, if at all, elsewhere. Those small, piercing moments of truth … It is connective tissue leaving us, the audience, to discern bones, flesh, and make the diagnosis. And a shocking break with playwrighting tradition.

It's hardly surprising that Russian audiences were, at first, doubtful, or that Chekhov complained of attempts to stereotype his characters. It is the playwright's cross to be crippled with constant fatigue in the search for truth, and then to be condemned as inept for finding it.

Chekhov, from the beginning, discovered and shared. He does not condescend. The work is mature. And he assumes that we are.

The realism that is in *Three Sisters*, *Vanya*, and *The Cherry Orchard* – the knowledge that fulfillment is beyond the grasp of the characters portrayed – chimes with Chekhov's own plight. He had his first hemorrhage in 1896.

In my own lifetime, people still died young from tuberculosis. My own maternal uncle died in six months from galloping consumption, leaving three small children. It is there in the play; the sense of time running out.

A further point … I wondered, pondering on the one physically violent event in *Three Sisters* (which happens offstage), why Chekhov was so little involved in the passionate revolutionary movements of the time. They were, after all, a major pastime of the bourgeoisie, then as now. He cannot have been unaware of – indeed, he was influenced early on by – Tolstoy, and the question has been much discussed.

There was, of course, his health, which made him an involuntary exile. Earlier, he was the mainstay of his family, in spite of being the third son. Then he was trained in the scientific method, which is particularly inductive when coupled with such an applied job as medicine. Practical work in the Russian provinces would have left little energy for idealism, or even political theory. You deal with patients one at a time, as individuals, rather than as members of a class or category.

Then there was the writing. Chekhov sold stories from his boyhood on, to supplement the family income. He became a journeyman at not one, but two of the most demanding crafts that have ever been devised. He referred to medicine as his wife, and writing as his mistress. Not much time left, you might say.

But there is another reason. The reason that makes writers so unreliable politically. You go where the writing takes you. Truth is not created by vote, or decision, but sought. You search and, when the page is full, you are surprised. It is not what you intended to say. It is not what you thought you thought.

Chekhov refers to this element often in letters to friends. You cannot guarantee the goods. Ibsen outraged first the political right, and then the political left with subsequent plays. Chekhov himself is impossible to pin down. He never overtly blames the regime for the failure of reforms. He notes the decay in provincial Russia; he records the stagnation, the savage plight of the peasants, the stifling pettiness of the middle classes. It is said that he is never, thereby, judgmental; that his kindness and sweetness are always present.

This certainly seems to have been true of him as a man. As a playwright, no. Writing to a friend about *Three Sisters*, he says: "This was written by someone very cunning and merciless."

I find him both. He is, both directly and indirectly, so wounding. He reveals people in their shallowness, in their pretensions. And he is without mercy. He is without mercy for falseness, dishonesty, laziness of thought, wilful refusal of life, of self-awareness. He has no patience with it, and he lets us have it – coldly and objectively. Like a doctor administering an emetic.

When you have a chest ailment, you can't breathe. For the tubercular doctor, Chekhov, who had toiled during epidemics, performed operations in filthy huts; who had travelled to remote Russia in order not to get soft, or spoiled by success, there was no patience with self-pity, with idleness, with self-deception.

He had strong hates: for the endless provinces of Russia, which had been his childhood background; for the so-called intellectuals of Moscow (cerebral, spiteful, and shallow) and, most of all, for despotism. He'd had a despotic father who beat him, and he never got over this. He was always shy, diffident … the penalty of sensitivity, of awareness, but also of that early brutalizing. You become untrusting, you don't feel secure in the world.

Chekhov wrote about love and truth, the stuff of life. And he couldn't bear the waste, the misuse of it.

Pam Gems

THREE SISTERS

CHARACTERS

ANDREI SERGEYEVICH PROZOROV	
NATALIA IVANOVNA	his bride, then wife
OLGA	his sister
MASHA	his sister
IRINA	his sister
FYODOR ILICH KULYGIN	Masha's husband, a schoolteacher
ALEKSANDER IGNATIEVICH VERSHININ	lieutenant colonel, battery commander
NIKOLAI LVOVICH TUZENBAKH	baron, lieutenant
VASILY VASILIEVICH SOLYONY	staff-captain
IVAN ROMANOVICH CHEBUTYKIN	military doctor
ALEKSEI PETROVICH FYODOTIK	second lieutenant
VLADIMIR KARLOVICH RODEI	second lieutenant
FERAPONT	an old man, a guard of the Zemstvo1
ANFISA	nanny, old woman, 80 years old

The action takes place in a provincial town.

THREE SISTERS

ACT ONE

<u>ACT ONE – SCENE ONE</u>

A drawing-room in the Prozorov house, with columns and a hall beyond, where the dining table is being laid.

OLGA, in the dark blue uniform of a teacher in a girls' school, is on her feet marking exercise books. MASHA, in black, with a little hat on her lap, sits reading. IRINA, in white, is standing, her mind elsewhere.

> OLGA

It's the fifth today. The fifth of May. Your name-day Irina. The day Daddy died – a year ago today. It was cold. There was snow. You were lying there, as white as a corpse. I thought we'd lost you. A year … and here we are. We talk about it now as though it was nothing. And you're in a white dress, your face shining.

The CLOCK strikes twelve.

> OLGA

Oh! And the clock striking just as it did then. The solemn music as they carried out the coffin, and the sudden noise of the guns – a volley of respect at the grave of a general in command of a brigade. But nobody there. Hardly anyone. And it was raining. It was so cold, the rain turned to snow.

IRINA

Don't. What's the point?

BARON TUZENBAKH, CHEBUTYKIN and SOLYONY appear in the hall, by the table.

OLGA

Today it's warm – so warm we can have the windows open. The birch trees aren't even out yet. In Moscow, in May, everything's in bloom. I remember Daddy getting his brigade in May and we left in sunshine. Eleven years ... it seems like yesterday. When I woke up this morning, saw the light – so bright it made your heart sing – I yearned to be back in Moscow.

CHEBUTYKIN

Like hell ...

TUZENBAKH

Rubbish.

MASHA, lost in her book, whistles to herself.

OLGA

Don't whistle indoors, Masha. It's bad luck. (*She looks at the book she is correcting.*) I'm getting a headache. Teaching all day, private lessons at night, I'm getting old before my time. Four years at that school has drained all the energy out of me. Only one dream gives me strength. Just one ...

IRINA

To go back. To go back to Moscow. Sell the house, finish everything here ...

OLGA

... and home to Moscow!

CHEBUTYKIN and TUZENBAKH laugh.

IRINA

Andrei will be a professor, he won't want to stay here.
There's only Masha.

OLGA

She can come to Moscow for the summers every year.

MASHA whistles quietly.

IRINA

It'll happen, God willing. (*She looks out of the
window.*) It's so lovely outside today – and it's my
saint's-day! When I remembered, first thing I felt –
such joy – I remembered when Mama was alive. Such
thoughts. Wonderful thoughts!

OLGA

You look lovely today. Shining. So beautiful – and
Masha too … and Andrei as well, if he wasn't so
fat. It doesn't suit him. I'm thinner, looking older, I
suppose, from having to put up with school. So tiring.
But today I'm home – no headache. I feel younger.
Everything's good and I'm only twenty-eight. I should
be married and able to stay at home. Oh, if I could be
at home all day, I'd love my husband.

TUZENBAKH

(*To SOLYONY*) Rubbish. Don't be such a bore. (*He
comes into the drawing room.*) Oh, I forgot! You'll be
getting a visit today from Vershinin, our new battery
commander. (*He sits at the piano.*)

OLGA

Oh, what a thrill.

IRINA

How old is he? Is he old?

TUZENBAKH

Not really. Forty, forty-five at the most. (*Playing quietly.*) Certainly no fool. Talks a lot.

IRINA

Is he interesting?

TUZENBAKH

Apart from having a wife – his second – a mother-in-law, and two little girls. Yes. You'll hear all about it from him. Wife's a bit touched. Wears her hair in plaits. Goes on and on about – I don't know what. Has a go at killing herself now and then, just to be annoying. I'd have got rid of her years ago, but he puts up with it. Just complains to everybody.

SOLYONY comes into the room with CHEBUTYKIN.

SOLYONY

With one hand, I can only lift 35 pounds but with two hands 300 even 400. That means two men are not twice as strong as one, but three times, five times, even more ...

CHEBUTYKIN

(*Reading from newspaper as he walks.*) If hair is falling out, dissolve four grammes of naphthalene in half a bottle of spirits and apply daily. (*He stops and writes it down*) Apply daily. (*To SOLYONY*) So, as I was saying – put the cork in the bottle, a glass tube through it. Then you take a pinch of colouring ...

IRINA

Ivan Romanovich ... dear Ivan Romanovich ...

CHEBUTYKIN

What is it, joy of my heart?

IRINA

Tell me, why am I so happy today? I'm in full flight.
Above me, big white birds in a blue sky. Why? Why?

CHEBUTYKIN

(*Kisses her hands tenderly*) My little white bird . . .

IRINA

When I woke up this morning, I got up – washed. All
of a sudden I felt . . . I began to feel that everything
was clear. That I knew how to live! I understand now,
dear Ivan Romanovich. A person must work, hard, all
the time, whoever he is. That alone can give his life
meaning, purpose, happiness . . . even ecstasy. How
right to be a worker – get up at dawn, break rocks on
the streets. Or a herdsman, or a teacher. Or a driver
on the railway. My God, better to be an ox – a horse
producing work – than a young woman who gets
up at noon, drinks coffee, and doesn't dress till two
o'clock. Oh, it's awful! I'm as thirsty as someone dying
of thirst in boiling hot weather. That's how much I
want to work. And if I won't . . . if I won't get out of bed,
then you must stop being my friend, beloved Ivan
Romanovich.

CHEBUTYKIN

(*Tenderly*) I will, I will . . .

OLGA

When we were small, we were out of bed by seven
o'clock. Papa's orders. Irina still wakes up – but she
lies there till nine thinking about the state of the

world with a face like this. (*She pulls a serious face, and laughs.*)

IRINA

Because I'm not a little girl any more. I'm twenty years old.

TUZENBAKH

A yearning for work. Occupation. God, I understand that! I've never done a stroke – never, ever. I was born in Petersburg – cold, pointless place – to a family that had never worked. Never wanted for anything. When I was a cadet, I'd come home every night and wait for a lackey to pull off my boots. My mother worshipped me – amazed if anyone found fault with me. As for work – doing anything useful – oh I was kept well away from that. Protected. Well, whatever the protection was <u>for,</u> it's not going to succeed. It's in the air – the storm that's coming – a huge overwhelming blast that will blow away all the lazy, idle meaningless lives spent with only the rot of boredom eating away people's souls. I'll work, and so will you all. Every one of us twenty years from now.

CHEBUTYKIN

Not me. I shan't be working.

TUZENBAKH

You don't count.

SOLYONY

You won't be here twenty years from now, thank God. Couple of years, you'll keel over from a stroke. Or I'll get furious, dear heart, and put a bullet in your nose. (*He takes out a scent bottle, and sprays himself with cologne.*)

CHEBUTYKIN

(*Laughs*) I haven't lifted a finger since I left
university. Haven't read a book . . . just the papers.
(*He takes another newspaper from his pocket.*) So I
know . . . What do I know? (*Looks at the paper*) Let's
see. I know about Dobrolyubov. He's a writer . . . of
something. God knows what.

KNOCKING from the floor below.

CHEBUTYKIN

Ah! Must be for me. Wonder who? Back in a minute.

CHEBUTYKIN exits, combing his beard in expectation of a visitor.

IRINA

What's he up to?

TUZENBAKH

Didn't you see his face? Probably got a present for
you.

IRINA

Oh no. That's so tiresome.

OLGA

Or he's doing something stupid.

MASHA

(*Sings quietly*) By the shore a golden chair
Around the oak
The oak so green
So gold the chair
So clear the light
The green and gold
Beguiling sight.

She rises, humming quietly to herself.

OLGA

Masha . . . you're unhappy today.

MASHA, still humming, puts on her hat.

OLGA

Where are you going?

MASHA

Home.

IRINA

You're going?

TUZENBAKH

Leaving Irina's saint's-day?

MASHA

It doesn't matter. I'll be back tonight. Goodbye darling. (*Kisses IRINA.*) Health and happiness, and good wishes again, to all. When Father was alive, thirty or forty officers at every saint's-day party. Now only one and a half. The place is like a desert. No-one's listening to me. I'm feeling low. So, I'm off. (*Laughing through tears.*) We'll talk later, but bye for now darling. I have to go.

IRINA

(*Upset*) Do you have to?

OLGA

(*With tears*) I understand, Masha.

SOLYONY

If a man philosophizes, that's philosophy. Sophistry at least. With two women, it's gab.

MASHA

What do you mean, you horrible man?

SOLYONY

Nothing. "He had no time to say hullo, Before the grizzly laid him low."

MASHA

(*Angry at OLGA*) Oh stop howling!

ANFISA and FERAPONT enter with a cake.

ANFISA

It's all right, Ferapont, old man. Your feet are clean. (*To IRINA*) From the Council, from Protopopov. It's a cake.

IRINA

Oh, thank you! Tell him thank you. (*She takes the cake.*)

FERAPONT

Eh?

IRINA

(*Louder*) Tell him thank you!

OLGA

Nanny, give him some. (*Louder, to FERAPONT*) Go on down! They'll give you a piece downstairs!

FERAPONT

Eh?

ANFISA

Downstairs ... cake downstairs, Ferapont Spiridonich.

ANFISA leads him off.

MASHA

I can't bear Protopopov. We shouldn't invite him.

IRINA

I <u>didn't</u>.

MASHA

Good.

CHEBUTYKIN comes in followed by a SOLDIER with a silver samovar. Murmurs of surprise and displeasure.

OLGA

A silver samovar ... oh no! *(She goes into the dining hall by the table.)*

IRINA

Ivan Romanovich, what are you doing?

TUZENBAKH

(Laughing) What did I tell you!

MASHA

My dear doctor, have you no shame at all?

CHEBUTYKIN

Beloved ones, you mean everything. You're all I have. I'm an old man, nearly 60. I'm nobody. Nobody at all, I have nothing. Nothing worth a damn, except my love for you. I'd have left this earth a long time ago if it weren't for that. *(To IRINA)* My darling little one, I've known you since the day you were born. I carried you in my arms, I loved your dear dead mother ...

IRINA

But why such expensive, extravagant presents?

CHEBUTYKIN

(Almost in tears, angry) Extravagant? Honestly. *(To the SOLDIER)* Take it in there. *(Teasing)* Expensive presents ...

The SOLDIER takes the samovar into the dining hall

ANFISA

(*Enters*) My dears, there's some colonel – I don't
know who he is – halfway up the stairs. I've never
seen him before. He's got his coat off already. Be nice,
Irinushka. Be polite to him. We're late with breakfast
already . . . oh Lord.

ANFISA exits.

TUZENBAKH

It must be Vershinin.

VERSHININ enters.

TUZENBAKH

Lieutenant-Colonel Vershinin!

VERSHININ

(*To MASHA and IRINA*) May I have the honour of
presenting myself: Vershinin. I'm delighted to be here
at last . . . good heavens – you've grown up!

IRINA

Do sit down. We're delighted to see you.

VERSHININ

The pleasure's all mine. But aren't there three of
you? I don't remember your faces but I do remember
Colonel Prozorov had three little girls. I saw them
with my own eyes. Time goes so quickly . . . so fast!

TUZENBAKH

Aleksander Ignatievich is from Moscow.

IRINA

From Moscow? Are you from Moscow?

VERSHININ

Yes. I was serving in his brigade when your father
was battery commander there. *(To MASHA)* I think I
remember your face a little.

MASHA

I don't remember yours.

IRINA

Olga! Olga! *(Calls to the dining hall)* Olga ... here!
(OLGA comes in to the drawing room.) Colonel
Vershinin is from Moscow.

VERSHININ

Ah, you must be Olga Sergeyevna – then you Maria –
and Irina, the youngest ...

OLGA

And you're from Moscow?

VERSHININ

Yes. I studied in Moscow, joined the service in
Moscow, served a long time there, and now here I am,
as you see, in charge of a battery at last. I don't really
remember you, but I do remember there were three
sisters, and I remember your father very clearly. I
used to visit you in Moscow.

OLGA

Vershinin ... ?

VERSHININ

Aleksander Ignatievich Vershinin.

IRINA

Aleksander Ignatievich?

VERSHININ

Yes.

IRINA

From Moscow?

VERSHININ

Yes.

IRINA

Oh, that's amazing!

OLGA

You see, we're moving back there.

IRINA

Most likely by the autumn. Going back to our home, where we were born, on Old Basmannaya Street.

IRINA and OLGA laugh with joy.

MASHA

(*Excited.*) And now we meet someone from Moscow! Now I remember! You remember, Olga – we used to call you "the lovesick major." You were a lieutenant then and you were in love with someone, and everybody teased you about it.

VERSHININ

(*Laughs*) Yes, that was me. The lovesick major.

MASHA

Only you had a moustache then. Of course you're older now. (*She becomes tearful at the realisation.*)

VERSHININ

Yes. I was still young then. In love. Not the same now.

OLGA

But you haven't got a single grey hair. You're older naturally. But not old.

VERSHININ

In my forty-third year. How long have you been away from Moscow?

IRINA

Eleven years. Masha, why are you crying? (*Tearful*) Now I'm crying!

MASHA

I'm all right. Which street did you live on?

VERSHININ

Old Basmannaya.

OLGA

But so did we!

VERSHININ

To get to the barracks, I had to walk over the huge bridge there. Water thundering under your feet. Not a place to be on your own. Saddens the soul. (*Pause.*) But here you have a fine river – wonderful!

OLGA

Cold though. Oh, and the mosquitoes!

VERSHININ

No. Good healthy Russian climate. The forest, the river, the birch trees. Of all the trees, I love birch trees. The most dear, modest things. A good place to live. Except, why is the railway station so far away? No-one seems to know why that is.

SOLYONY

I know.

They all look at him.

SOLYONY

Because, if the station were near, then it wouldn't
be far and, since it's far, it can't be near, can it? An
awkward silence.

TUZENBAKH

A joker, Vasily Vasilievich.

OLGA

Oh, now I remember you. I remember you!

VERSHININ

I knew your mother.

CHEBUTYKIN

A fine woman, God rest her soul.

IRINA

Mama is buried in Moscow.

OLGA

In the Novo-Devichy churchyard.

MASHA

I'm beginning not to remember her face. Dreadful.
Well, who'll remember us? We'll all be forgotten in
time.

VERSHININ

Yes, forgotten. Nothing to be done there. All the
things that mean so much to us – all forgotten.
Unimportant in the end. (*Pause.*) What's interesting
is not knowing what will last – remain, become
significant – and what won't. Probably Copernicus ...

Columbus were laughed at when they were alive. Perhaps our lives will seem ridiculous, primitive. Even sinful.

TUZENBAKH

Who knows? Or the other way round. We'll be remembered with reverence and respect. There's no torture now. Public executions are banned. Of course, a good deal of suffering still goes on ...

SOLYONY

(*High voice*) Cheep, cheep, cheep! Here, some birdseed, baron. Let's hear you philosophise.

TUZENBAKH

Vasily Vasilievich, leave off! (*He moves to another seat.*) You're being tedious.

SOLYONY

(*High voice*) Cheep, cheep, cheep!

TUZENBAKH

(*To VERSHININ*) So much suffering everywhere. But at least we're aware of it nowadays. Progress there, surely?

VERSHININ

Oh, of course.

CHEBUTYKIN

If you think we'll be remembered with respect, baron, I can't agree. We're down there – way down. Look at me (*He stands up.*) An inconsequential midget. But go on, tell me what a fine specimen stands before you. Cheer me up.

A VIOLIN is heard offstage.

MASHA

That's Andrei, our brother.

IRINA

The scholar of the family. Papa was a military man, but Andrei's an academic.

MASHA

Papa wanted it.

OLGA

We've all been teasing him today. We think he's a little bit in love.

IRINA

With a certain young lady who'll probably come through that door at any minute.

MASHA

You should see the way she dresses. Not that they're hideous, her clothes – or unfashionable. They're just ... weird. Bright yellow with fringes and a red blouse! She must scrub her cheeks raw, they're so red. Andrei's not in love. He can't be. I won't have it! He's got taste. He's just doing it to tease us. Someone said yesterday that she's after Protopopov, the chairman of the District Council. Very suitable. *(Calls)* Andrei, come here! Just for a minute.

ANDREI enters, holding a newspaper.

OLGA

This is my brother, Andrei Sergeyevich.

VERSHININ

Vershinin.

ANDREI

Prozorov. (*Wiping the sweat from his face.*) You're the new battery commander?

OLGA

Aleksander Ignatievich comes from Moscow, Andrei!

ANDREI

Congratulations. Now my sisters will never leave you alone.

VERSHININ

I've been boring them already, I'm afraid.

IRINA

Look what Andrei gave me today – a picture frame. He made it himself.

VERSHININ

Yes, it's ah ...

IRINA

And the one on the piano. He made that too.

ANDREI waves a hand and moves away.

OLGA

He's the family scholar, and a musician, and he makes things. He can do anything. Don't go, Andrei! He always disappears. Come here!

MASHA and IRINA, laughing, pull him back.

MASHA

Come on!

ANDREI

Please, leave me alone.

MASHA

Don't be silly! When we called the Colonel the lovelorn major he didn't mind at all.

VERSHININ

Not a bit!

MASHA

And you're the lovesick fiddler!

IRINA

Or the lovelorn professor!

OLGA

He's in love! Andrusha's in love!

IRINA

(Applauding) Bravo, bravo! Encore! Andrusha's in love!

CHEBUTYKIN

(Holding ANDREI by the waist from behind, still holding his newspaper.) Nature forms us for what? For love alone! (Roars with laughter.)

ANDREI

All right ... enough. (Wipes his face.) I didn't sleep last night. Read till four. Thought about this and that till the sun came in the bedroom. While I'm here this summer there's a book I want to translate from the English.

VERSHININ

You read English?

ANDREI

Yes. Papa, God rest his soul, burdened us with oh, so much education. The year after he died, I filled out. It was as if my body had escaped from prison. Thanks to my father, my sisters and I know French, German and English – and Irina knows Italian. Oh, it cost us, believe me!

MASHA

Knowing three languages! What's the point of that here? Useless – like having a sixth finger.

ANDREI leaves, unnoticed.

VERSHININ

Useless knowledge? There's no such thing. The town that doesn't need intelligent, educated people doesn't exist. Let's say that, in a backward town like this, there are only three people like you. All right, the life will suffocate you here but you won't disappear. You'll have some influence. And there'll be more of you to follow – and more, and more – until, in the end, you'll be in the majority and life will be astonishing. Beautiful. Amazing. If such a life doesn't exist yet, work for it. Dream of it. Learn more to prepare for it. (*Laughs*) And you complain of knowing too much!

MASHA

(*Taking off her hat*) I'll stay for breakfast.

IRINA

(*Sighs*) We should write all this down.

TUZENBAKH

You say it will be amazing in the future. True. But we must work for it. Work towards it.

VERSHININ

(*Stands up*) Yes. So many flowers in this room! (*Looks around*) Wonderful. I envy you. I've spent

my life in rooms with two chairs, a sofa and a smoky
stove. This is what I've been missing all my life –
flowers. (*Rubs his hands.*) Well ... anyway.

TUZENBAKH

Yes – work, we must work. Oh, he's German. All that
feeling. But I'm not, I'm Russian, I don't even speak
German. My father was Orthodox.

Pause.

VERSHININ

(*Moving about the stage*) I often think ... suppose
we could start our lives again? Use the first life as
something to learn from. At least we would have
rooms such as these, filled with light and flowers.
I've two girls. My wife's a sick woman and so on. Next
time round I'd avoid marriage. Absolutely!

KULYGIN enters in a tailcoat uniform.

KULYGIN

(*Approaches IRINA*) My dear sister, allow me to
congratulate you on your saint's-day, and to wish
you, from my soul, health, and all a girl of your
age could wish for. I'd like to present you with this
(*Gives her a book*). The history of our school's fifty
years, written by me. Nothing in it. I wrote it from
the lack of anything better to do, but read it anyway.
Gentlemen!

IRINA

(*To VERSHININ*) Kulygin. Teacher at our school.
Town councillor.

KULYGIN

(*To IRINA*) In this book, you'll find a list of all who
graduated here in the last fifty years. Feci, potui,
faciant meliora potentes. I did what I could. Let him
who can, do better.

IRINA

But you gave me this book at Easter.

KULYGIN

(*Laughs*) Oh well, give it back. Better still, give it to
the Colonel. Colonel – something to read when you're
bored and there's nothing else to read.

VERSHININ

Thank you. (*Rises*) I'm so pleased to have met you ...

OLGA

Oh, you're not leaving!

IRINA

Stay and have breakfast with us, please!

OLGA

Yes, you must!

VERSHININ

(*Bowing*) I didn't realise it was your saint's-day.
Forgive me. I didn't congratulate you.

VERSHININ leaves with OLGA – into the dining hall beyond.

KULYGIN

Sunday today. Day of rest and contentment –
depending on age and position. Time to put the
carpets away till winter in mothballs. Remember
the Romans. Mens sana in corpore sano. As our
headmaster puts it: the secret to a successful life

is order. Order and form. Without that – phtt! (*He laughs, his arm around MASHA'S waist.*) Masha loves me. My wife loves me. And the curtains too. Away with the carpets! Oh, I'm in a fine mood today! Off to the headmaster's at four, Masha. He's organising a walk for the teachers and their families.

MASHA

No thank you.

KULYGIN

My dear, why not?

MASHA

We'll talk about it later. Oh, all right, I'll come. Leave me alone now, please. (*She moves away.*)

KULYGIN

And then we'll spend the evening with him. He's not a fit man, but he never ceases to put himself out. Wonderful. He said to me yesterday, after the staff meeting, 'I'm exhausted Fyodor Ilich – exhausted!' (*He looks at the wall clock and then his own.*) Your clock is seven minutes fast. Yes, he said: 'I'm exhausted.'

A VIOLIN can be heard offstage.

OLGA

Breakfast is ready. We're having pie!

KULYGIN

Olga! Dear, dear Olga! Yesterday, I worked from morning till eleven at night. Went to bed worn out. Today? Today, I'm happy.

KULYGIN goes into the dining hall.

KULYGIN

(*Offstage*) My dear ... ?

CHEBUTYKIN

(*Putting his paper in his pocket and stroking his beard.*) Pie? Excellent.

MASHA

(*To CHEBUTYKIN, sternly*) Only don't drink anything today, d'you hear? It's bad for you.

CHEBUTYKIN

Rubbish. I haven't had a binge for two years. Anyway, what difference does it make?

MASHA

Don't you dare. (*Out of her husband's hearing.*) Another boring, endless evening.

TUZENBAKH

Simple answer. Don't go.

CHEBUTYKIN

Don't go, darling.

MASHA

Oh yes. 'Don't go.' Oh, this cursed life!

CHEBUTYKIN

(*Following her to the dining hall*) Never mind ...

SOLYONY

(*Following them*) Cheep, cheep, cheep ...

TUZENBAKH

That's enough, Vasily Vasilievich. Enough!

SOLYONY

Cheep, cheep, cheep ...

KULYGIN

(*Happily*) Your health, Colonel! I'm a teacher. Masha's husband, and really well looked after. Dear Masha's so good!

VERSHININ

I'll have the dark vodka. (*He drinks*). Your health! I feel at home here.

Only IRINA and TUZENBAKH are left in the living room.

IRINA

Masha's low today. She married at 18 when he seemed the most interesting person in the world. But it turned out he wasn't. He is very kind, but not clever.

OLGA

Andrei, are you coming?

ANDREI

(*Off*) Yes!

ANDREI enters and makes for the table.

TUZENBAKH

What are you thinking about?

IRINA

I don't like that Solyony of yours. He frightens me. Nothing he says makes sense.

TUZENBAKH

He's an odd man. Can be irritating. I think he's shy. When we're together, just the two of us, he's clever, tender even. In company, he gets aggressive. Don't go in. Stay. For a moment? Tell me, what are you thinking? (*Pause.*) You're twenty. I'm not thirty yet.

So many years ahead of us. Long, long rows of days
full of my love for you.

IRINA

Nikolai Lvovich, please don't talk about love to me.

TUZENBAKH

(*Not listening*) I have a desperate hunger for life and
experience – for battle, work and this … this thirst in
my soul that's grown, Irina, into my love for you. It's
as if you're wonderful to make life wonderful for me.
What are you thinking about?

IRINA

Make life wonderful? What are you saying? Our life,
the three of us, it's … For us life has … it's as though
we're drowning in weed and mud. (*She wipes her
face, smiling.*) Oh, now I'm crying. Work, that's the
the solution. We're unhappy – miserable – because
we don't have an occupation. We don't work. We were
brought up to despise work.

NATALIA IVANOVNA(Natasha) enters wearing a pink dress with
a green belt.

NATASHA

They're sitting down to eat already. I'm late.
(*Prinking before the glass.*) I think my hair's all
right. (*Sees IRINA*) Irina Sergeyevna! Best wishes!
(*Gives IRINA a firm, long kiss.*) You've so many
guests. I feel shy. No, I do, baron!

OLGA enters the drawing room.

OLGA

Natalia Ivanovna! Hello, my dear!

They kiss.

NATASHA

Happy Saint's-Day. You've so many people here ... I
feel quite ...

OLGA

Nonsense. Only friends and family. (*Nervous
undertone*) You're wearing a green belt. Oh dear.

NATASHA

Why, is it bad luck?

OLGA

No, no, it's just ... It doesn't go with the dress.

NATASHA

(*Daunted*) Oh but it's not really green. It's a much
duller colour.

OLGA exits into the dining hall. NATASHA follows her.

They all sit down to eat. The drawing room is empty.

KULYGIN

Here's to Irina and a handsome fiancé. Time you were
married!

CHEBUTYKIN

And for Natalia Ivanovna a little fiancé too.

KULYGIN

Natalia Ivanovna already has a little fiancé.

MASHA

(*Taps fork against plate*) A toast! To life, wherever it
went!

KULYGIN

Masha! C-minus for bad behaviour.

VERSHININ

This tastes very good. What's it made from?

SOLYONY

Cockroaches.

IRINA

Ugh! Don't be disgusting!

OLGA

For dinner tonight: roast turkey and sweet apple
pie. I'm at home all day today, thank God, <u>and</u> this
evening, gentlemen. This evening please.

VERSHININ

May I?

IRINA

Of course – please!

NATASHA

All very informal here.

CHEBUTYKIN

And here for love and love alone. (*Laughs.*)

ANDREI

(*Angry*) Oh stop it. You never leave off!

FYODOTIK and RODEI enter with a large basket of flowers.

RODEI, loud-voiced, has a lisp.

FYODOTIK

They're already eating.

RODEI

Wait a minute! (*He takes a photo.*) One. Hang on.
(*Takes another*) Two? Right – after you.

They take the flowers into the dining hall, where they are greeted.

RODEI

Congratulations and best wishes. The weather's fine.
I've been out with the boys. I teach gymnastics at the
school.

FYODOTIK

(*Takes a picture.*) You can move now, Irina
Sergeyevna. It's all right! You're looking very pretty
today, if I may say. I've got a spinning top for you, it
makes the most amazing noise.

IRINA

Oh, lovely.

MASHA

Near the shore a green oak grows,
Around the trunk, a golden chair
Around the trunk, a golden chair
(*Tearful*) Why do I keep saying that? It's been in my
head all morning.

KULYGIN

Thirteen at table!

RODEI

(*Loud*) Who believes that, eh? (*Laughter.*)

KULYGIN

Thirteen at table means someone's in love. Not you by
any chance, Ivan Romanovich?

Laughter.

CHEBUTYKIN

Oh, I may be an old dog, but why is Natasha here
blushing I wonder?

Loud laughter. NATASHA runs into the drawing room, followed by ANDREI.

ANDREI

Takes no notice. Ignore them ...

NATASHA

I shouldn't have left the table like that, but I was embarrassed. I just can't ... (*Buries her face in her hands.*)

ANDREI

Don't be upset. They were only joking. They mean no harm. They're good people and they love me – and you. Come to the window. They can't see us here.

NATASHA

I just don't know how to be with other people!

ANDREI

Oh, my dear, you're so young – wonderful! Don't worry. Don't be upset! Trust me. It's all right, they can't see us. They can't see us! Why do I love you? When did I ... ? I don't understand any of it. Oh, my beloved! Sweet darling girl. Marry me! I love you. I love you ... as no-one's ever loved ever before.

They kiss.

The OFFICERS enter and – seeing them – leave in amazement.

Fade to black.

ACT TWO

Evening. The same scenery as the first act.

The drawing room in darkness. From the street, an ACCORDION plays.

NATASHA in her dressing-gown, enters with a candle. She stops at the door to ANDREI'S room.

NATASHA

Andrei, what are you doing? Are you reading? Don't worry. (*Opens and closes another door.*)

ANDREI

(*Enters, book in hand*) Natasha . . . ?

NATASHA

Oh look, the servants haven't lit the candles. They're all excited with the Lent Carnival. You have to watch them. I found a candle alight at midnight yesterday. No one's owned up of course. (*Puts her candle down.*) What time is it?

ANDREI

(*Looks at his watch*) A quarter past eight.

NATASHA

And Olga and Irina still at work. Olga's at a meeting, Irina's still at the post office. (*Sighs*) Poor things. I was saying to your sister this morning: 'My dear, you must look after yourself.' But she doesn't listen. A quarter past eight. I'm worried about little Bobik. He's not at all well. Yesterday, a temperature – today he's freezing cold. I worry. I can't help it!

ANDREI

He's all right, Natasha. Nothing wrong with the boy.

NATASHA

He should be on a diet. Now all these people coming.
Can't you put them off?

ANDREI

Well hardly – they've been invited.

NATASHA

I leaned over him this morning, and he woke up and
gave me this beautiful smile. He knew me. I said,
'Hullo, Bobik, hullo, my pet.' And he laughed. Children
know. They understand. We can't have all these
people tonight. I'll tell them it's off.

ANDREI

(*Uncertain*) It's really up to my sisters. It's their
house.

NATASHA

And yours. I'll tell them. They'll understand. (*Going*)
I've ordered thick soured milk for supper. It's for
you or you'll never lose weight. (*Stops*) He was cold.
That room's too cold for Bobik. We must put him in a
warmer room. Irina's room's perfect. It gets the sun
all day. I'll tell her. She can sleep with Olga. She's only
here at night, after all. (*Pause.*) Andrei? You're very
quiet.

ANDREI

Just thinking. No, nothing.

NATASHA

I wanted to say something. Oh yes. Ferapont's come
round from the Council. He wants a word with you.

ANDREI

(*Yawns*) All right, let's have him in.

NATASHA exits.

ANDREI bends to the candle she has left, and reads his book.

FERAPONT enters, wrapped up in an old threadbare coat, with a book and papers.

ANDREI

Hullo my friend, what can I do for you?

FERAPONT

A book and some papers from the Chairman. (*He hands them over.*)

ANDREI

Thanks. Why so late? It's past eight o'clock.

FERAPONT

Eh?

ANDREI

I said it's late!

FERAPONT

I know. I've been hanging about. They said you were busy. Well, I'm in no rush. (*Thinks Andrei said something.*) Eh?

ANDREI

I didn't say anything. (*Looks at the book.*) Day off tomorrow. I'll go in anyway. Nothing to do here. (*Pause.*) Funny, isn't it, old friend? The way things turn out. I was feeling bored. Picked up this book today. (*Laughs briefly*) My university lectures. You have to laugh. What am I now? Secretary of the district council – under Protopopov for God's sake. I get to be a member of the council. Me – the man who dreams every night that he's a professor at Moscow University. A famous scholar, the pride of Russia!

FERAPONT

I wouldn't know. I don't hear very well.

ANDREI

I don't suppose I'd be saying all this if you could. I need someone to talk to. My wife ... (*Shakes his head*) she doesn't understand. My sisters ... I don't know. I'm afraid of them. That they'll poke fun at me. Be ashamed of me. I don't drink, I don't like bars. But what I wouldn't give now to be sitting at Testov's, or the Grand Moscow.

FERAPONT

One of the contractors in the Council was telling us the other day about these merchants eating pancakes. One of them ate forty at one go, and dropped dead. Either forty or fifty – can't remember.

ANDREI

You sit in Moscow, in the huge hall of a restaurant. You don't know anybody, and nobody knows you. But you don't feel like a stranger. Here you know everyone, everyone knows you, but you're a stranger ... a total stranger. And lonely.

FERAPONT

Eh? The same builder was saying – could have been lying – there's a cable stretched across the whole of Moscow.

ANDREI

What for?

FERAPONT

No idea. That's what he were saying.

ANDREI

Rubbish. *(He reads.)* You ever been to Moscow?

FERAPONT

Eh? *(Pause.)* No. Wasn't God's will. *(Pause.)* Can I go?

ANDREI

Yes.

FERAPONT goes.

ANDREI

Look after yourself. *(Reading.)* Come back tomorrow
for the papers. Off you go. *(Pause.)* He's gone.

A BELL RINGS.

ANDREI

Ah ... things to do ...

ANDREI stretches, and ambles off to his room.

Offstage, NANNY sings, rocking the baby.

MASHA and VERSHININ enter.

Behind them, the MAID lights the lamp and candles.

MASHA

I don't know. *(Pause.)* Perhaps it's what one's used
to. It took us ages to get used to not having orderlies
after Papa died. But I ... I do believe ... Well,
perhaps ... it's different in other places. But, in this
town, most certainly, the most decent, generous, well-
educated people are the military.

VERSHININ

I'd love some tea.

MASHA

(*Looks at her watch*) They'll bring it soon. I was married off at eighteen. I'd only just finished school, and my husband was a teacher – who, of course, seemed incredibly intelligent at the time.

VERSHININ

Mmm . . . yes.

MASHA

Oh, I'm not just . . . it's not just my husband. I'm used to him. But being with his colleagues, the other teachers, is unbearable. There are so <u>many</u> people who are crude, un-educated, uncouth. Rudeness worries me. It upsets me. I'm upset when someone is unsubtle, lacking politeness, ill-mannered.

VERSHININ

The military are just as bad as the civilians. At least in this town. Talk to anyone educated – he's either sick of his wife, or fed up with his home, his estate, and his horses. Russians are capable of complexity, aspiration, yet they set their sights so low. Why?

MASHA

Why indeed? You're very down today.

VERSHININ

I haven't eaten. One of my daughters is ill. It upsets me when that happens. I blame myself for landing them with their mother. Ridiculous woman. We started swearing at each other at seven. At nine, I slammed the door and left. (*Pause.*) I never talk about this. Odd. I only complain about it to you. (*He kisses her hard.*) Don't be angry with me. I have no- one apart from you. No-one at all . . .

MASHA

What a noise that stove's making. There was a noise like that in the pipes just before Papa died … just the same.

VERSHININ

Are you superstitious?

MASHA

Oh yes.

VERSHININ

Strange. (*Kisses her hand.*) You're a wonderful, lovely woman. Lovely, wonderful. It's dark in here, but I can see your eyes shining.

MASHA

(*Moves*) It's lighter over here …

VERSHININ

I love you, I love you, I love you … I love your eyes, the way you move, you are in my dreams … wonderful, lovely woman!

MASHA

(*Laughing quietly*) When you say things like that it makes me laugh. I don't know why. It frightens me. Please, don't do it again. (*Whispers*) Yes do, say it. I don't mind. (*She covers her face with her hands*) I don't mind. (*Urgently.*) Someone's coming, talk about something else.

IRINA and TUZENBAKH enter.

TUZENBAKH

I have this triple-barrelled surname, I'm the Baron Tuzenbakh-Kroner Altschauer, but I'm as Russian as you. Russian Orthodox. Hardly any German left in me. Patience perhaps, or is it persistence? I know I get on your nerves walking you home every night.

IRINA

I'm so tired.

TUZENBAKH

And I shall go on doing it. Walking you home every night for ten, twenty years until you chase me off. (*He sees MASHA and VERSHININ.*) Oh hello, it's you!

IRINA

Here I am at last. (*To MASHA*) A woman came in to send a wire to her brother in Saratov. To say her son died today. But she couldn't remember the address. So, she just put Saratov, and stood there crying. I said "I haven't got time for this." I was so stupid. Are the players still coming?

MASHA

Yes.

IRINA

(*Sits in an arm chair*) Oh, I must sit down.

TUZENBAKH

(*Smiling*) When you come home from work, you look so tiny.

IRINA

I'm tired! I hate working in the post office.

MASHA

You're thinner. It makes you look like a boy. (*She starts to whistle a tune.*)

TUZENBAKH

It's her new hair-cut.

IRINA

I must find another job. This one's no good. There's no
poetry in it – just mindless routine.

A KNOCK.

IRINA

The doctor is knocking. *(To TUZENBAKH)* Can you
knock, my dear? I can't, I'm tired.

TUZENBAKH knocks on the floor.

IRINA

We must do something. They were playing cards
again last night. They said Andrei lost two hundred
roubles.

MASHA

(Indifferent) Well if it's gone, it's gone.

IRINA

He lost two weeks ago, and in December. I wish he'd
lose everything and we could get out of this town.
God, I dream of Moscow every night. I'm mad. I know
we're moving in June, but that still leaves February,
March, April, May … nearly six months.

MASHA

Don't tell Natasha he lost.

IRINA

Why not? Why should she care?

CHEBUTYKIN, risen from a nap, comes into the dining hall. He
combs his beard, sits at the table, and takes out his newspaper.

MASHA

Oh, here he is. Has he paid his rent?

IRINA

(*Laughs*) No, not a Kopek in eight months. He's obviously forgotten.

MASHA

(*Laughing*) Look at him there. At peace with the world!

They laugh. Pause.

IRINA

Why so quiet, Aleksander Ignatievich?

VERSHININ

I don't know. Tea. Half my life for a cup of tea! I haven't eaten since this morning.

CHEBUTYKIN

Irina Sergeyevna!

IRINA

What do you want?

CHEBUTYKIN

Come here. Venez ici.

She goes, and sits at the table.

CHEBUTYKIN

I can't do without you.

IRINA sets out the cards for Patience.

VERSHININ

Well if there's to be no tea, what about some high-flown discussion?

TUZENBAKH

Yes! Let's do it.

VERSHININ

Life in the future? In three hundred years?

TUZENBAKH

Mmm ... life in the future. Well, they'll all be flying
about in balloons. Jackets will change. They'll
discover, perhaps, a sixth sense – and develop it. But
life will stay the same. Full of difficulties, fortune
or misfortune. And, in a thousand years, man will
sigh in just the same way: "Oh how hard life is!" And,
exactly the same, he'll be frightened and not want
to die.

VERSHININ

(*Thinks for a moment*) How to explain it? I think
that everything on earth will change little by little.
Already it's changing, in front of our eyes. In two
hundred, three hundred, finally a thousand years, a
new happy life will be here. We won't be a part of it, of
course, but we can work towards it. Suffer – and help
to create it.

MASHA laughs quietly.

TUZENBAKH

Why are you laughing?

MASHA

I don't know. I've been laughing all day. I don't know
why.

VERSHININ

I was a student like you. Didn't go on to the academy,
but I read a lot. Probably useless books but I can't
help wanting to know more. I'm getting old. Look, I've
got grey hairs. But I've learned one important fact.

There's no such thing as happiness. Not for us. We can only work towards it – for our children, and our children's children.

FYODOTIK and RODEI appear in the dining hall, and start singing quietly to the guitar.

TUZENBAKH

Can't we even dream about happiness? What if I <u>do</u> feel happy?

VERSHININ

No.

TUZENBAKH

(*Claps his hands, laughs*) How can I convince you? We're obviously at cross purposes.

MASHA laughs quietly.

TUZENBAKH

You may laugh. Listen, even in a million years, life will be just the same. Following its own laws. Birds migrating to and fro. That's the way it is.

MASHA

There must be some meaning to it. What does it all mean?

TUZENBAKH

Mean? Look, it's snowing. What does that mean?

MASHA

(*After a pause.*) We must have faith or life is empty. We may not know why cranes fly, why children are born, or the sky adorned with stars but, if you don't know why you're alive, your life means nothing.

Pause.

VERSHININ

All the same, I'm sorry to say goodbye to my youth.

MASHA

Gogol says: "Life is a bore, my friends."

TUZENBAKH

Can't argue with that, gentlemen.

CHEBUTYKIN

(*Reading a newspaper.*) Balzac got married in Berdichev.

IRINA starts to sing quietly.

CHEBUTYKIN

I must write that down in my notebook. (*He writes*) Balzac got married in Berdichev. (*He reads the newspaper.*)

IRINA

(*Laying out the cards. Pensively*) Balzac got married in Berdichev.

TUZENBAKH

The die is cast. (*To MASHA*) I'm resigning my commission, Maria Sergeyevna.

MASHA

So I heard. But I don't like civilians.

TUZENBAKH

I'm not handsome enough for a soldier. I'm going to work. For at least one day in my life, I'm going to work so hard that I'll fall asleep as soon as my head hits the pillow. (*Goes to dining hall.*) Workers sleep soundly enough.

FYODOTIK

(*To IRINA*) I bought you some coloured pencils in Moscow Street ... and this little knife ...

IRINA

I'm not a child any more. (*Takes them*) Oh, they're lovely!

FYODOTIK

I bought a knife for myself, another knife, and another one, this one for cleaning your ears, and these are scissors for the nails ...

RODEI

(*Loudly*) How old are you doctor?

CHEBUTYKIN

Me? Thirty-two.

Laughter.

FYODOTIK

Let me show you another Patience.

The SAMOVAR is brought in. ANFISA stands by it with a letter.

NATASHA enters and arranges the table.

SOLYONY enters, greets everyone, and sits at the table.

VERSHININ

My God, the wind!

MASHA

Oh, I'm so sick of winter. I can't even remember the summer!

IRINA

(*Playing Patience*) It's going to come out. We're off to Moscow.

FYODOTIK

No, it's not coming out. See the eight on the two of spades? That means you won't go to Moscow.

CHEBUTYKIN

(*Reading the paper*) Tzitzikar. Smallpox. An epidemic . . .

ANFISA

Mashenka, some tea . . . (*To VERSHININ*) Sir, please? I'm sorry, your Honour, I've forgotten your name . . .

MASHA

Can I have it here, Nanny?

IRINA

Nanny!

ANFISA

Coming!

NATASHA

(*To SOLYONY*) Babies understand you know. They understand perfectly. I said to Bobik: "Hello, my darling." And his little face lit up. Of course, you'll say it's because I'm his mother, but he really is an exceptional child.

SOLYONY

If that child were mine, I'd dip him in butter and fry him in a pan, and eat him.

SOLYONY Takes tea to the drawing room and sits in the corner.

NATASHA

You are a vile, vulgar creature!

MASHA

Summer and winter, what's the difference if you're
happy? In Moscow, I wouldn't even notice the
seasons.

VERSHININ

Remember the Cabinet Minister jailed over the
Panama affair? Kept a diary about the birds outside
his prison window – about the joy they gave him. As
soon as they freed him, he stopped noticing the birds.
You won't notice Moscow when you're living there.
Happiness is a state you hope for. It doesn't exist.

TUZENBAKH

(*Picks up a box*) Where are the sweets?

IRINA

Solyony ate them.

TUZENBAKH

All of them?

ANFISA

(*Serving tea*) A letter for you, sir.

VERSHININ

For me? (*Takes it.*) Ah. From my daughter. (*He
reads.*) Yes of course. Excuse me, Maria Sergeyevna, I
must slip away.

Shakes his head at the proffered tea, and rises, shaken.

VERSHININ

The old story.

MASHA

What is it? Can you say?

VERSHININ

(*Quietly*) My wife's taken poison again. I must go. All so unpleasant. (*He kisses MASHA'S hand.*) Dear, dear Masha. I'll go out this way.

VERSHININ leaves.

ANFISA

Where is he? I've just poured his tea. He's an odd sort of . . .

MASHA

(*Angry*) Oh leave it! And stop following me around. You're getting on my nerves! Silly old woman!

ANFISA

What are you upset about? Mashenka?

ANDREI

(*Offstage*) Anfisa!

ANFISA

(*Imitating him*) "Anfisa!" He just sits there!

ANFISA goes.

MASHA

(*By the table, angry*) Oh let me sit down. Cards all over the table . . .

IRINA

We're playing!

MASHA

Drink your tea.

IRINA

Mashka, what are you upset about?

MASHA

Keep out of my way. Just leave me alone!

CHEBUTYKIN

(*Laughing*) Don't touch her, don't touch her!

MASHA

Sixty years old! For God's sake, act your age or shut up.

NATASHA

(*Sighs*) Masha, dear Masha, must you? With your looks, you could be a real success in society. If it weren't for ... 'je vous en prie, pardonnez-moi, Marie, mais vous avez des manières un peu grossières.'

TUZENBAKH

(*Trying not to laugh*) Could you ... ? I ... I think I need a cognac ...

NATASHA

Il paraît que mon Bobik déjà ne dort pas. He's woken up. He's not well today. I must go, excuse me ...

NATASHA goes.

IRINA

Where did the Colonel go?

MASHA

Home. His wife again. (*Pulls a face.*)

TUZENBAKH

(*Crosses to SOLYONY with cognac*) You're always on your own with your thoughts. Come on, let's make up. Have a brandy.

They drink.

TUZENBAKH

I dare say they'll have me at the piano all night
playing rubbish. Never mind.

SOLYONY

What do you mean, make up? I haven't said anything.

TUZENBAKH

You always make me feel something's wrong between
us.

SOLYONY

(*Declaiming*) Didn't they tell you? Didn't you know?
That I am different, Aleko?

TUZENBAKH

What's Aleko got to do with it?

Pause.

SOLYONY

When I'm just alone with someone else, I'm fine. But,
in company, I tighten up. Then I talk a lot of rubbish.
Doesn't mean anything. I'm a lot straighter than
many, and I can prove it.

TUZENBAKH

I don't like the way you go on at me in front of people.
Still, I like you. Let's get drunk. I want to get drunk
today.

SOLYONY

Right.

They drink.

SOLYONY

I've never had anything against you, Baron, but
I'm like Lermontov. Nothing I can do about it. They

tell me I even look like him. (*He takes out a bottle of cologne, and sprinkles his hands.*)

TUZENBAKH

I've resigned my commission. Finita! Been thinking about it for five years. Done it at last. I'm going to work. I've made up my mind.

SOLYONY

(*Declaiming*) "Forget your dreams, Aleko."

ANDREI enters quietly with a book, and sits by the candles.

TUZENBAKH

I shall work.

CHEBUTYKIN goes into the drawing room with IRINA.

CHEBUTYKIN

And they served us genuine Caucasian food. Soup with onion followed by chekartma, a meat dish.

SOLYONY

Chereshma isn't meat, it's a plant like an onion.

CHEBUTYKIN

No, dear heart. Chekartma is a meat, like lamb.

SOLYONY

And I'm telling you that cheresma is onion.

CHEBUTYKIN

And I'm telling you that chekartma is lamb.

SOYONY

And I'm telling you that cheresma is onion.

CHEBUTYKIN

I'm not going to argue with you. You've never been to the Caucasus, and you haven't eaten chekartma.

SOLYONY

Because I can't bear it. It smells like garlic.

ANDREI

Gentlemen, please!

TUZENBAKH

When are the players coming?

IRINA

Nine o'clock. They're due now.

TUZENBAKH

(*Embracing ANDREI, sings*) "Here's a doorway made
of maple."

He hums a folksong, and leads ANDREI into the dance that goes
with it. CHEBUTYKIN joins in. Laughter.

TUZENBAKH

(*Kisses ANDREI*) A drink, Andrusha! To our
friendship! And to both of us in the university – in
Moscow!

SOLYONY

Which one? There are two in Moscow.

ANDREI

There's one university in Moscow.

SOLYONY

And I'm telling you two.

ANDREI

Three. The more the merrier.

SOLYONY

Two! The old one and the new one. If you don't want to
know, to hell with you. I'm off.

SOLYONY Goes out.

TUZENBAKH

Bravo, bravo! (*Laughs*) Gentlemen ... music! Never mind Solyony.

He sits at the piano and plays a waltz

MASHA

(*Dancing alone*) The Baron is drunk, is drunk, is drunk!

NATASHA enters.

NATASHA

(*To CHEBUTYKIN*) Ivan Romanovich!

She speaks to him quietly, and leaves.

CHEBUTYKIN touches TUZENBAKH on the shoulder, and whispers to him.

IRINA

What?

CHEBUTYKIN

We'd better be off. Goodnight.

TUZENBAKH

Time to go. Goodnight.

IRINA

But what about the players?

ANDREI

(*Embarrassed*) We've had to put them off. Natasha says Bobik's not well. I really don't know. It's all the same to me.

IRINA

(*Shrugs*) Oh well, if Bobik's not well ...

MASHA

She's throwing us out. (*To IRINA*) It's not Bobik who's ill, it's <u>her</u>! (*Taps her forehead.*) Petit- bourgeoise!

ANDREI exits to his room.

CHEBUTYKIN follows, they say goodbye in the back room.

FYODOTIK

What a shame. I was looking forward to being here for the evening, but of course if the baby's ill … I'll bring him a little toy tomorrow.

RODEI

(*Loudly*) I had a good long sleep. I'd thought I'd be dancing half the night. It's only nine o'clock.

MASHA

Let's go outside and decide what to do.

We hear them say goodbye, and TUZENBAKH'S laugh.

ANFISA and the MAID clear the table, and put out the candles.

NANNY can be heard singing.

ANDREI, in hat and coat, enters quietly with CHEBUTYKIN.

CHEBUTYKIN

I never got round to marrying. Life flashed by so quickly and, in any case, I was hopelessly in love with your mother who was married already.

ANDREI

Why marry? It's boring.

CHEBUTYKIN

What about loneliness? Say what you like, dear boy, it's a terrible state, loneliness. Ghastly. Well, what difference does it make in the end?

ANDREI

Let's go.

CHEBUTYKIN

Why? What's the hurry?

ANDREI

Natasha. She'll try and stop me.

CHEBUTYKIN

Ah!

ANDREI

I shan't play cards tonight. I'll sit and watch. I've
been feeling short of breath. Doctor, what ... ?

CHEBUTYKIN

Oh, don't ask me, dear boy. I don't remember. No idea
of medicine these days.

ANDREI

Let's go through the kitchen.

They leave.

A BELL RINGS, and again. VOICES and LAUGHTER.

IRINA enters.

IRINA

(*To ANFISA*) Who is it?

ANFISA

The players, from the carnival.

ANOTHER RING.

IRINA

You'll have to say we're not at home, Nanny. Say we're
sorry.

ANFISA exits.

IRINA walks about deep in thought. She seems anxious.

SOLYONY enters.

> SOLYONY

Where is everybody?

> IRINA

They've gone home.

> SOLYONY

Strange. Are you on your own?

> IRINA

As you see. (*Pause.*) Good night.

> SOLYONY

I apologize for earlier. I wasn't myself. Very tactless.
I'm sorry. But you see, you're not like the others.
You're pure, splendid. you see the truth. Only you –
only you can understand me. I love you, deeply,
endlessly ...

> IRINA

Goodbye. Please – leave ... you must.

> SOLYONY

I can't live without you. (*Approaches.*) Oh, bliss! Your
eyes! Those wonderful eyes, I've never seen such
eyes!

> IRINA

(*Coldly*) Stop, please.

> SOLYONY

It's the first time I've ... I haven't spoken of my love
before. It's as though I'm no longer on earth. On

another planet. (*Rubs his forehead.*) Anyway, no matter. Obviously, I can't make you ... But I swear I'll kill any other man who comes near you. Oh, wonderful!

NATASHA comes through with a candle, and looks in doors for her husband.

NATASHA

Andrei? Oh! Captain Solyony. I'm sorry, I didn't see you there. Forgive me. I'm not dressed for visitors.

SOLYONY

No matter. Goodbye.

SOLYONY leaves.

NATASHA

My poor girl, you're tired. (*Kisses IRINA.*) You should have been in bed hours ago.

IRINA

Is Bobik asleep?

NATASHA

Yes, but he's very restless. By the way, I've been meaning to say ... But I can't seem to catch you. Bobik's nursery is so cold and damp, and your room would be perfect for him. Could you move in with Olga?

IRINA

(*Not comprehending*) What?

The sound of a TROIKA, with bells.

NATASHA

You'll be in with Olga and Bobik in your room. He's such a darling. Today I said "Oh Bobik my little one!

My little one!" He looked up at me with those teensy little eyes.

DOORBELL.

NATASHA

That must be Olga. She's terribly late.

The MAID approaches and whispers in NATASHA'S ear.

NATASHA

Protopopov? What an odd fellow! He wants me to go riding with him in his troika. (*Laughs.*) These men!

A BELL.

NATASHA

He should have been here fifteen minutes ago. (*To the MAID*) Tell him I'm coming.

NATASHA exits.

The MAID goes.

IRINA sits, wrapped in thought.

KULYGIN, OLGA and then VERSHININ enter.

KULYGIN

What's all this? Isn't there a party?

VERSHININ

When I left half an hour ago, you were waiting for the players.

IRINA

Everyone's gone.

KULYGIN

And Masha? Where's Masha? Why's Protopopov down below in a troika? Who's he waiting for?

IRINA

Oh don't. I'm tired.

KULYGIN

I'm sorry I spoke.

OLGA

My meeting's only just finished. I've been deputising
for the headmistress. Ohh, my head. *(She sits)*
Yesterday, Andrei lost two hundred at cards. The
whole town's talking about it.

VERSHININ

Sorry to disappear. My wife tried to put the wind
up me by taking poison. It's all right. She's all right.
They got her through it. Well, time to go, I suppose.
May I wish you all the best? *(To KULYGIN)* Fyodor
Ilich, could we go somewhere? I really can't go home
just now – I just can't.

KULYGIN

I'm sorry. I'm tired. *(Stands.)* So tired. My wife gone
home has she?

IRINA

She must have.

KULYGIN

(Kisses IRINA'S hand.) Goodbye then. Tomorrow, and
the day after, I have all day to rest. I was counting
on some pleasant company tonight. Oh fallacem
hominem spen! Accusative case for exclamations.

VERSHININ

Well, I refuse to go home alone.

VERSHININ exits with KULYGIN, whistling.

OLGA

Oh, my poor head. I'll go and lie down. No work
tomorrow, thank God. Or the day after. Oh my head …

She goes.

IRINA

(*Alone*) All gone. Nobody here.

The sound of an ACCORDION on the street.

The NANNY sings a song, off.

NATASHA enters in her fur coat and hat followed by the MAID.

They cross the back room.

NATASHA

I'll be back in half an hour. I'm just going for a drive.

NATASHA and the MAID exit.

IRINA

(*Alone and sad*) To Moscow! To Moscow! To Moscow!

Fade to black.

ACT THREE

OLGA and IRINA'S room. Two o'clock at night.

Beds left and right, bordered by screens. Offstage a repeating ALARM BELL rings – a fire alarm.

MASHA is on the sofa in her usual black dress.

OLGA and ANFISA enter.

ANFISA

They're all sitting down below, under the stairs. I said 'come up,' but they won't. They keep saying: "Where's Papa? Where is he? Is he burned to bits?" People everywhere in the courtyard, only half- dressed …

OLGA

Here, take this grey one, (*Taking dresses from the cupboard.*) And this – and the blouse. Here, a skirt, Nanny. My God, what a thing to happen! Kirsanovsky Alley, burnt to the ground! (*Throwing the skirt at NANNY.*) The Vershinins got a terrible fright, poor things. Nearly lost their house! They must stay here tonight. They can't go back there. Poor Fyodotik. Nothing left. Every stick in the world gone. Poor man!

ANFISA

I can't carry all this Olyusha. You'll have to call Ferapont.

OLGA

(*Ringing the bell*) I keep trying. (*Opens the door*) Is anybody there? Can somebody come please?

Through the open door, a red glow of fire. The SOUND OF A FIRE BRIGADE PASSING.

OLGA

What a nightmare! I've had enough!

FERAPONT enters.

OLGA

Here, take these down. Give them to the Kolotilin girls. You'll find them under the stairs. (*Piles him with clothes.*) And these.

FERAPONT

Yes mum. It was Moscow was on fire in 1812. That gave the Frenchies a shock.

OLGA

Go on! Move!

FERAPONT

Yes'm.

FERAPONT leaves.

OLGA

Give it all away, Nanny. We don't need it. God, I'm so tired I can hardly stand. The Vershinins can't possibly go home. We'll put the girls in the living room. The Colonel with the Baron and Fyodotik – or he can sleep in the hall. Of course, the doctor's drunk, today of all days. We can't put anyone with him. He does it on purpose. Vershinin's wife can go in with the girls.

ANFISA

(*Exhausted*) Olyusha dearest, you won't turn me out, will you?

OLGA

Nanny don't talk nonsense. Nobody's going to turn
you out.

ANFISA

(Lays her head on OLGA'S breast.) Oh my own
precious. I do work hard, I do. But when I get weak it'll
be 'Go!' But where will I go? I'm eighty – in my eighty-
first year ...

OLGA

Sit down, Nanny, poor love. You're tired out. Sit down.
Have a rest. You're white as a ghost.

She helps ANFISA to a seat.

NATASHA enters.

NATASHA

They're saying we must form a relief committee
for people who've lost their homes in the fire. Very
good idea. It's the duty of the rich to help the poor.
Bobik and Sofochka are fast asleep, as if nothing had
happened! So many people in the house. Nowhere to
turn. Now they say flu's spreading in the town. I'm
scared the children might get it.

OLGA

(Not listening) You can't see the fire from this room.
It's so peaceful in here.

NATASHA

Oh dear, I must look a fright. *(In front of the mirror)*
People say I've put on weight. No. No, I haven't. Oh,
look at Masha. Fast asleep, exhausted, poor thing. *(To
ANFISA, coldly)* How dare you sit in my presence! Get
up! Get out!

ANFISA leaves.

NATASHA

Why do you keep that old woman? I don't understand you.

OLGA

(*Taken aback.*) I'm sorry. I don't understand you.

NATASHA

What is she here for? She's no use to us. She's a peasant. Waste of money. Send her back to her village. I like a house in order, not full of useless servants. Oh, you poor thing, you're tired. Our headmistress is tired. Mind you, when Sofochka's big enough to go to school, I shall be scared of you.

OLGA

I shan't be headmistress.

NATASHA

You will, Olechka. It's been decided.

OLGA

I shall say no. I can't. I don't have the strength. (*Drinks water*) You were so rude to Nanny just now. I'm sorry, it made me feel quite ill.

NATASHA

(*Worried*) I didn't mean to upset you.

MASHA rises, takes up her pillow and leaves in a rage.

OLGA

It's the way we were brought up. When people are rude, unkind, it makes me feel ill.

NATASHA

I'm sorry, I'm sorry ... (*Kisses her.*)

OLGA

Just the slightest – a harsh word to a servant – and
I ... I can't ...

NATASHA

I know I speak out of turn sometimes, but you must
agree, she should be back in the village where she
belongs.

OLGA

But she's been with us for thirty years!

NATASHA

I know, but she can't work anymore! Either I don't
understand you, or you won't understand me. She's
incapable. She just sleeps or sits.

OLGA

So, let her sit.

NATASHA

(Surprised) How can I do that? She's a servant!
(Tearful) I don't understand you, Olya. I have a
nanny, a wet-nurse, a maid, a cook. Why do we need
this old woman? What for?

The FIRE ALARM is sounding outside.

OLGA

I've aged ten years tonight.

NATASHA

No, we must have this out once and for all. You're at
school – I'm at home. You teach – I run this house.
And, if I say something about the servants, I know
what I'm talking about. I know what I'm talking
about. I want that thieving old hag – that old
witch – out of here! (Stamping her feet.) Don't you

dare irritate me like this. Don't you dare! *(Controls herself.)* You'll have to move downstairs. We can't go on like this. Impossible.

KULYGIN enters.

KULYGIN

Where's Masha? We should be getting home. The fire's dying down they say. *(Stretches)* Only one block gone. The wind made it look bad for a time, as if the whole town was burning. *(Sits.)* I'm exhausted. Oh Olya, if it weren't for Masha I'd have married you. Such a good person. I'm worn out.

He listens.

OLGA

What?

KULYGIN

The doctor. Drunk again. On one of his ... You'd think it was deliberate. *(Stands up)* I think I can see ... Yes. That's him – the old so-and-so. I think I'll ... *(He secretes himself in a corner.)* God, he's a waste of time.

OLGA

He hasn't had a drink for two years. All of a sudden, this.

OLGA goes with NATASHA to the back of the room.

CHEBUTYKIN enters, and crosses the room with a deliberately steady gait. He looks around, then crosses and washes his hands.

CHEBUTYKIN

(Gloomily) Blast the lot of them. I'm the doctor, I can
cure everything – wrong! If I knew anything once ...
all forgotten. Nothing left ... all gone.

Unnoticed by him, OLGA and NATASHA leave.

CHEBUTYKIN

That woman at Zaseep last Wednesday. She's dead
and I feel guilty because she died. Twenty-five years
ago, I knew something. A few ... Now, nothing. My
head is empty. My soul is cold. Am I a man? Do I
have arms, legs, a head? Do I walk, eat, sleep ...
exist? *(Cries)* If only I didn't! *(Stops crying)* Who
in hell knows. At the Club, that stuff about Voltaire,
Shakespeare ... all sitting there as though we'd
read ... knew all about ... Seedy bloody lot. All I could
remember was the woman lying dead. That's all I
could think of. I'm repulsive. Get drunk. What else is
there?

IRINA, VERSHININ and TUZENBAKH enter, the latter in smart
new civilian clothes.

IRINA

This will do. Nobody comes here.

VERSHININ

If it weren't for the soldiers, the whole town would
have gone up. Fine boys!

KULYGIN

(Approaches) Does anyone have the time?

TUZENBAKH

After three. It's getting light.

IRINA

Everyone's in the back room. Nobody wants to leave.
Your precious Solyony's there too. *(To CHEBUTYKIN)*
You'd better be getting to bed, Doctor.

CHEBUTYKIN

I'm fine, thank you. *(Stroking his beard.)*

KULYGIN

(Laughing) Well tanked up, eh? *(Claps him on the
shoulder)* Good lord. In vino veritas, yes?

TUZENBAKH

I keep being asked to organise a concert – for the fire
victims.

IRINA

Who'd be in it?

TUZENBAKH

I could organise something. Maria Sergeyevna, on the
grand piano . . .

KULYGIN

She plays wonderfully.

IRINA

Masha hasn't played in years.

TUZENBAKH

Nobody in this town knows anything about music
apart from me. I can assure you, Masha is a
magnificent pianist. Almost gifted.

KULYGIN

Quite right, Baron. I adore Masha. Splendid woman.

TUZENBAKH

To play like that, knowing that there's nobody –
nobody around to appreciate it.

KULYGIN

(*Sighs*) Mmm. But would it be all right, d'you think
for Masha ... as my wife ... to take part in a public
concert? (*Pause.*) I mean, I ... it might be acceptable,
but our headmaster – his views are ... Very clever
man of course. It's not his business but ... I'll have a
word with him if you like.

CHEBUTYKIN picks up a porcelain clock and examines it.

VERSHININ

I'm filthy. Dirty work, fighting fires. I don't look
human. (*Pause.*) I heard yesterday that we may be
transferred. The brigade's going off somewhere.
Poland – Siberia – long way anyway.

TUZENBAKH

I heard that. The town will be empty without the
army.

IRINA

And we'll be leaving too!

CHEBUTYKIN drops the clock, which smashes.

CHEBUTYKIN

Whoops!

Pause. Everyone is upset.

KULYGIN

(*Picking up the pieces.*) Ivan Romanovich! How could
you? Something so valuable! Z minus for behaviour!

IRINA

That was Mama's clock.

CHEBUTYKIN

All right, if it was Mama's, it was Mama's. Maybe I
didn't break it. It only seems that I did. Maybe we
only seem to exist when in fact we don't ... I don't
know anything. Who does? *(By the door.)* Why look
at me like that? Natasha's having a little affair with
Protopopov, but you don't see that. You don't see
anything. You just sit there and you see nothing.
(Sings to himself as he leaves.)

VERSHININ

Yes. *(He laughs.)* What a strange night! *(Pause.)*
I ran home as soon as the fire started. The house
was fine, but the girls were on the doorstep in their
nightclothes. No sign of their mother. People, horses,
dogs running about – and the looks on their faces! I
thought, my God, what will they have to live through
in the years to come? I grabbed them and ran. And all
I could think of was: what will my girls have to live
through?

A FIRE BELL

VERSHININ

(After a pause.) When I arrived, who do I see? Their
mother – screaming and shouting.

MASHA enters with her pillow and sits on the sofa.

TUZENBAKH falls asleep

VERSHININ

When my girls were on the doorstep in their
nightdresses, and the street was lit by the flames,

I stood there thinking: this is how it must have been before – when there was looting and burning. But think of the difference between then and now. Another two, three hundred years, and they'll look back on u̲s̲ with horror and amazement. It'll all seem primitive. What a life it'll be. Oh what a life! (*Laughs*) Forgive me, I'm off again. Indulge me if you can. I'm in the mood for it. (*Pause.*) It's as if the whole world is asleep. Hasn't woken up yet. So that all we can do is imagine how it will be when it does. Here, in this town – how many people like you? Two? Three? But, in the future, there'll be more and more. Better and better. Leaving you behind. (*Laughs*) God, I'm in a bizarre mood today. I'm in the mood for life! (*Sings*)

"Love will triumph, love will triumph,
Love will make the choice,
Lovers bow to love's command,
True love's beguiling voice."

MASHA

Tra la la.

VERSHININ

Tra la.

MASHA

Tra la la?

VERSHININ

Tra la la. (*He laughs.*)

FYODOTIK enters.

FYODOTIK

(*Dancing*) All gone! Burnt to the ground!

Laughter.

IRINA

What's so funny? How can you laugh?

FYODOTIK

(*Laughs*) Everything gone. Nothing left! The guitar burnt. The photographs burnt. All my letters. The book I wanted to give you – burnt.

SOLYONY enters.

IRINA

No, please go away, Vasily Vasilievich. You can't come here.

SOLYONY

Why the Baron and not me?

VERSHININ

We must be going anyway. How's the fire?

SOLYONY

Dying down, they say. (*To IRINA*) Why the Baron and not me? (*He sprays himself with cologne.*)

VERSHININ

(*Sings*) Tra-la-la!

MARSHA

(*Sings*) Tra-la-la!

VERSHININ

(*Laughs, to SOLYONY*) Shall we go into the hall?

SOLYONY

Good, write this down. 'Make it an engaging piece, Sharp enough to tease the geese.' (*Looking at TUZENBAKH.*) Chirp, chirp, chirp . . .

VERSHININ and FYODOTIK leave.

IRINA

Wretched Solyony. The room stinks of smoke. The Baron's gone to sleep. Baron! Baron!

TUZENBAKH

(*Waking*) Mmm, yes. The bricky and ... I'm not raving. I'm going to work in a brickyard. I've made up my mind. I've started some arrangements. The manager says ... (*Tenderly to IRINA*) Oh you are so splendid. Your skin so white. You shine like a candle in the dark air. Like a star. Why be unhappy? Come away with me. We'll leave together – work together!

MASHA

Nikolai Lvovich, go away.

TUZENBAKH

(*Laughing*) Oh are you here? I can't see you. (*Kisses IRINA'S hand.*) I'm going. I remember a morning, a long time ago. It was your birthday. You were so full of life. Talked about the joy of working. Life seemed so possible, so promising then. What's happened? Where has it gone? (*Kisses her hand.*) You're crying. Go to bed. It's getting light. Oh, if only you would let me devote my life to you!

MASHA

Nikolai Lvovich, go away. I mean it.

TUZENBAKH

I'm going.

TUZENBAKH goes.

MASHA

(*Lying down.*) Are you asleep, Fyodor?

KULYGIN

Mmm?

MASHA

You should go home.

KULYGIN

Masha, my darling Masha ...

IRINA

She's exhausted, Fodya. Let her rest.

KULYGIN

I'll go in a minute, my wonderful wife. My one and only. I love you.

MASHA

(*Angry*) Amo, amas, amat, amamus, amatis, amant.

KULYGIN

(*Laughing*) No, it's true. She's amazing. I've been married to you for seven years. It's as though it was yesterday morning. No, it's true! You're an astonishing woman. I'm happy, I'm happy, I'm happy!

MASHA

And I'm fed up, fed up, fed up! (*She sits up.*) No, I can't keep quiet any longer. I can't get it out of my head. It's Andrei. He's mortgaged this house to the bank, and his wife's sitting on the money. The house doesn't belong to him! It belongs to all four of us. If he'd an ounce of decency, he'd remember that.

KULYGIN

He owes money to half the town, Masha.

MASHA

Well, it's infuriating! Disgusting! (*She lies down.*)

KULYGIN

We're not poor. I teach, I tutor. I'm honest. Omnia mea
mecum porto, as they say.

MASHA

I don't need anything. But it isn't right, and he knows
it. (*Pause.*) Go home, Fyodor.

KULYGIN

(*Kisses her.*) You're tired. Have a rest for half an
hour. I'll wait for you in there.

KULYGIN goes.

KULYGIN

I'm happy … I'm happy … I'm happy …

IRINA

It's true. Andrei's not the same since he married that
woman. All his ambition is gone. At one time, he was
going to be a professor. Yesterday, he was over the
moon because he's finally on the local council. He's a
member and Protopopov is the Chairman. The whole
town's laughing. He's the only one who doesn't see
it! What does he do when everyone else is out on the
street fighting the fire? He's in his room. Sitting in
his room playing the violin. The violin! (*Nervously*)
Oh, it's awful! (*Cries*) I can't bear it anymore! I can't!

OLGA enters to clear up her little table, but is arrested by IRINA'S
distress.

OLGA

Darling, what is it? What's the matter?

IRINA

(*Sobbing*) Where's it all gone? Where did it go? Oh my
God, I've forgotten everything! It's all a muddle in my

head. I don't remember the Italian for window. I've forgotten everything. More and more every day. Life slips away, and it won't come back. We'll never go to Moscow. I see that. We won't, we won't ... we won't ...

OLGA

Darling, darling ...

IRINA

(*Restrains herself.*) I'm so unhappy. I can't work. I can't bear the post office. I hate it! Everything about it. I'm twenty-four and my brain's drying up. I'm getting stupid. I'm getting old. And there's nothing – nothing. No satisfaction. I seem to be going further and further away from life. Falling into a pit. Into the abyss. Why I haven't killed myself? God only knows. I don't.

OLGA

Don't cry, darling, don't. I can't stand it ...

IRINA

I'm not crying, I'm not. I've stopped. Look, I've stopped.

OLGA

Listen. Listen darling. I'm talking to you as your sister. Your friend. Take my advice, marry the Baron.

IRINA weeps quietly.

OLGA

You like him. You respect him. True, he isn't handsome. But he's a decent, honourable man. People don't marry for love you know.

IRINA

Then why?

OLGA

For duty. I'd marry without love as long as he was
decent. Even if he was old.

IRINA

I kept waiting for when we went to Moscow, where I'd
meet the man of my dreams – and love him. It's all
rubbish. I'm such a fool.

OLGA

(*Embraces IRINA*) My darling, beautiful sister, I
do understand. When the Baron left the army, and
came here in a suit, I thought "Oh! He isn't handsome
anymore." And I cried! When he asked me what was
wrong, what could I say? But if God wants you to
marry him, I'd be happy.

NATASHA crosses with a candle in silence.

MASHA

(*Sits*) Walking about as though she started the fire.

OLGA

Masha, you are idiotic. You really are.

MASHA

(*After a pause.*) Oh, darling sisters, I'm going to tell
you something. I can't keep it to myself any longer.
I'm in agony. I'm going to tell you. Nobody else – ever.
It's my secret, I can't stay silent any longer. (*Pause.*) I
love him. Oh, it's no use. I love him. Vershinin.

OLGA

(*Goes behind a screen.*) Don't! In any case, I can't
hear you.

MASHA

What can I do? (*Holds her head.*) I thought he was odd
at first. Then I pitied him. Then I fell in love with him.
With his voice – everything he said. His unhappiness.
His daughters . . .

OLGA

(*Behind the screen.*) I can't hear you, whatever you're
saying, I can't hear it.

MASHA

You're being stupid. Can't you understand, I love him?
That's how it is. That's my lot. And he loves me. It's
terrifying. And wonderful. (*She pulls IRINA down
to herself.*) Oh, my dear, we'll get through our lives
somehow. Not like a novel, where everything makes
sense and is resolved. I'm in love. And it's all strange.
Different. I don't know what to say. Or do. Oh, my dear
sisters! Now you know. You mustn't tell anyone. And
no more from me. Like Gogol's madman, I shall hold
my tongue. Sssh!

ANDREI enters, followed by FERAPONT.

ANDREI

(*Angry*) I don't understand. What do you want?

FERAPONT

Andrei Sergeyevich, I've explained it to you ten times
now!

ANDREI

In the first place, I'm not Andrei Sergeyevich to you.
I'm Your Honour!

FERAPONT

The firemen want to know if they can get to the river
through the garden. Otherwise, they'll have to break
their backs going the long way round.

ANDREI

All right, all right. Tell them yes. All right.

FERAPONT leaves.

ANDREI

I'm sick of the sight of them! Where's Olga?

OLGA appears from behind the screen.

ANDREI

I can't find the key to the cupboard. Can I have yours,
the little key ... ?

OLGA gives him the key. IRINA goes behind the screen.

ANDREI

God, what a fire! Enormous! Dying down now.
Damned Ferapont irritated me so much, I was yelling
at him to call me your Honour. (*Pause.*) What's the
matter, Olga? (*Pause.*) We're all here. Let's have it out.
Now. Once and for all. What is it? What have you got
against me?

OLGA

Not now, Andrusha. Tomorrow. (*Getting upset.*) Oh,
what a night!

ANDREI

(*Embarrassed*) Look, there's no need to get upset.
Just tell me. What have you all got against me? Just
say it!

VERSHININ singing offstage.

VERSHININ

Tra-la-la!

MASHA

Tra-la-la. (*To OLGA*) Good night, Olya. God be with you. (*Goes to screen, and kisses IRINA.*) Sleep well. Night, Andrei. Leave it for now. They're exhausted. We'll sort it out tomorrow.

MASHA goes.

OLGA

Andrusha, leave it till tomorrow. Time for bed. (*Goes behind screen.*)

ANDREI

I'll just say this and then I'll go. I know you've got something against Natasha. I've been aware of it since the day we married. Natasha is a wonderful person. I love my wife and I respect her, and I expect others to respect her too. (*Pause.*) The other thing. I'm sorry to disappoint you. I'm not a professor, nor an academic now. I'm a member of the local council and proud of it. (*Pause.*) There's something else. I did mortgage the house without asking you, and I apologise. I apologise for that. I'm sorry. I had to do it. I was in debt. But I've given up cards now, and I can say, in justification, that you girls get an annuity, whereas I ... that's to say, I don't have an income.

Pause.

KULYGIN

(*At the door.*) Is Masha here? That's odd. Where is she?

KULYGIN goes.

ANDREI

You're not listening. Natasha's a wonderful woman. *(He paces the stage. And stops.)* When I got married, I thought we'd all be happy but … my God! *(He cries).* Oh, my dear sisters! It's not true. Don't believe a word of it!

ANDREI leaves.

KULYGIN

(At the door.) Where's Masha? Why isn't she here? I don't know.

KULYGIN goes.

The stage is empty. The ALARM sounds.

IRINA

(Behind the screen.) Olya? Who's knocking?

OLGA

It's the doctor. He's drunk.

IRINA

Oh, what a night. *(Pause.)* Olya! *(Looks out.)* Did you hear? The brigade's being transferred. Somewhere far away.

OLGA

It's only a rumour.

IRINA

We'll be all on our own. Olya!

OLGA

What?

IRINA

Darling, I do respect the Baron. He's a fine man. All right, I will marry him. Only we must, we _must_ go to Moscow! Please . . . please . . . it's the only place in the world. We must go Olya. We must!

Fade out.

ACT FOUR

The old garden by the Prozorov house. Midday.

An alley of fir-trees, a river beyond. Beyond that, forest. There's a verandah on the right, with bottles on the table. Champagne has been drunk. PEOPLE pass in the background. A squad of SOLDIERS march by.

CHEBUTYKIN, genial throughout the act, is in an armchair, waiting to be called. He carries a stick, and wears a military cap.

IRINA, KULYGIN, wearing a medal around his neck, without his moustache, and TUZENBAKH stand on the verandah waiting to say goodbye to FYODOTIK and RODEI, who approach in campaign uniform.

TUZENBAKH
(*Embracing FYODOTIK*) Good man. We've been good friends. (*Kisses RODEI*) And you, Rodei – goodbye!

IRINA
Au revoir!

FYODOTIK
Adieu. We won't meet again.

KULYGIN
Who's to say? Oh look, I'm crying!

IRINA
We'll meet again.

FYODOTIK
In ten … fifteen years? We won't know each other.
We'll be strangers. One more. (*Takes a photo.*)

RODEI

(*Embraces TUZENBAKH.*) We'll never meet again.
(*Embraces him.*) Never again. (*Kisses IRINA'S hand.*)
Thank you for everything. Everything!

FYODOTIK

(*Cross*) Stand still!

TUZENBAKH

God willing we'll see each other again. Write. Be sure
to write!

RODEI

(*Looks around.*) Goodbye, trees! (*Calls*) Hup! Hup!
(*Pause.*) Farewell, echo!

KULYGIN

Who knows? You might get married in Poland. Find a
little Polish wife to call Kokhane – beloved!

FYODOTIK

(*Glancing at his watch.*) We'll be off in an hour.
Solyony's the only one from our battery going on the
barge. The rest of us are marching. Three batteries go
today. Tomorrow another three, and then peace and
quiet all over town.

TUZENBAKH

And a deadly boredom.

RODEI

(*To KULYGIN.*) Your wife?

KULYGIN

Masha? In the garden.

FYODOTIK

We must say goodbye to her.

RODEI

Goodbye. Must be off, or I'll be in tears. (*Hugs TUZENBAKH and KULYGIN, and quickly kisses IRINA'S hand.*) It's been wonderful here.

FYODOTIK

(*To KULYGIN*) A little book and a pencil, to remember us by. We'll go by the river.

They leave, looking around them.

RODEI

(*Shouts*) Hup-hup!

KULYGIN

(*Shouts*) Goodbye!

FYODOTIK and RODEI, upstage, bid MASHA farewell.

They exit together.

IRINA

They're gone. (*She sits on the verandah's lowest step.*)

CHEBUTYKIN

They didn't say goodbye to me.

IRINA

What about you? You didn't say ...

CHEBUTYKIN

No, I forgot somehow. Anyway, I'll be seeing them soon. I'm off tomorrow. One more day, and that's it. A year's time I'll be retired (*Puts his newspaper away, takes out another.*) A changed man. Quiet. Sober. A decent fellow.

IRINA

A very good idea. Advisable.

CHEBUTYKIN

I agree. *(Sings)* Tarara boomdeay, I'm on the fence
today.

KULYGIN

Ivan Romanovich, you're incorrigible!

CHEBUTYKIN

Yes, I should have listened to you. You'd have made a
new man of me.

IRINA

Why did you shave off your moustache? I can't bear
to look at you.

KULYGIN

Why not?

CHEBUTYKIN

Do you want to know what you look like? No, better
not.

KULYGIN

Why? It's the way to look now – a la mode. The
headmaster shaved his off. He's always ahead, so
when I became an inspector – off. Nobody likes it, but
I'm happy with or without a moustache. *(Sits.)*

ANDREI appears apart, pushing a pram.

IRINA

Ivan Romanovich. Dear Doctor, you were on the
boulevard yesterday. What happened?

CHEBUTYKIN

What happened? Nothing. *(Reads his paper.)* Just
some nonsense. Nothing important.

KULYGIN

The way I heard it, the Baron and Solyony bumped
into each other outside the theatre ...

TUZENBAKH

Please. That's enough. (*He waves a dismissive hand,
and goes into the house.*)

KULYGIN

Solyony started on the Baron. He took offence and
said something.

CHEBUTYKIN

It was nothing. Nonsense.

KULYGIN

There was a teacher who wrote 'nonsense' on a boy's
essay. Only, his writing was so bad the boy thought it
was a Latin word meaning 'excellent.' You know what
they're saying? That Solyony's in love with Irina, so
he hates the Baron. Understandable. She's a terrific
young woman, Irina. Like Masha, she has depth. But
you're more gentle, Irina. Of course, Masha can be ...
She's extremely ... I love her.

Calls of greeting from the garden.

IRINA

(*Shivers*) I don't know why, I'm jumping at everything
today. (*Pause.*) Everything's packed, ready to be
sent on after lunch. The Baron and I will get married
tomorrow and set off for the brick factory. The day
after that, I start a new life at the school. God give me
strength. When I took my exams for teaching, I cried
for joy. I felt blessed. (*Pause.*) The horse and cart will
be here after lunch for my things.

KULYGIN

All very fine. All these ideas. No matter, I wish you well, from the bottom of my heart.

CHEBUTYKIN

My golden girl. I'm losing you. You're flying away from me. I'm left behind like a bird that's too old to spread its wings anymore. Fly away, my darling. God be with you. (*Pause.*) You shouldn't have shaved off that moustache, Fyodor Ilich.

KULYGIN

Oh, leave it. (*Sighs.*) Off today, the soldiers. It'll all quieten down now. She's a fine woman, Masha. I don't care what they say. Honest. A good woman. I love her very much. I'm grateful for what I've got. Each to his own destiny. Hah! There's a man at the excise office, Kozyrev. We were at school together. He got thrown out for not understanding the ut consecutivum. Whenever I see him, I say: "Hullo, ut consecutivum." And he says it back, with a cough. Dreadfully poor, and not well at all these days. I'm fine. I've been lucky all my life. Even awarded the Order of St Stanislav ... second class. Now I'm teaching the ut consecutivum. I'm an intelligent man of course. But that's not the secret of happiness.

In the house, someone plays *The Maiden's Prayer* on the piano.

IRINA

At least I shan't have to put up with The Maiden's Prayer any more ... or Protopopov. (*Pause.*) He's in there. In the drawing room. Even today.

KULYGIN

Is the headmistress here?

MASHA walks apart.

IRINA

No. They've sent for her. I hate living here alone now she's at the school. I wish I was busy like Olya. There's nothing to do. I hate this house. My room. If I'm not destined for Moscow, then I'm not. So be it. What can I do? He's proposed to me and I've made up my mind. It's God's will. He's a good man, Nikolai Lvovich. Surprisingly good and kind. A good human being. And, suddenly, I've come alive. It's as if I've grown wings. I'm happy, and everything's become easy for me again. Suddenly I want to work, work, work. Only, yesterday, something happened. Something mysterious. I felt ... *(She shudders.)*

CHEBUTYKIN

Oh, nonsense.

NATASHA

(At the window) The headmistress!

NATASHA goes.

KULYGIN

Ah, the headmistress ...

He ushers IRINA inside.

CHEBUTYKIN

(Reading the paper.) "Tarara boomdeay ... I'm on the fence today ... "

MASHA approaches. Further off, ANDREI pushes the pram.

MASHA

There you are, sitting away.

CHEBUTYKIN

What if I am?

MASHA

Oh, nothing. (*Sits. Pause.*) You loved my mother.

CHEBUTYKIN

Very much.

MASHA

Did she love you?

CHEBUTYKIN

(*Pause.*) I don't remember now.

MASHA

Is my man here? We had a cook who used to call her
policeman friend 'my man.' Is mine here?

CHEBUTYKIN

Not yet.

MASHA

When you lose the little bit of happiness you've ever
had, it starts to destroy you. You become bitter. It's …
I'm seething inside. (*Points at her breast.*)

ANDREI wheels the pram past them.

MASHA

Look at him. He's finished. Like the bell. So much
money raised. So much effort. Thousands of people's
efforts. Up it went, the great bell. And was dropped.
Shattered. Just like Andrei. Why?

ANDREI

Oh, for some peace and quiet! This house is so noisy.

CHEBUTYKIN

Not long now. (*Looks at his watch.*) This old watch
has a bell. Listen. (*Winds, and the watch strikes.*) The
first, second, and fifth batteries will leave on the dot
of one. (*Pause.*) And I'm off tomorrow.

ANDREI

For good?

CHEBUTYKIN

No idea. May be back in a year. Who knows? What
does it matter?

The sounds of a HARP and a VIOLIN in the distance.

ANDREI

The town will be like a birdcage with a cloth over
it. (*Pause.*) Something happened yesterday – I don't
know what. Outside the theatre.

CHEBUTYKIN

It's nothing. Just some nonsense. Solyony started on
the Baron, who lost his temper and humiliated him,
and Solyony felt obliged to challenge him to a duel.
(*Looks at his watch*) About now, I should think. In
the woods over by the river – bang bang. (*Laughs*)
Solyony thinks he's Lermontov. Even writes poetry. I
mean, a joke's a joke, but this is his third duel.

MASHA

Whose?

CHEBUTYKIN

Solyony.

MASHA

What about the Baron?

CHEBUTYKIN

What about the Baron?

MASHA

(*After a pause.*) I'm sorry, I don't ... No, it mustn't be allowed! He could wound the Baron. Even kill him!

CHEBUTYKIN

Oh, he's a good man. But what's one baron more or less? Let them!

VOICE

(*Beyond the garden*) "Aie! Hup-hup!"

CHEBUTYKIN

That was Skvortsov shouting. He'll be waiting in the boat. He's the second.

ANDREI

(*After a pause.*) I think that taking part in a duel, even as a doctor, is immoral.

CHEBUTYKIN

Moral, immoral, what's the difference? We're here. Are we here? We exist. Do we exist? Anyway, does it really matter?

MASHA

Talk, talk, talk. (*Moves to go.*) It'll be snow soon. Having to listen to ... (*Stops.*) No, I can't go inside. Let me know when Vershinin comes (*Looks up.*) The birds are already going. Swans ... geese ... off you go, my loves.

MASHA Exits.

ANDREI

There'll be nobody here. The officers are leaving.
You're going. My sister's getting married. I'll be the
only one left.

CHEBUTYKIN

What about your wife?

FERAPONT enters with papers.

ANDREI

A wife is a wife. This one's a respectable, honest
woman, and kind. At the same time, there's
something that … that reduces her to a petty, blind
animal. I can say this to you. You're my friend. The
only one I can tell. I love Natasha, but sometimes she
seems so surprisingly vulgar. Such a squalid human
being that I can't remember why I love her. Or, at
least, loved her once.

CHEBUTYKIN

(Stands) My friend, I'm leaving tomorrow. And we
may never see each other again. Take my advice. Put
on a hat, take a stick in your hand, and leave. Leave
and go without a backward look. The further the
better.

SOLYONY, crossing with TWO OFFICERS, sees CHEBUTYKIN, and
breaks off to join him.

SOLYONY

(Greets ANDREI.) Doctor, it's time. Half-twelve
already.

CHEBUTYKIN

I'm coming, damn you. (To ANDREI) If anyone wants
me, say I'll be back directly. (Sighs) Ohhh!

ANDREI goes.

SOLYONY

"He didn't have time to say hullo, before the bear had laid him low." What are you groaning for, grandpa?

CHEBUTYKIN

Oh, shut up.

SOLYONY

Fighting fit, eh?

CHEBUTYKIN

Like a dead dog.

SOLYONY

Don't get worked up, old man. I'll just wing him. (*Sprinkles his hands with cologne.*) I've poured a whole flask on today (*Sniffs his hands.*) They still smell like a corpse. (*Pause.*) Remember Lermontov's poem? "And he, rebellious, seeks the storm, As if in storms relaxes Peace."

CHEBUTYKIN

He didn't have the time to care, before it squashed him, Grizzly Bear."

CHEBUTYKIN leaves with SOLYONY.

Shouts are heard – "Huy Ai!" *ANDREI and FERAPONT enter.*

FERAPONT

You must sign these papers.

ANDREI

Leave me alone. Please . . .

ANDREI exits with the pram.

FERAPONT

But they're for signing. That's what they're for! (*He goes upstage.*)

Enter IRINA and TUZENBAKH in a straw hat.

KULYGIN

(*Crossing*) Hey Masha! Hey!

TUZENBAKH

The only man in town glad to see the back of the soldiers.

IRINA

That's understandable. (*Pause.*) The town will be deserted.

TUZENBAKH

I'll be back in a moment.

IRINA

Where are you going?

TUZENBAKH

Just into town to … ah … see my friends off.

IRINA

Tell me the truth, Nikolai. What's the matter? (*Pause.*) What happened yesterday outside the theatre?

TUZENBAKH

(*Moves, impatient.*) I'll be with you again, in an hour. (*Kisses her hands.*) Oh, my beloved. (*Looks into her face.*) I've been in love with you for five years, and I still can't get used to it. You're more wonderful to me every day. Your hair … those amazing eyes. Tomorrow, I'm going to take you away with me. We'll

work, we'll be rich. All our dreams will come true.
Well, except for one thing – that you don't love me.

IRINA

I can't help it. I'll be your faithful and obedient wife,
but love? What can I do? (*Cries*) I've never been in
love. Not once in my life. I dream of it day and night,
but my soul is like our beloved grand piano. All locked
up and no key. (*Pause.*) What's the matter?

TUZENBAKH

I didn't sleep last night. No key. That's what tears me
to shreds. (*Pause.*) Say something.

IRINA

What is there to say? It's all a mystery. Look at these
trees, standing there, silent and still.

TUZENBAKH

Tell me something.

IRINA

What? Tell you what?

TUZENBAKH

Anything.

IRINA

Oh stop. Stop. (*Pause.*)

TUZENBAKH

Funny how stupid things can suddenly seem
important. You think no, this is absurd but you
can't … Oh, never mind. Today I'm happy. These
firs, maples, birch trees. It's as though I've never
been aware of them before. Looking at me – all alive
and waiting to see what's going to happen. Such

beautiful trees. The life around them should be just as beautiful.

VOICES

(*Off*) Hullo! Hup, hup!

TUZENBAKH

I must go, I'm late. Look at that tree. It's dead but it's still swaying with the others in the wind. It'll be the same with me if I die. I'll still be part of life somehow. Goodbye, my dear. (*Kisses her hands*) The papers you gave me are on my table, under the calendar.

IRINA

I'll come with you.

TUZENBAKH

(*Alarmed*) No, no! (*Goes quickly, stops in the avenue.*) Irina!

IRINA

What?

TUZENBAKH

(*Not knowing what to say*) I haven't had my coffee. Get them to make me some.

TUZENBAKH goes quickly.

IRINA pauses, thoughtful, then goes upstage, and sits on the swing.

ANDREI enters with the pram.

FERAPONT appears.

FERAPONT

Look, these aren't my papers. I didn't make them up. They're official.

ANDREI

What's happened? Where did it all go? When I was
young and clever, I was full of ideas and hope. Why,
when we've hardly started, does it all go dull? Grey,
mindless, and useless. This town's been here for two
hundred years. A hundred thousand inhabitants.
And not one – not one – hero, past or present. Not a
scholar, not an artist. No-one to inspire the desire to
emulate. No-one to arouse even one stab of envy. Eat,
drink, sleep, die. Next lot the same. Generation after
generation. Vodka, cards, petty lawsuits, and love-
affairs to stifle the boredom. The children end up the
same. How could they not? The same as their parents.
(To FERAPONT) What do you want?

FERAPONT

The papers.

ANDREI

Go away.

FERAPONT

(Hands him the papers.) The doorman at the Revenue
Office was telling me they had two hundred degrees
of frost in Petersburg last winter.

ANDREI

Disgusting as it all is, somehow – when I think of
the future – I feel light. There's a feeling of space, of
freedom. I can see myself – and my children – freed
from a life of doing nothing but drinking, eating goose
with cabbage, and falling asleep after lunch. Freed
from this vile sponging off other people.

FERAPONT

He said two thousand people froze. People were horrified, he said. It was either Petersburg or Moscow.

ANDREI

(*With emotion*) Oh my dear sisters, my wonderful sisters. (*Through tears*) Masha . . .

NATASHA

(*At the window*) Who's making all that noise? Is it you, Andrusha? You'll wake Sofochka. Il ne faut pas faire du bruit. La Sophie est dormée déjà. Vous êtes un ours. (*Angry*) If you want to talk, give the pram to someone else. Ferapont take the pram from his Honour!

FERAPONT

Eh? Yes ma'am. (*Takes the pram.*)

ANDREI

(*Embarrassed*) I was talking quietly.

NATASHA

(*Outside, talking to Bobik*) Bobik . . . naughty Bobik . . . Wicked boy!

ANDREI

(*Glancing at papers*) All right, I'll have a look and sign what's necessary, and you can take them back to the Council.

ANDREI Goes inside, reading the papers.

FERAPONT pushes the pram off.

NATASHA

(*Beyond the window.*) What's Mama called, Bobik?
Who's this? This is Auntie Olya. Say hello, Olya.
Auntie Olya!

Two wandering musicians – a MAN and a WOMAN – enter playing
violin and harp.

VERSHININ, OLGA and ANFISA come out and listen quietly for a
moment.

IRINA approaches.

OLGA

Our garden is like a public courtyard. People
walk through it,. Drive through it. Nanny give the
musicians something.

ANFISA

Off you go, with God's blessing good people.

The MUSICIANS bow and leave.

ANFISA

Poor things! They must be in a bad way to be doing
that. (*To IRINA*) Irisha! (*Kisses her.*) Oh child, look
at me. Alive and well in an official flat along with
Olushka. A room and a bed all to myself. Everything
official from the Government! Never in my life have
I lived like this, old sinner that I am. I sleep through
the night. Dear Lord, Mother of God, there's not a
happier soul in the whole world!

VERSHININ

(*Looks at his watch. To OLGA*) Time for me to go.
(*Pause.*) Where is Maria Sergeyevna?

IRINA

She's in the garden somewhere. I'll go and find her.

VERSHININ

If you would. I'm pressed for time.

ANFISA

I'll go. (*Shouts*) Mashenka, hey!

She and IRINA go into the garden.

ANFISA

He-ey, he-ey!

VERSHININ

Everything comes to an end. (*Looks at his watch.*)
Time to go. The town laid on food for us. Champagne.
A speech. I sat there and ate and drank and listened.
But my heart was here, with you. (*Looks round at the
garden.*) I've grown so used to you all.

OLGA

Will we see each other again sometime?

VERSHININ

Probably not. (*Pause.*) My wife and daughters will
stay on for another two months. If anything should
happen or be needed . . .

OLGA

Yes, yes, of course. You can rely on us. (*Pause.*) By
tomorrow, there won't be a soldier left in town. Just
memories. For us, obviously, the beginning of a new
life. (*Pause*) Nothing happens as you think it will. I
didn't want to be a headmistress, yet here I am. No
question now of going to Moscow.

VERSHININ

Well ... thank you for everything. Forgive me for ...
if I was ever ... I've talked a good deal. Forgive me for
that. Don't remember me badly.

OLGA

(Wiping her eyes.) Where is Masha? Why isn't she ...?

VERSHININ

What else can I say in farewell? What precious piece
of information? *(Laughs.)* Life's hard. Hopeless
sometimes, and yet we have to agree, things are
improving. They're getting better. Things are bound
to become clearer before long. *(Looks at his watch.)*
It's time I went. In the past, life was filled with war,
campaigns, raids, conquests. All over, that. Leaving a
big empty space needing to be filled. We're searching.
Searching passionately. It will come. It'll happen. If
only it could be soon! *(Pause.)* You know, if we could
just add education to ... *(Looks at his watch again.)*
It's time to go.

OLGA

Here she is.

MASHA enters.

VERSHININ

I came to say goodbye.

OLGA moves apart discreetly.

MASHA

(Looks into his face.) Goodbye ...

A long kiss.

OLGA

Come on, come on . . .

MASHA weeps bitterly.

VERSHININ

Write to me. Don't forget! Let me go . . . it's time now. (*To OLGA*) Olga Sergeyevna, take her. It's already time for . . . I'm late. (*Moved, he kisses OLGA'S hands, then embraces MASHA again, and leaves quickly.*)

OLGA

Stop it, darling . . . Masha, come on . . .

Enter KULYGIN.

KULYGIN

(*Embarrassed.*) That's all right. Let her cry. My dear, good kind Masha. I'm happy. No matter what's gone on. I've no complaints. Let Olga be my witness. No reproaches. We'll go back to where we were. Nothing to be said. All over.

MASHA

(*Restraining her sobs.*) In the creek, there's a green oak. A golden chair on a green oak . . . a golden cat . . . a golden oak . . . I'm getting confused. (*Drinks water.*) An unfortunate life. I don't need anything. I'll be all right soon. What does it mean 'the creek?' Why do I have that word in my head? My thoughts are all mixed up.

IRINA enters.

OLGA

Sssh, Masha, that's enough . . . let's go in.

MASHA

(*Angry*) I'm not going in there! (*Cries, but stops suddenly.*) Not in that house. Not any more.

IRINA

Let's sit together. Even if we don't say anything. I'm going tomorrow, remember?

Pause.

KULYGIN

Look. (*Puts on a false beard and moustache.*) I took it away from a boy yesterday. I look like the teacher in the German class. They are funny, those boys.

MASHA

Yes, you do look like the German.

OLGA

(*Laughs*) Yes.

MASHA cries.

IRINA

Come on, Masha …

KULYGIN

Very much like him.

Enter NATASHA.

NATASHA

(*To the MAID.*) Look, Protopopov is upstairs with Sofochka, and Andrei Sergeyevich here with Bobik! Honestly, children! They're such a nuisance. (*To IRINA*) Such a shame you're leaving tomorrow, Irina. Stay another week at least.

She shrieks at the sight of KULYGIN. He laughs and takes off the beard.

NATASHA

You gave me such a fright! *(To IRINA)* I've got so used to you. It's not going to be easy not having you here. I'll get them to put Andrei into your room with his violin. He can scrape away in there, and we'll put Sofochka in his room. Gorgeous, little girl. She's really incredible. Today, she looked at me, eyes like this and said "Mamma!"

KULYGIN

True, she's a beautiful child.

NATASHA

So, I'll be all on my own here tomorrow. *(Sighs.)* The first thing I'm going to do is have that avenue of fir- trees chopped down. Then the maple. It's so ugly. *(To IRINA)* My dear, that belt doesn't suit your face at all. You need something lighter, more tasteful. And I'm going to have flowers here ... there ... and there. Lots of flowers for their smell. *(Stern)* Why is there a fork on the bench here? *(To the MAID)* What is a fork doing out here on the bench? I'm asking you a question. *(Shouts)* Be quiet! Who said you could speak?

KULYGIN

She's off!

Offstage, a BAND plays a march. They all listen.

OLGA

They're leaving.

CHEBUTYKIN enters.

MASHA

Our boys are off. Well, there we are. Bon voyage. (*To KULYGIN*) We must go home. Where are my hat and cape?

KULYGIN

I took them in. I'll go and fetch them.

KULYGIN goes in.

OLGA

Yes, we can all go home now. Time to go.

CHEBUTYKIN

Olga Sergeyevna!

OLGA

What?

CHEBUTYKIN

It's all right. I don't know how to say it to you. (*He whispers in her ear.*)

OLGA

(*Frightened*) No, it can't be! It's not true!

CHEBUTYKIN

I know. (*Sits upstage.*) I'm exhausted. I can't talk anymore.

MASHA

What's happened?

OLGA

(*Hugs IRINA*) Today is a terrible day. I don't know how to tell you, my dear . . .

IRINA

(*Crying*) What is it? Quick, for God's sake, what is it?

CHEBUTYKIN

The Baron has been killed in a duel.

IRINA

I knew it … I knew it!

CHEBUTYKIN

(On a bench in the background.) I'm worn out. (Takes out his paper.) Let them cry. (Sings quietly) Tarara boomdeay. I'm on the fence today. (Opens his paper.) Oh, what difference does it make?

The THREE SISTERS stand, clinging to one another.

MASHA

Listen to the music! They're going. Leaving us. Here we are. Left behind to start a new life. We have to live. What else can we do? We have to live.

IRINA puts her head on OLGA'S chest.

IRINA

There will come a time when we understand. When everyone knows what it's all for. All this suffering and deprivation. No more mysteries. No more things unexplained. Until then, we have to live. Work. We have to work. That's all there is – work! I'll go off tomorrow. I'll teach. Teach children in the school. I'll dedicate my life to whatever's needed. It's already autumn. Winter will be here soon, and we'll be smothered in snow. But I shall be working. I'll be working.

OLGA hugs both her SISTERS.

OLGA

Listen to the music. So bright. Alive. It makes you want to live! Dear God, life will go on. Time will pass and we'll leave it and be forgotten. Our faces. Our voices. How many of us there were. But our sufferings will turn to joy for those who come after us. We will be remembered with a kind word. There will be peace and happiness. And those of us now alive will be blessed. Dear sisters, our life isn't over. We'll live. And the band is playing so joyfully. I feel soon … so soon … we shall begin to understand why we live. Why we suffer. If only we only knew. If we only knew!

The MUSIC plays more and more quietly.

KULYGIN enters, smiling happily, with Masha's hat and cape.

ANDREI pushes the pram, in which Bobik is sitting up.

CHEBUTYKIN
(Sings quietly) Tarara boomdeay … (He whistles the tune, then reads his paper.) What difference does it make, eh? What difference?

OLGA
If we only knew. If we only knew!

CURTAIN

STANLEY

A new play by Pam Gems

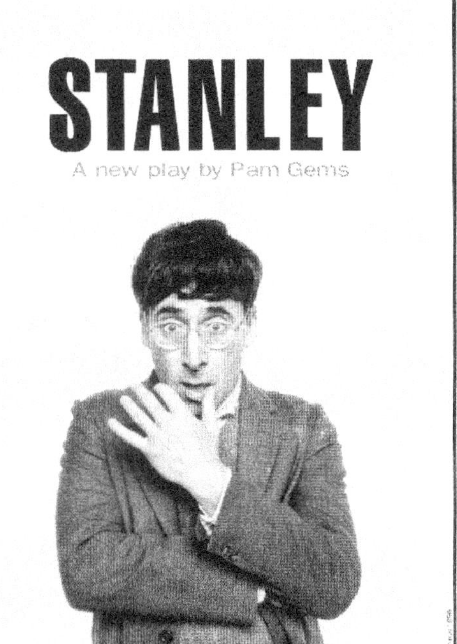

STANLEY'S WOMEN

screenplay by PAM GEMS
and JONATHAN GEMS

based on the play
"Stanley" by Pam Gems

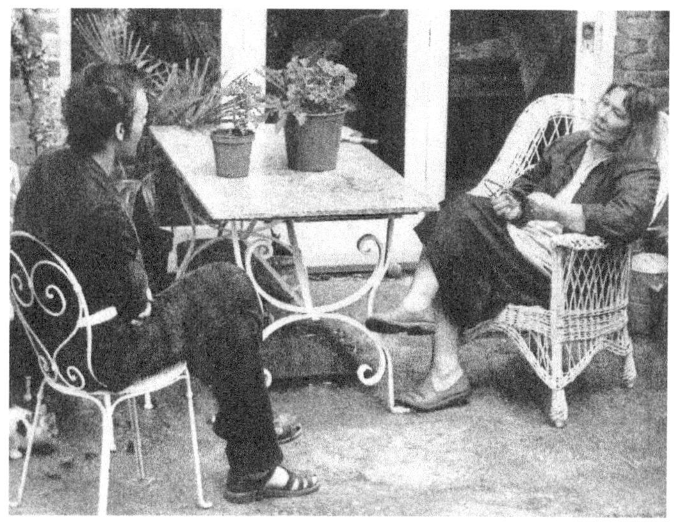

Pam Gems and Jonathan Gems. 1982.

STANLEY'S WOMEN

STANLEY'S WOMEN is a screen adaptation of STANLEY, the Pam Gems play first presented at the Cottesloe by the National Theatre, in London, UK, on February 1st, 1996, starring Antony Sher, directed by John Caird.

STANLEY won an Olivier Award for 'Best Play,' and a Writer's Guild award for 'Best West End Play.' The production was subsequently transferred to The Circle In the Square Theatre in New York City.

The stage play is published by Nick Hern Books, 14 Larden Road, London W3 7ST. www.nickhernbooks.co.uk

STANLEY SPENCER (1891–1959)

English painter, one of the most original figures in 20th-century British art. He lived for most of his life in his native village of Cookham, which played a large part in the imagery of his paintings. His education was fairly elementary, but he grew up in a family in which literature, music, and religion were dominant concerns and his imaginative life was extremely rich. He said he wanted 'to take the inmost of one's wishes, the most varied religious feelings … and to make it an ordinary fact of the street,' and he is best known for pictures in which he set biblical events in his own village. His visionary attitude has been compared to that of William Blake. Spencer was a prize-winning student at the Slade School (1908–12) and served in the army from 1915 to 1918, first at the Beaufort War Hospital in Bristol, then in Macedonia.

Text source: *The Oxford Dictionary of Art and Artists*
(Oxford University Press)

FOREWORD

Why write a play about Stanley Spencer? There have been books, biographies, picture reproductions of varying fidelity, and at least two excellent television documentaries – all based on fact – and as accurate as data and human memory allow.

But a play is different. Drama comes from feeling rather than thinking. Plays tend to arrive like blocks of marble, ready to be chiseled out.

Two years ago, I set out for Italy to work on a play about Giuseppe Garibaldi, the Italian patriot. Sickness intervened and France became home for several months. In France, there was time to read, look at paintings, and time to dwell on a conversation I had with James Roose-Evans, theatre director and eminence grise of British Theatre. He lent me a book on Spencer on firm promise of return. (I did.)

In France, roaming the art galleries, it seemed that British painting was not appreciated as it should be. The dominance of France, and then America, has led to our native work being undervalued – at least until the arrival of the American collectors, Robert and Ann Summers.

As for Stanley Spencer, there was reaction early against forms that seemed bizarre or misshapen. His nudes shocked. Then, in the Fifties, after the war, people had a need for warmth, light … wine and peaches. For colour. Also, much of Spencer's iconography is Christian and, after six years of slaughter and destruction, Christianity seemed to be a flop. People had had enough pain. Impressionism and post-impressionism reigned, and impasto graced domestic walls. True, a lot of painting from the British Isles does not burn the retina. The light in northern Europe does not make for the spectacular. But it does make for complexity.

Apart from admiration, and a wish to celebrate, there are other reasons for using a well-known character as premise for a play. A famous protagonist brings glamour. Characters from a bygone era, another country – distant in time and space – are exotic. That which is strange excites us. And excitement is the stuff of drama.

It's a matter of technique, similar to choice of key and tempo in music, or colour and dimension in painting.

It can be more exciting to create one's own characters. Indeed, it's often regarded as especially potent to write of the now – to throw light on the contemporary. Chekhov did it, and so did Ibsen. On the other hand, Shakespeare and Brecht both made use of historical characters, and there are advantages to this.

Firstly, you start, as it were, one act in. This helps when writing a new play because, nowadays, plays are no more than two hours long. You only have two hours in which to say your piece. Plays used to be much longer – three, four, even five acts. They were full of explication. Film, and then television, have created audiences more attuned to pace of exegesis. Audiences have become more sophisticated, and used to jump cuts in time and space. So, with two hours, max, there is an advantage in starting with familiar characters and a known milieu. Then one plays a different game. You pull the rug. Drama is, by its nature, subversive. It seeks to influence indirectly. You use known data as a springboard. Or a lure.

There's another argument against dealing with the contemporary. It can work brilliantly, but often doesn't. The danger is superficiality. The shallow take. Look close enough and the view is blurred.

And there is a third reason. When I began in the theatre, it had become fashionable for actors to go about in jeans – mock workman's clothes. 'Look,' said the actor. 'I'm just a feller like you. I'm real.' Well ... leaving aside the low salaries that actors earn, (the whole of theatre runs on actors' goodwill and generosity of spirit) that, of course, is not true.

Most people, for most of their lives – if they are lucky enough to have a paid occupation – are doing what they wouldn't do, if they had freedom of choice. Most people's lives, in the West, lack drama. We are protected by the fruits of industry ... by warmth, light, transport ... in order to serve industry. Gone are the days of my childhood when there was the drama of sepsis, pneumonia, diphtheria, and galloping consumption. Now, our anxieties are in free fall, and our imaginations, urban and suburban, deprived of air and trees, birds, weather, water and animals, are stultified.

The Situationists were right. Where would we be without the stimulation and pacification of the media? Entertainment fills the imagination. Which is why actors should *not* seek to disguise what they are – which is glamorous. They are the other; the creatures of our imagined scenarios. To be revered not just for their skills, but because their work is special, dealing as it does with our hearts and souls. Glamour doesn't mean wearing sequins – although it might. It *does* mean fulfilling a bond. Promising respite from dullness; presenting us with richer and fuller lives.

It used to be fashionable to say that art changes nothing. I don't believe that. We modify all the time. We respond to stimuli. What those stimuli depend on is the quality of the art. And, if we are lucky, the best art.

Like the painting of an English genius, Stanley Spencer.

PAM GEMS.
January 1996

STANLEY'S WOMEN

MAIN CHARACTERS

STANLEY SPENCER

HILDA CARLINE

PATRICIA PREECE

DOROTHY HEPWORTH

SUPPORTING CHARACTERS

ELSIE, the maid

AUGUSTUS JOHN

GWEN JOHN

DORELIA

DUDLEY TOOTH

HENRY LAMB

MRS CARLINE – Hilda's mother

PANSY PACKENHAM

THE VICAR

MODDOM

SUMMERS, a Times reporter

COLONEL

COLONEL'S WIFE

SCHOOLBOYS #1 and #2

STANLEY'S WOMEN

MUSIC: *VaughanWilliams "Floss Campi" for solo viola.*

OPENING CREDITS over a series of paintings by Stanley Spencer.

EXT. HIGH STREET – COOKHAM VILLAGE – DAY.

A sunny day. Cookham village is ancient, rural and picturesque. The high street is crooked and lined with quaint shops and antiquated street lamps. It looks like a Stanley Spencer painting.

SUPERIMPOSE CAPTION: "Cookham Village – 1949".

EXT. COOKHAM COMMON – DAY.

A MAN in a dirty coat is seated on a little stool, painting a canvas set up on an easel. This is STANLEY SPENCER – aged about 57. He looks mad, his coat stained with paint, his hair sticking up. Next to him is an old pram filled with paints, brushes, paper, rags etc. He squints at the sky, then sits back patiently.

ELSIE, a pretty, plump, middle-aged woman in a print dress, comes across the green, carrying a basket.

> ELSIE
>
> Morning, Stan.

> STANLEY
>
> Morning, Elsie.

She looks at him in enquiry as he is not working.

> STANLEY
>
> I'm waiting for the sun on that puddle.

ELSIE looks at the puddle. HER POV: the puddle – in shadow.

ELSIE looks back at STANLEY.

ELSIE

We're ever so pleased. All of us. Puts Cookham Village
on the map, eh?!

STANLEY

I'm still the same, me.

ELSIE

Still, Sir Stanley Spencer . . .

ELSIE savours the moment, then:

ELSIE

Well, I must get on.

STANLEY nods and smiles. He watches her walk away down the
path, her bottom bouncing under her dress.

STANLEY

(Mutters) Never did get that arse right.

TWO SCHOOLBOYS run up to him.

SCHOOLBOY #1

'Ere! My mum said you 'ad two wives, Stan!

STANLEY

(Eyes glittering.) That's right, I did!

SCHOOLBOY #2

But you're only allowed one. That's the law!

STANLEY

King Solomon had a thousand wives.

SCHOOLBOY #2's mouth drops open.

SCHOOLBOY #1

Only in the Bible.

                    SCHOOLBOY #2
(Nods) In the Bible.

They look at him sternly, and dash off.

STANLEY chuckles, and looks up at the sky. HIS POV: a beautiful sky, but a cloud is blocking the sun.

                    STANLEY
What I need is a good English wind to blow that cloud away.

HIS POV: the sun comes out from behind the cloud.

                    STANLEY
Thank you, God. Thank you. Thank you. Thank you. Thank you.

ON: STANLEY – mixing colours.

ON PUDDLE: the shadow is chased away, and the puddle shimmers with sunlight.

EXT. BATTLEFIELD – FIRST WORLD WAR – NIGHT. (B&W)

SOUND OF SHELLS EXPLODING, gunfire, and men screaming.

A mob of ENGLISH INFANTRYMEN is crossing No-Man's-Land – bent low, negotiating the rolls of barbed wire.

FLASHES OF LIGHT from explosions illuminate the soldiers.

A SOLDIER falls face-down in the mud.

An EXPLOSION nearby.

SMOKE.

As the smoke clears a DISORIENTATED SOLDIER appears, seen dimly in the darkness, staggering towards us.

                                        DISSOLVE TO:

EXT. STREET – HAMPSTEAD – DUSK.

It is dusk.

ON: a Georgian/Victorian Hampstead street with Hampstead Heath in the background. A LAMPLIGHTER is lighting the gas lamps.

SUPERIMPOSE CAPTION: "Hampstead Village, London – 1921."

STANLEY SPENCER (30), in a brown suit and yellow tie, comes into view, and walks briskly up the street. He is freshly-washed and shaved, and holding a bunch of wildflowers.

EXT. CARLINE HOUSE – DUSK.

STANLEY knocks on the front door of a Georgian house.

Lights glow through the curtained windows. The house is warm and welcoming. STANLEY is a little nervous. He brushes his hair back.

The front door opens revealing HILDA CARLINE (24).

It's love at first sight.

> STANLEY
> Hullo, uh ... I'm Stanley Spencer. One of the painting group. Mrs Carline invited me for dinner.

> HILDA
> That's my mother. Come in.

She stands back.

> STANLEY
> Thank you very much.

He goes past her into the house. She closes the door. They exchange another look, fascinated by each other.

DISSOLVE TO:

EXT. CHURCH - HAMPSTEAD - DAY.

The road outside the small church is crowded with MOTOR CARS.

THREE LATECOMERS hurry down the path.

These are: AUGUSTUS JOHN - tall and bearded, in a moleskin suit, with a cane, wearing a wide-brimmed velvet hat, and a flowing scarf thrown around his shoulders.

GWEN JOHN, his red-haired sister - tall, thin and bleak.

And DORELIA - 22, slim, long-necked, beautiful.

AUGUSTUS JOHN
What's all this marrying about!

MUSIC can be heard faintly from inside the small church.

INT. CHURCH - DAY.

STANLEY and HILDA CARLINE are standing together in front of the altar. Behind them, the church is filled with GUESTS. In the front row are:

MRS CARLINE (Hilda's mother) - eccentric in a vast hat.

DUDLEY TOOTH - a charming, immaculately-suited art dealer.

HENRY LAMB - an upper-class painter - attractive, sardonic.

PANSY PAKENHAM - pretty, aristocratic.

NANCY CUNARD, attractive, bobbed hair, both arms covered with bangles, next to her BLACK BOYFRIEND, in a business suit.

A MAN IN A GREEN JACKET with a GINGER CAT on his shoulder.

A BALD OLD WOMAN.

A FEROCIOUS WOMAN SCULPTOR.

AUGUSTUS JOHN, GWEN JOHN and DORELIA.

VICAR

And do you, Hilda Carline, take this man to be your
lawful wedded husband – to have and to hold from
this day forth so long as ye both shall live?

HILDA

I do.

HILDA and STANLEY look at each other and grin.

INT. ELEGANT LONDON INTERIOR – DAY.

The Wedding Reception.

The walls are covered in PRE-RAPHAELITE PAINTINGS and
pictures by Augustus John, Gwen John, Henry Lamb and Stanley
Spencer.

Loud hubbub of conversation.

HENRY LAMB pours some poisonous blue liquid from a jug into a
vast silver punch bowl. GWEN JOHN throws in some exotic fruit.

CUT TO: The elegant DORELIA standing under a large portrait of
her, champagne glass in hand.

ON: STANLEY and HILDA – surrounded by THE MAN with the
GINGER CAT on his shoulder, the BALD OLD LADY, and the
FEROCIOUS WOMAN SCULPTOR.

STANLEY

We're going to live in Cookham and paint.

HILDA

And have babies.

STANLEY chokes on his drink. The others react variously.

CUT TO: MRS CARLINE and DUDLEY TOOTH.

MRS CARLINE

Mr Tooth? Mr Dudley Tooth, the art dealer?

DUDLEY

(Bows) And you are Mrs Carline?

MRS CARLINE

Yes. The bride's mother.

DUDLEY

And her father? (He looks around.)

MRS CARLINE

Gone to the Devil, Mr Tooth.

CUT TO: STANLEY introducing HILDA to AUGUSTUS JOHN.

STANLEY

Augustus John.

AUGUSTUS gives HILDA the eye. DORELIA immediately appears
at his side, guarding her property.

AUGUSTUS

(To HILDA) Divorce him!

He gooses her. She squeaks. DORELIA glares.

CUT TO: *HENRY LAMB feeling up GWEN JOHN.*

GWEN JOHN

(Bored) Oh Henry . . .

HENRY

Play your cards right, I'm yours for the night.

GWEN

Shove off.

WIDESHOT OF PARTY. *Everyone* is getting drunk and talking loudly.

CUT TO: STANLEY and HILDA talking with DUDLEY TOOTH.

GWEN JOHN comes up, and kisses HILDA.

> HILDA

Stan – d'you know … ?

> GWEN

(To STANLEY) Gwen John. Hullo Dudley. (To HILDA) Sorry we were late. My sainted brother was painting Lawrence.

> HILDA

D.H.?

> GWEN

T.E. – Lawrence of Arabia.

> AUGUSTUS

(Looms up) Bugger was late. His magneto packed up.

HENRY LAMB barges up, drunk, and puts his arm around STANLEY.

> HENRY

(Raises his glass) Stan, I salute you! Here's to old Cookham. The last noble peasant of the art world!

> STANLEY

(To HILDA) If I'm a peasant, so's Caravaggio. You're all the same. Ooh, mustn't be old hat! Got to be avant-garde!

The OTHERS react: "Here we go. He's off."

STANLEY

What's this toilet stuck to the wall? "Marvellous!" All
this fashion for ideas. Ideas! You think that's what
it takes to fill a canvas? Here! (He bangs his chest.)
Anybody can do it from the mind . . . but from the
heart . . .

AUGUSTUS

(Sardonic) Bravo Spencer, bravo!

AUGUSTUS JOHN, with DORELIA clinging to his arm, is clapping.

STANLEY

Bravo yerself – you snooty coot!

STANLEY leaps at him. They fight.

PEOPLE watch the fight. HENRY LAMB hands his drink to GWEN,
and pulls STANLEY off AUGUSTUS.

AUGUSTUS turns and grabs one of STANLEY'S legs.

STANLEY struggles with AUGUSTUS and HENRY. A chair and a
lamp go over.

ON: DORELIA, NANCY CUNARD and PANSY PAKENHAM seated on
a sofa. They draw up their legs to avoid the fight.

The drinks table collapses with a crash.

Loud cheers.

EXT. SPENCER COTTAGE – COOKHAM VILLAGE – DAY.

A pretty cottage with a garden and a large shed in the garden.

HILDA comes out of the back door. She crosses the garden to the
shed.

INT. SHED – DAY.

STANLEY is painting a large canvas. He paints demonically, eyes gleaming.

HILDA comes in. STANLEY looks round. His expression alters and becomes tender.

EXT. RIVER – DAY.

STANLEY and HILDA walk by the river. He holds up a branch for her.

EXT. MEADOW – DAY.

They cross a meadow, hand in hand.

EXT. SMALL STONE BRIDGE – DUSK.

STANLEY and HILDA on a small stone bridge. They kiss.

EXT. COOKHAM STREET AND LINDWORTH HOUSE – DAY.

WIDESHOT of Cookham Village.

STANLEY and HILDA come into view, walking hand in hand.

HILDA stops and looks at the comely Georgian facade of Lindworth House. They stand, looking at it together, then smile. They like it.

> STANLEY

I'll buy it for you.

HILDA laughs. He kisses her.

EXT. COOKHAM HIGH STREET – DAY.

A "crocodile" of TEN 'INCURABLES,' in bright blue hospital uniforms, shuffle down the street – tended by TWO NURSES.

STANLEY and HILDA appear from around the corner. HILDA sees the INCURABLES and tries to hold STANLEY back. But STANLEY approaches them and stands still, looking at them, his face expressionless.

A PATIENT, prone in a WICKER CARRIAGE, leers up with a wild, mad expression.

HILDA pulls STANLEY back as he panics. The 'crocodile' goes past. STANLEY points at the last TWO MEN – both missing a leg. He starts to laugh. The NURSES, affronted, shoo the MEN forward.

STANLEY, hysterical, is pulled away by HILDA.

NEW ANGLE: *Further down the street, A WOMAN emerges from a shop.*

CLOSER ON: WOMAN as she comes out of the shadow. She has striking good looks. This is PATRICIA PREECE (late twenties).

Behind her, coming out of the shop, is her companion, DOROTHY HEPWORTH (about thirty-five).

PATRICIA looks scornfully at the INCURABLES as they pass. DOROTHY tugs at PATRICIA'S sleeve.

DOROTHY

Patricia! Isn't that Hilda Carline?

PATRICIA looks round.

EXT. COOKHAM HIGH STREET – DAY.

STANLEY, HILDA, PATRICIA and DOROTHY meet.

HILDA

Patricia!

PATRICIA

Hilda!

HILDA

What are you doing here? (To STANLEY) Patricia and
I were at the Slade together!

STANLEY looks at PATRICIA with interest. Her gaze is cold and
dismissive.

PATRICIA

We're living at Moor Thatch cottage down the road.

HILDA

Oh, that's marvellous.

DOROTHY shakes STANLEY'S hand vigorously.

DOROTHY

Dorothy Hepworth. I was recently in London and saw
your Apple Gatherers at the Tate. Quite wonderful.

PATRICIA

(To DOROTHY) He's Stanley Spencer?

STANLEY

Yes.

PATRICIA

(Accusingly) You're Stanley Spencer?

PATRICIA turns on DOROTHY, enraged.

PATRICIA

Why didn't you tell me?

Laughter from the others. STANLEY looks at PATRICIA. They
walk off down the middle of the road together, forcing the traffic
round them.

EXT. OUTSIDE MOOR THATCH – LATER.

DOROTHY and PATRICIA go up the garden path to their front door.

                    DOROTHY

... the best painter in England. Without question.

She holds open the door for PATRICIA.

                    PATRICIA

(Entering) How did she get him? She's not even
good-looking.

EXT. STREET, MONUMENT AND COMMON - COOKHAM - DAY.

ON: 1914-18 War Monument. STANLEY and HILDA look at it.

                    HILDA

Bury the bits? What do you mean?

                    STANLEY

Before I volunteered for the infantry, that was my job.
Medical orderly.

                    HILDA

You never told me.

They stroll onto the Common.

                    STANLEY

I had to pick up the amputations from the surgical
tents, dig a hole and chuck them in.

                    HILDA

Why didn't they incinerate them?

                    STANLEY

Dunno. (Short laugh.) They gave you a check list. Tent
number one, three arms, two legs, half a shoulder and
a penis.

Then they both start to laugh. They try to stop but they can't.

EXT. COUNTRY LANE AND WOODS – DAY.

STANLEY and HILDA walk down lane through the woods.

> STANLEY
>
> I remember once on a forced march . . .

FLASHBACK (B&W)

MEN stumbling, exhausted over frozen and dreadful ground.

EXT. LANE, WOODS AND LAKE – DAY.

STANLEY and HILDA are sitting on a bank overlooking a pretty lake in the woods.

> STANLEY
>
> . . . trying to walk between the frozen ruts . . . men moaning, dropping . . .

> HILDA
>
> Oh Stanley – awful – come here. (She opens her arms.)

> STANLEY
>
> No!!

He jumps up.

His shout startles her. She looks up at his ecstatic face, astonished.

> STANLEY
>
> No. In the middle of . . . (He shakes his head) . . . of . . .

CLOSE ON STANLEY.

FLASHBACK (B&W)

The forced march. STANLEY has stopped. Other MEN stumble past him as he gazes up at the sky with an ecstatic face.

> **STANLEY (V/O)**
> All of a sudden, the stars up above seemed to turn
> warm! The snow had little flames, licking up all
> around me. I felt … I felt … I felt … 'It's all right!'

The MEN push past him, exhausted, wounded.

EXT. LANE, WOODS AND LAKE – DAY.

ON: STANLEY

> **STANLEY**
> I was surrounded by horror … and yet there was
> light. Everything moving and glowing around me, as
> if I was in a great big church. A church of the whole
> world!

HILDA gazes at him in wonder.

STANLEY squats at the mossy base of a LARGE OAK TREE, and
takes her hand.

> **STANLEY**
> I felt … unselfish. I thought: if I can just hang on to
> this. Carry this blinding moment of worship inside
> me, like the arc of the covenant, then I'll get there – to
> pure imagination.

> **HILDA**
> Through bliss?

> **STANLEY**
> Exactly.

STANLEY gazes at her, full of love. She returns his gaze.

> **STANLEY**
> I know it can't be like that all the time. Still, I got the
> point. I know what he meant.

                    HILDA

He?

                   STANLEY

God. God's unselfish because he has no self. That's the
way to paint, don't you see?

They kiss. It is a long kiss, deep and passionate.

INT. STANLEY'S STUDIO – NIGHT.

STANLEY, standing on a table, is painting the huge, unfinished
'Resurrection.'

He moves and knocks over a paint box – which clatters to the
ground – breaking the spell.

He looks down. HIS POV: *HILDA is standing below. She wears his
old jacket over naked shoulders,* and is eating beans from a tin. She
smiles up at him and gives him a spoonful. He bends and eats, then
jumps down beside her. HILDA looks up at the painting.

HER POV: HILDA is portrayed among the other figures.

She smiles. He looks at her and is pleased at her pleasure. They
both look up at the painting like two children.

                    HILDA

Oh yes.

INT. STANLEY'S STUDIO – NIGHT.

HILDA, naked to the waist, is posing for STANLEY. Silence – but
for the scrape of a pencil.

                   STANLEY

Can you bend forward?

ANGLE ON: STANLEY sketching HILDA.

STANLEY

I want your breasts sort of hanging.

HILDA bends forward.

INT. STUDIO – NIGHT – LATER.

STANLEY and HILDA are drawing each other. The floor is littered with sketches.

STANLEY

I couldn't have married anyone else.

He draws, rubs out, and blows on the paper.

STANLEY

First time I saw you I thought: "There she is!"

They look at each other – smile. He opens his arms.

INT. SPENCER BEDROOM – NIGHT.

HILDA, naked by the wash-stand, reaches for her nightgown. STANLEY, in bed, watches her.

STANLEY

I love sending my thoughts to you. It's like sending
them home.

HILDA smiles. She throws the nightgown away, and slides into bed, into his waiting arms.

INT. SPENCER BEDROOM – DAY.

ELSIE, the maid, is changing the bedlinen.

STANLEY appears in the doorway and watches her with pleasure as she leans over, showing her thighs.

ELSIE

Shan't be long Mr Spencer.

STANLEY

No hurry.

He dodges around the bed, to help her tuck in the clean sheets. He sniffs her as he passes.

STANLEY

Mmmm, carbolic. (Across the bed.) I'll do you in your pinnie, Elsie – under the tree.

ELSIE

Not tonight you won't. I've got a date with Clark Gable.

She smooths the cover and scoops up the dirty bed linen, exposing her hairy armpits.

STANLEY

(Excited) Oooh!

ELSIE smiles and goes.

STANLEY

(Quiet pleasure) Oooh ...

EXT. WOODS AND LAKE – DAY.

WIDESHOT. *STANLEY, with easel and painting-case strapped to his back, traipses up a vast, wide hill.*

EXT. WOODS AND LAKE – DAY.

STANLEY is setting up his easel. He freezes. HIS POV: A WOMAN is swimming in the lake.

ON: STANLEY, watching.

ON: PATRICIA, naked, swimming in the lake. Sunlight bounces on the surface of the water. PATRICIA looks beautiful, like a water nymph.

CU: STANLEY SPENCER – transfixed. He grabs his large sketchpad and starts drawing.

INT. SPENCER KITCHEN – NIGHT.

STANLEY has spread his sketches of PATRICIA all over the table.

STANLEY

What do you think?

HILDA is at the stove, making dinner. She wipes her hands, comes over, and looks at the sketches.

HILDA

(Nods) Mmm. Did she see you?

STANLEY

Don't know.

HILDA

I expect so. She probably liked it.

She sits suddenly. STANLEY looks at her, puzzled.

She smiles faintly and very slowly keels over sideways.

INT. DOCTOR'S SURGERY.

HILDA sits in front of the DOCTOR'S desk. The DOCTOR takes off his glasses.

DOCTOR

Well, Mrs Spencer, congratulations!

HILDA looks at him, baffled.

DOCTOR

It appears that we are expecting!

CU: HILDA'S mouth opens.

                    HILDA

When?

                    DOCTOR

In about six months.

He beams. HILDA is stunned.

INT. STUDIO – DAY.

STANLEY is painting. HILDA comes in, nervous.

                    HILDA

Stan?

He turns, annoyed at being interrupted.

                    STANLEY

What is it?

ON: *HILDA, very nervous.*

                    HILDA

Er ...

INT. BEDROOM – NIGHT.

STANLEY is in bed, HILDA beside him.

                    STANLEY

It won't make any difference, will it?

                    HILDA

Of course not.

They lie side by side. Outside a fox calls.

                    STANLEY

Do I have to do anything?

                    HILDA

Just love us both, that's all.

> STANLEY

I can manage that. I think.

He turns away from her.

> HILDA

Stan, nothing could ever come between us. How could
it? We're one. One flesh. Us. You and me. It's sacred.
We're sacred.

She kisses his shoulder.

> HILDA

I love you. I love every part of you. It's wonderful
never to be shy. To know and be known. To be open.
Stan? Stan? Have you gone to sleep?

He grins and jumps on her. He was fooling.

> HILDA

Stan, no, be careful!

> STANLEY

Why?

> HILDA

We might hurt something.

Rebuffed, STANLEY draws back. They lie, awkward, side by side.

INT. TEA SHOP – COOKHAM – DAY.

DOROTHY and PATRICIA are at a table.

As the WAITRESS arrives with the tea, DOROTHY looks up and
sees

STANLEY standing at the door, looking awkward.

PATRICIA crosses to him and talks to him by the door.

DOROTHY pours tea for herself, and sips grimly as PATRICIA flirts.

INT. MOOR THATCH COTTAGE – DAY.

PATRICIA is on the chaise longue, wearing a loose pink wrap, which keeps falling off one shoulder.

STANLEY struggles in with logs and stacks them round the fire. He builds up the fire with a couple of logs. Then he gets up, noticing a PAINTING OF AN OLD MAN.

> STANLEY
>
> (Points) By you?

> PATRICIA
>
> (Turns her head. Languid) No – Dorothy.

> STANLEY
>
> Anything of yours?

> PATRICIA
>
> Nothing I could possibly show you.

> STANLEY
>
> What does your agent say?

> PATRICIA
>
> (Indignant) We're not represented! We live in hopes.

She gazes up at him mesmerically. The fire burns up.

CUT TO:

Later.

The outside door bangs as STANLEY leaves. PATRICIA enters the room, and gazes reflectively at the burning logs. Then turns at a sound.

> PATRICIA
>
> Hullo. Having a snoop?

DOROTHY

(At the door to the kitchen, cigarette in mouth) No –
just looking for a saucepan to hit you over the head
with.

INT. SPENCER BEDROOM – NIGHT.

HILDA

(Puzzled) Mmm, you smell of smoke!

STANLEY

I took some logs round to Moor Thatch. (He leans up
on his elbow) Hilda, they haven't got two ha'pennies
to rub together. She was wearing a sort of pink
wrap . . .

HILDA

(Nuzzling) Patricia?

STANLEY

Pink. (He lies back on the pillow as she caresses him.)
Sort of creamy pink silk – Hilda! (He sits up crossly.)

HILDA

It's all right, so long as we're careful . . .

She jumps on top of him. He pushes her off roughly.

HILDA

Stan!

He leaps out of bed, getting tangled up in the sheet.

STANLEY

I don't know why you're always after me when I
particularly don't want you!

HILDA looks at him, and tries not to laugh.

HILDA

I know. It's Patricia.

STANLEY

You can't help yourself. She ...

HILDA

Oh, all right. All right, Stanley. If you must.

He beams at her gratefully.

INT. SPENCER KITCHEN – DAY.

HILDA serves up a dreadful burnt pie. STANLEY eats up manfully, looks at HILDA, waiting for permission. She looks at him drily. He jumps up, and rushes out.

HILDA, unable to eat, empties away the pie.

EXT. MOOR THATCH COTTAGE – DAY.

A thin wisp of smoke comes out of the chimney.

INT. MOOR THATCH COTTAGE – DAY.

PATRICIA stretches out on the chaise longue in her peignoir. STANLEY sketches her.

EXT. SPENCER GARDEN – DAY.

HILDA is seated in front of an easel. In front of her is an iris in a vase which she is painting.

INT. DOROTHY'S STUDIO – A SHED – DAY.

DOROTHY is doing a portrait of PATRICIA. PATRICIA is restless.

DOROTHY

Keep still.

She paints in silence.

> DOROTHY

(Painting intently) And I wish you'd stop flirting with
Stanley Spencer.

PATRICIA takes an apple from the table at her elbow, spoiling
DOROTHY'S composition, and starts to eat.

> PATRICIA

He does have his uses. Dudley Tooth's his agent for
one.

DOROTHY paints, nose to canvas.

> DOROTHY

Mmm. Not fair to lead him on though, Pixie.

> PATRICIA

(Throws away core) Dreadful little oik. Gives me the
horrors.

> DOROTHY

So, you won't sit for him again?

> PATRICIA

Are you mad? You saw his sketches. He's drawn me
all crooked!

INT. SPENCER STUDIO – DAY.

Paintings everywhere – vibrant and alive. STANLEY, up on the
table, is finishing a picture of Cookham Village. He works in a
frenzy, mixing colours frenetically.

MUSIC – Bach, loud.

He blows out his cheeks, drops the brush, leaps down, steps back,
and prowls back and forth assessing the work. He stands – gazing
up. It satisfies him. He looks outside the window, where HILDA,

heavily pregnant, walks up and down. His face is neutral. He turns back to the canvas, and feels reassured.

EXT. COOKHAM – DAY.

WIDESHOT of Cookham Village. It looks like the painting.

EXT. LINDWORTH HOUSE – DAY.

A smart motor car is parked outside the house. STANLEY and DUDLEY TOOTH go down the path through the front garden.

HILDA, very pregnant, stands by the front door.

> STANLEY
>
> I said I'd get it for her.

> DUDLEY
>
> Splendid, Stanley.

> HILDA
>
> Dudley . . .

> DUDLEY
>
> Hilda darling.

He kisses her on the cheek.

> DUDLEY
>
> When are you due?

> HILDA
>
> (Nervous, smiling) Well, last week actually.

                                        DISSOLVE TO:

EXT. LINDWORTH GARDEN – DAY.

CLOSE ON: BABY sleeping in a pram.

Not far away, HILDA is picking violets from a grassy bank.

PAN TO: High window in house. STANLEY'S face is in the window.

INT. MOOR THATCH COTTAGE – DAY.

PATRICIA takes a large bowl of violets through to her bedside table. She looks down at the violets thoughtfully.

INT. STANLEY'S LINDWORTH STUDIO – DAY.

The Lindworth studio is much bigger than the previous one. STANLEY is up high on scaffolding, working and whistling.

HILDA comes in with the baby in the pram.

> HILDA
> Where are my violets, the ones I picked this morning?

STANLEY keeps painting.

> HILDA
> I left them on the draining board.

HER POV: He looks down at her.

> STANLEY
> She wanted them for her room.

HILDA picks up a paint jar and throws it at him. He yells and dodges.

INT. CHURCH – COOKHAM – DAY.

The Christening.

CU: *AUGUSTUS JOHN'S face.*

HIS POV: STANLEY, betweeen HILDA, and PATRICIA (godmother) who, by tradition, holds the BABY.

STANLEY looks soppily at PATRICIA. She and the BABY make a dazzling composition. PATRICIA catches AUGUSTUS's eye.

VICAR

They brought young children to Christ that he should touch them, and his disciples rebuked those that brought them.

AUGUSTUS JOHN glances round at the back of the Church.

HIS POV: Stanley Spencer's painting 'The Resurrection' is hanging on the back wall, over the entrance.

VICAR (V/O)

But when Jesus saw it, he was much displeased, and said unto them: suffer the little children to come unto me, and forbid them not …

SERIES OF SHOTS of people in the congregation:

ELSIE, standing next to STANLEY.

HENRY LAMB and his wife, PANSY – arm in arm.

GWEN JOHN with DUDLEY TOOTH.

DORELIA and MRS CARLINE.

DOROTHY.

VICAR (V/O)

… for such is the kingdom of God. Verily I say unto you, whosoever shall not receive the kingdom of God as a little child, he shall not enter therein. And Jesus took up the children in his arms, and put his hands upon them and blessed them.

ON: STANLEY looking down at the BABY in PATRICIA'S arms.

HILDA flicks him a mildly troubled look.

INT. CHURCH – DAY – LATER.

CLOSE ON: THE VICAR'S hand trickling water on the BABY'S head.

NEW ANGLE: STANLEY, flanked by PATRICIA and HILDA, HENRY LAMB and GWEN JOHN, gives a little shiver, as if <u>he</u> is being christened.

ON: THE BABY crying.

EXT. BACK GARDEN – LINDWORTH HOUSE – DAY.

Garden Party.

A wind-up gramophone is playing a ragtime tune. THREE COUPLES are dancing.

Linen covered tables decked with simple food have been set out in the garden. ELSIE is serving drinks. ELEGANT PEOPLE, including AUGUSTUS JOHN, DORELIA, STANLEY, HILDA, PANSY LAMB, MRS CARLINE and FRANCIS BACON mill about.

ON: *PATRICIA, standing with DOROTHY and DUDLEY TOOTH –* drinks in their hands.

> PATRICIA
>
> You were looking into the possibility of a show for us.

> DUDLEY
>
> I'm still making enquiries. (Smiles politely) Not easy, as you know.

> PATRICIA
>
> You manage it for other people.

> DUDLEY
>
> (To DOROTHY) I gather the work shown under Miss Preece's name is actually yours, Miss Hepworth. Is that true?

> DOROTHY
>
> (Slight pause) Yes.

DUDLEY

I see. (He backs away) Well, I'll see what I can do.

PATRICIA

I think you should, otherwise...

The MUSIC stops so that her raised voice is loud in the sudden silence.

PATRICIA

... I shall have to marry that dirty little Stanley
Spencer.

DUDLEY and DOROTHY are dumbfounded. SEVERAL PEOPLE look round at PATRICIA.

INT. SPENCER LINDWORTH STUDIO – DAY.

STANLEY is painting on the scaffolding. HILDA is sitting on a rug, feeding the BABY. STANLEY stops working and glares down at her resentfully. She bends over the BABY, unaware of him. He watches, then jumps down, stands and watches.

HILDA bends over the BABY, whispering softly to her. This makes STANLEY irate.

HILDA

What's the matter?

STANLEY sits by her, pulling at her arm like an importunate child.

STANLEY

I need you.

HILDA smiles vaguely and bends over the BABY.

HILDA looks up at STANLEY, her face tired. She puts her breast away.

> STANLEY

If I'm to work I have to feel right!

HILDA gets up with the baby and goes, to put him down to sleep.

> STANLEY

I need you!

EXT. MOOR THATCH GARDEN – DAY.

PATRICIA strolls in the garden. DOROTHY, smoking, leans at the studio door, watching her.

INT. SPENCER HOUSE STUDIO – DAY.

From outside, the sound of women's laughter. STANLEY, in the studio, broods, biting his nails.

EXT. GARDEN, LINDWORTH HOUSE – EARLY EVENING.

ELSIE clears a line of washing, and puts it in a basket.

HILDA is playing with the BABY. ELSIE goes over and looks down at the BABY.

> ELSIE

Look at her little fingers. Ahh!

> HILDA AND ELSIE

Ahhh!

STANLEY comes out of the studio, with his bicycle. He looks at the WOMEN. They don't notice him.

> ELSIE

Ah! That wasn't wind ... that was a smile.

> HILDA

You know she can lift her head now?

ELSIE

Can she?

HILDA

And she can say "ih"!

STANLEY goes away up the path and out of the gate.

HILDA kisses the BABY'S foot.

INT. MOOR THATCH COTTAGE – NIGHT.

PATRICIA is lying naked, except for a pair of shoes, on the chaise longue. STANLEY is drawing her.

STANLEY

Keep still.

PATRICIA

You know I hate being looked at.

STANLEY stops drawing.

STANLEY

All right. I'll do you when you're not looking.

PATRICIA crosses – winds up the gramophone, puts on a record and begins to dance for him.

STANLEY lies back on the chaise longue and watches her, fascinated.

She grabs a cigarette and puts it in a holder, without stopping dancing.

He gets up and lights her cigarette for her. He throws himself back on the sofa.

She dances round, jumps on the sofa and puts a foot on his crotch.

He kisses her foot.

> STANLEY

I must buy you red shoes. With heels.

> PATRICIA

I'd prefer some decent jewellery.

STANLEY thinks she's joking.

> STANLEY

Diamonds?

> PATRICIA

If you like.

STANLEY gazes up at her.

INT. SPENCER LINDWORTH STUDIO – DAY.

STANLEY is painting. HILDA is rocking the pram.

> STANLEY

You're out in that garden all day. You don't paint What
do you think you're doing?

The BABY in the pram starts to cry. STANLEY picks up the BABY
and goes on painting with the BABY under one arm.

> STANLEY

I'm telling you Hilda Carline. Treat God's gift with
reverence or it'll come back to you like a bullet and
smash you in the face!

HILDA looks at him resentfully and takes the BABY from him. She
walks up and down with the BABY – who won't stop crying.

> STANLEY

You've made use of me – now I'm not wanted.

> HILDA

That's not true!

STANLEY throws off his shirt from the heat. Then he takes off his trousers and kicks them down.

He is wearing an ancient grey vest, and old, sagging underpants.

HILDA rocks the BABY in her arms. The BABY stops crying.

STANLEY

How am I supposed to feel like having sex with you if you don't make yourself more attractive!

HILDA looks at him in his terrible underwear.

HILDA

Stanley! Oh, never mind.

STANLEY stomps out.

HILDA

Where are you going? (Calls after him) I've told you! Have her if you want, if that's what you need!

EXT. LONDON – DAY.

WIDESHOT of London street (early 1930s).

INT. ELEGANT LINGERIE SHOP – MAYFAIR – DAY.

STANLEY, in his funny, shapeless hat, is sitting on a small gilt chair, looking eager and nervous.

The MODDOM of the shop is showing embroidered and lace-edged lingerie to PATRICIA.

MODDOM

Apricot? Or there's chartreuse ... Eau de Nil?

PATRICIA scoops all of it into her arms and goes into the changing room.

STANLEY clears his throat. The MODDOM looks at him. He is indicating a piece of frilly black lingerie in a box on the counter, which PATRICIA has forgotten.

MODDOM

Of course, sir.

The MODDOM clacks across the floor to the changing room, with the black lingerie.

INT. ELEGANT LINGERIE SHOP – MAYFAIR – DAY – LATER.

STANLEY sits waiting.

The MODDOM is packing stuff away.

PATRICIA comes out from the changing room.

PATRICIA

I'll have all of them.

MODDOM

Of course, Moddom.

STANLEY blinks.

EXT. COOKHAM RAILWAY STATION – DUSK.

The TRAIN pulls in.

THREE PASSENGERS get off the train. STANLEY helps PATRICIA alight. She looks round nervously as he gives her the elegant shopping bags. She offers him her cheek. He kisses it – and they part – going separate ways.

NEW ANGLE: PATRICIA is pleased with her purchases.

STANLEY thunders up behind her. She turns, surprised.

Breathless, he can't speak, but thrusts a small package at her.

He leaves her standing – the package in her gloved hand.

INT. BEDROOM – MOOR THATCH – NIGHT.

PATRICIA, in a nightdress, opens the packet from STANLEY.

Inside a velvet box is a DIAMOND PENDANT of striking modern design. She holds it to her neck and looks at herself in the mirror.

The door clicks. She turns. DOROTHY is at the door.

PATRICIA holds out the necklace. DOROTHY puts it on for her.

They regard the effect in the mirror. PATRICIA looks challengingly at DOROTHY. DOROTHY looks stricken.

EXT. MOOR THATCH COTTAGE – NIGHT.

The small cottage windows glow warmly. A thin column of smoke issues from the chimney.

INT. MOOR THATCH COTTAGE – NIGHT.

PATRICIA, lying on the sofa, in front of a roaring fire, is startled by STANLEY'S face at the window.

It disappears.

She looks.

His face reappears again.

INT/EXT. MOOR THATCH COTTAGE – NIGHT – LATER.

PATRICIA opens the front door and looks out.

                    PATRICIA
        Stanley?

HER POV: There is no sign of him.

EXT. STREET – COOKHAM – NIGHT.

STANLEY runs down the street. He stops – panting, sweating – and leans on a wall.

INT. KITCHEN – LINDWORTH – NIGHT.

A big farmhouse kitchen.

HILDA is making cocoa. She is wearing a sloppy old nightdress and looks young and vulnerable. She turns as STANLEY pads in quietly.

> HILDA
> What happened?

He just looks at her.

> HILDA
> Did you sleep with her?

He shakes his head and goes out through the kitchen door, into the garden.

HILDA puts a jug of cocoa, two mugs and a tin of biscuits on a tray.

INT. SPENCER LINDWORTH STUDIO – NIGHT.

STANLEY is sitting despondently at one of the trestle tables.

HILDA comes in with tray.

HILDA sits across from STANLEY – putting the tray down. She pours the cocoa.

> HILDA
> Was she annoyed?

She hands him the cup of cocoa.

> STANLEY
> What?

HILDA

Because you didn't sleep with her?

STANLEY

I don't know. I didn't ask.

He takes a biscuit.

STANLEY

I saw her through the window. She has these long
fingers, I must do them. And just the one light on, so
her shoulders stood out like peeled pears.

HILDA

Oh Stan!

HILDA looks at him, sad-eyed.

INT. MOOR THATCH COTTAGE - NIGHT.

PATRICIA and DOROTHY are cuddling on the sofa.

PATRICIA

It won't make any difference between us.

DOROTHY

Won't it?

PATRICIA

Not in the slightest. You'll see.

PATRICIA goes to the fire, which is blazing up, and opens her
peignoir so she can warm her body. DOROTHY watches her, then
gets up and goes to the door.

She bangs a fist to the side of her head, infuriated and helpless.

EXT. THE BRIDGE - DAY.

STANLEY and PATRICIA walk hand in hand across the bridge.

THE VICAR cycles towards them.

STANLEY tries to kiss PATRICIA. She laughs – pushing him away.

THE VICAR looks surprised.

He raises his hat as he cycles past.

INT. SPENCER STUDIO – LINDWORTH – NIGHT.

STANLEY is on the floor, drawing HILDA, who is sitting on a stool with her legs apart, posing for him. He hums, drawing rapidly.

> STANLEY
>
> She let me kiss her.

> HILDA
>
> You're making a fool of yourself.

He draws, head down.

> HILDA
>
> Patricia may not be what she seems.

> STANLEY
>
> (Head down) What do you mean?

> HILDA
>
> She and Dorothy have lived in Paris. They're
> sophisticated.

> STANLEY
>
> I know. You never see her going about like an old dish
> rag.

HILDA frowns at STANLEY.

> STANLEY
>
> Could you squat down? I want to get the inside of your
> thighs.

HILDA squats. STANLEY draws.

STANLEY

Damn!

HILDA

What is it?

STANLEY

I'm getting an erection.

HILDA rises, unbuttoning her blouse.

HILDA

Do you want to ... ?

STANLEY

No, I've got to get this right.

STANLEY turns over a new sheet of paper and begins again.

HILDA

All right, I'll go to London! If you want me to go to
London – stay in London, I'll go!

STANLEY, head down, sketches rapidly.

HILDA

I'll take the baby to mother's.

STANLEY keeps sketching.

HILDA

Give you some time on your own.

STANLEY sketches demonically. He doesn't look at her.

INT. MOVING TRAIN – DAY.

HILDA and the BABY in a train compartment – looking out of the
window.

INT. TRAIN STATION – LONDON – DAY.

MRS CARLINE, Hilda's mother, opens her arms as HILDA arrives, carrying the BABY.

A PORTER follows carrying her suitcases.

INT. KITCHEN & LIVING ROOM – MOOR THATCH COTTAGE – NIGHT.

DOROTHY is in the kitchen, grimly washing brushes and hearing sounds. She listens, goes into sitting room – then climbs the stairs.

At the top of the stairs she hears laughter.

She listens at a door.

INT. BATHROOM – NIGHT.

PATRICIA is in the bath. The room is lit by candles. STANLEY watches as PATRICIA pours scent into the water, and smiles at him.

PATRICIA
(Mouths) I love you.

He is bewitched.

EXT. STREET AND CARLINE HOUSE – HAMPSTEAD – DUSK.

ON: a Hampstead street, with Hampstead Heath in the background.

A LAMPLIGHTER is lighting the gas lamps.

The door of HILDA'S MOTHER'S house opens, revealing HILDA. She looks up and down the street.

CLOSER ON HILDA – looking lost.

EXT. FIELD – DAY.

It is a glorious day.

STANLEY is lying on the grass, sketching PATRICIA. He picks up his rubber.

PATRICIA

What are you doing?

STANLEY

I'm trying ... (rubbing out) ... to find a difficult problem.

PATRICIA

Why?

STANLEY

Because easy problems aren't exciting.

PATRICIA lies back, eyes closed.

STANLEY looks around at the views.

STANLEY

God! Beautiful!

PATRICIA

Me?

STANLEY

Everything! You – the trees – everything! Look around you!

But she lies back, watching him work. STANLEY draws in silence, absorbed.

PATRICIA

You should do more landscapes.

STANLEY

I'll do the landscapes of your legs.

He approaches her.

STANLEY

I want to crawl all over you like an ant.

PATRICIA

Then you must. (She lets him.) Darling ...

He looks up.

PATRICIA

Why don't I take over your affairs?

She lets him fondle her.

PATRICIA

Landscapes sell! Yours are wonderful!

EXT. COUNTRY LANE. DAY.

STANLEY and PATRICIA are walking. He carries everything.

She is at his ear.

PATRICIA

... all you have to do is concentrate on what you do
best.

He looks at her in enquiry.

PATRICIA

Paint!

They walk out of sight.

PATRICIA (V/O)

You don't need that big house. Sell it! Better still, put
it in my name until after the divorce, then it'll belong
to both of us.

A FLOCK OF CROWS fly up.

INT. LIVING ROOM – CARLINE HOUSE – NIGHT.

HILDA is seated at a table, writing a letter.

> HILDA (V/O)
>
> I don't understand. You're my husband. We took vows before God to be together forever. Didn't you mean it?

EXT. MEADOW – DAY.

STANLEY and PATRICIA are lying together in the grass.

STANLEY is trying put his hand up PATRICIA'S skirt.

> PATRICIA
>
> Don't.

> STANLEY
>
> I can't help it. My feelings have all come alive!

He thrusts himself at PATRICIA. She pushes him away.

INT. LIVING ROOM – CARLINE HOUSE – NIGHT.

HILDA is writing.

> HILDA (V/O)
>
> Stanley, please! I don't want to leave you. I want to come home. Please. Can't I be near you? See you? Nothing feels right. You can't make me not want to love you.

EXT. THE RIVER – DAY.

STANLEY and PATRICIA, in each other's arms, watch the water move slowly by. PATRICIA talks softly into his ear.

> PATRICIA
>
> Why should you spend the rest of your life paying for Hilda? She has a perfectly well- placed family.

She pulls away and looks at him with a big honest stare.

PATRICIA

You're an artist. You must be free. Your loyalty must
be to the work. And me of course.

INT. MOOR THATCH COTTAGE – NIGHT.

PATRICIA and STANLEY are kissing on the sofa. STANLEY looks
drunk with kisses.

PATRICIA

Did you sign the papers?

STANLEY

You're so beautiful.

PATRICIA

Stanley! I asked you a question.

STANLEY looks away.

PATRICIA

You didn't sign them, did you?

STANLEY

Why can't I ... ?

PATRICIA

Why can't you what?

STANLEY

Why can't I have both of you?

He looks at her pleadingly.

Her gaze is impenetrable.

INT. LIVING ROOM – CARLINE HOUSE – NIGHT.

HILDA is writing a letter.

INT. SPENCER STUDIO – LINDWORTH – DAY.

STANLEY and PATRICIA are naked. He is painting them both using mirrors, squirting colours and mixing.

HILDA (V/O)

I love you! A hundred children couldn't replace one Stanley.

INT. KITCHEN – CARLINE HOUSE – DAY.

MRS CARLINE, HILDA and the CHILD (in a high chair) are having breakfast. HILDA hands an opened letter to MRS CARLINE who reads it to herself and looks up, shocked.

MRS CARLINE

(Reads) "Do you think you could manage on two pounds a week? I've been losing commissions. No, it's not that …

The Maid (MAISIE) comes in with fresh toast, puts it on the table and leaves.

MRS CARLINE

(Resuming) I need the money to spend on Patricia."

The TWO WOMEN look at each other, wide-eyed.

HILDA faints.

MRS CARLINE

Oh my God …

MRS CARLINE gets up and goes to HILDA.

MRS CARLINE

(Calls out) Maisie! Maisie!

THE MAID hurries in, alarmed.

EXT. HAMPSTEAD HEATH – DAY.

DIFFERENT ANGLES ON: *HILDA* sitting on a park bench. All around, PEOPLE play with their CHILDREN and DOGS romp.

> HILDA (V/O)
>
> I'm sorry Stanley. I've been ill. There's something wrong with me. I seem to have lost the knack of living. (She watches sadly as CHILDREN play.) I feel I don't belong in this world. That I've no proper place. That I must keep very still and small or something awful will happen to me and the baby.

She looks around at the views and the people. They are distorted.

> HILDA (V/O)
>
> (Pause) I seem to be in a moon-world full of ash and flint and cold hostile stars. Not on this loving earth at all.

INT. SITTING ROOM – LINDWORTH – DAY.

STANLEY is seated at a table – writing a letter.

He looks mesmerised. PATRICIA is standing over him, dictating.

> PATRICIA
>
> Please discontinue writing.

STANLEY writes.

> PATRICIA
>
> Your letters will be returned unopened. In future address all correspondence to my solicitor.

STANLEY writes and puts down the pen. But she hasn't finished.

> PATRICIA
>
> I wish no further connection with you.

At this, he falters and looks up at her.

Her face is implacable.

He writes.

INT. HILDA'S BEDROOM – NIGHT.

HILDA is sitting at her desk, writing to him.

> HILDA (V/O)
>
> Am I not worth keeping as a friend? I've made no fuss. Surely, I'm worth something for that. All I've wanted is for you to be happy. Oh, Stanley, how can you be happy when you know I'm in such a plight?

INT. LIVING ROOM – MOOR THATCH COTTAGE – DAY.

DOROTHY is standing in the kitchen doorway.

Very excited, STANLEY takes a ring box out of his pocket.

He takes out the RING and gestures to PATRICIA to offer her hand.

He puts the ring – a beautiful sapphire – on her finger.

She looks pleased and displays it to DOROTHY.

DOROTHY makes no expression.

INT. HILDA'S BEDROOM – DAY.

HILDA is in bed looking very pale. MRS CARLINE comes in with soup, but HILDA shakes her head.

INT. REGISTRY OFFICE – DAY.

STANLEY, in his brown suit and his old hat, and PATRICIA, in a pale snaky dress, face the REGISTRAR – a small, ghoulish man in black.

>REGISTRAR
>
>And do you take this man to be your lawful wedded
>husband . . .

Behind them, standing in the chair-rows of the dull, unadorned room, are DUDLEY TOOTH, DOROTHY, HENRY LAMB and PANSY LAMB.

>REGISTRAR (OFF-SCREEN)
>
>. . . to have and to hold, from this day forth, so long as
>ye both shall live?

CU: PATRICIA – grim with triumph.

>PATRICIA
>
>I do.

EXT. REGISTRY OFFICE – DAY.

PATRICIA and STANLEY come down the registry office steps, followed by DUDLEY, HENRY and PANSY.

They blink in the sunshine. DOROTHY stands slightly apart, grasping a large handbag.

INT. HALLWAY – CARLINE HOUSE – DAY.

GWEN JOHN and MRS CARLINE are talking in the hall. GWEN has just arrived and is wearing her coat. They look up as HILDA appears on the landing, in her white nightdress.

HILDA'S knees give way.

They rush up the stairs to her aid.

EXT. LINDWORTH HOUSE – COOKHAM – DAY.

A car drives up. The CHAUFFEUR gets out and opens the door.

PATRICIA and STANLEY get out.

DOROTHY makes to get out as well, but then realises she is not wanted, and puts her leg back in.

The CHAUFFEUR closes the door.

ON: STANLEY and PATRICIA going up the path. Behind them, the CHAUFFEUR gets into the driving seat and the car drives off.

STANLEY opens the front door. Then he turns, picks PATRICIA up, and staggers through into the hall with her.

INT. LIVING ROOM – LINDWORTH HOUSE – DAY.

STANLEY carries PATRICIA into the living room.

He dumps her on to the large sofa, throws off his jacket, and pulls off his shoes.

>PATRICIA

What are you doing?

>STANLEY

I thought we ...

>PATRICIA

But ...

>STANLEY

Surely now we ... ?

He starts unbuttoning his trousers.

>PATRICIA

No.

>STANLEY

Why not?

>PATRICIA

It's too soon.

STANLEY

Soon? What do you mean?

STANLEY looks at her, bewildered, his trousers around his ankles.

Pushing past him, she runs out of the room, leaving him open-mouthed.

EXT. STREET – COOKHAM – DAY.

PATRICIA runs down the street. PASSERS-BY watch her with curiosity.

INT. LIVING ROOM – MOOR THATCH COTTAGE – DAY.

DOROTHY, huddled in an easy chair, is weeping softly.

Suddenly there is a loud banging on the door. She turns.

PATRICIA (V/O)

Dorothy!

DOROTHY jumps to her feet and leaps towards the door.

PATRICIA falls into her arms.

EXT. MOOR THATCH COTTAGE – LATER – DAY.

STANLEY is knocking on the front door.

He peers through the windows.

INT. BEDROOM – MOOR THATCH COTTAGE – DAY.

PATRICIA and DOROTHY are in bed together, making love.

STANLEY

(From below, outside) Open the door! Open the door!

He bangs on the front door. They look up briefly.

EXT. MOOR THATCH COTTAGE – DAY.

STANLEY bangs hopelessly on the front door.

Passing VILLAGERS watch with interest and enjoyment.

STANLEY, defeated, sits on the step.

INT. MOOR THATCH BEDROOM – DAY.

PATRICIA and DOROTHY are safe in each other's arms.

Below the bedroom window, the crowd drifts away.

STANLEY gets up wearily and follows them down the road.

EXT. COUNTRY ROAD – DAY.

A SINGLE-DECKER BUS winds its way along the road.

As the bus comes closer, we see HILDA in a seat by the window, sitting alone.

EXT. BUS STOP – COOKHAM VILLAGE – DAY.

The bus pulls up in the centre of Cookham.

A MAN and a WOMAN get out – followed by HILDA.

She is carrying nothing except her handbag.

EXT. LINDWORTH HOUSE – DAY.

HILDA approaches the house. Making up her mind, she goes through the front garden and up the steps.

She knocks at the front door, and turns to look at her neglected garden. She knocks again, tries the door and goes in.

INT. HALL – LINDWORTH HOUSE – DAY.

HILDA, timid, looks into the sitting room.

HER POV: There is no-one there and the room is a mess.

                    HILDA

  Elsie?

She goes towards the kitchen.

                    HILDA

  Cooeee!

EXT. BACK GARDEN AND STUDIO – LINDWORTH HOUSE – DAY.

HILDA comes out of the kitchen door into the back garden.

She crosses the back garden and goes into the studio.

INT. STUDIO – DAY.

HILDA enters the studio.

                    HILDA

  Elsie? Coooeee! Elsie?

There's a noise from up on the scaffolding, which makes her jump
and let out a small scream. She stumbles back and looks up.

HER POV: STANLEY is gazing down at her from the scaffolding.

                    HILDA

  (Angry) You frightened me!

                    STANLEY

  Hilda?

                    HILDA

  (Disorientated) I'm sorry. I didn't know you'd be here.
  You frightened me. Elsie said she'd packed my things.

STANLEY looks at her with shining eyes and dashes down the
ladder.

STANLEY

Hilda!

HILDA backs away.

HILDA

Why aren't you on your honeymoon? Where's
Patricia?

STANLEY

With Dorothy.

STANLEY grabs both of HILDA'S hands and draws her forward.
He sits her down on a chair.

HILDA

(Nervous) What is it? What's the matter?

STANLEY

I've been waiting for you.

He lifts a hand to keep her in her seat. Then he dashes around the
many canvasses, and pulls out three of them. He sets them down in
front of her. They are paintings of Patricia in the nude.

He waits, very tense, for her opinion.

STANLEY

Dudley says people will think them dirty.

HILDA doesn't reply. She looks from one picture to another.

STANLEY

What do you think?

HILDA

They're lovely, Stanley. Truthful.

STANLEY

I knew you'd understand. I've missed you so much.

> HILDA

I've missed you!

> STANLEY

I'm sorry. I didn't mean any of it. Patricia said I had
to, for the divorce.

> HILDA

That's no excuse.

> STANLEY

I know. I'm sorry. I'm sorry Hilda. I'm so sorry. I don't
know what came over me.

He starts to steer her into the garden, with an arm around her.

They go out.

EXT. GARDEN LINDWORTH HOUSE – LATER – DAY.

STANLEY finishes laying out a picnic under the apple tree. A rug
with dishes of food, decorated with flowers.

HILDA is standing – melancholy.

> STANLEY

There you are. All your favourites. Spanish cheese,
marmite toast ... oh ...

He puts his hand in his pocket and takes out a big pork pie.

> HILDA

I'm sorry. I'm not very ...

He kneels down in front of her. Reluctantly, she sinks down on the
rug and takes a piece of marmite toast.

Watched by STANLEY, she tries to eat, but has trouble swallowing.

> HILDA

Could I ... could I have a drink of water?

STANLEY jumps up.

STANLEY

Oh! I forgot! Barley water!

STANLEY dashes into the house.

HILDA looks around at her beloved garden.

STANLEY comes out brandishing a jug and two glasses.

EXT. GARDEN – LINDWORTH HOUSE – LATER – DAY.

HILDA, now relaxed, sits side by side with STANLEY on the grass.
There are half-drunk glasses of barley water in front of them.

HILDA

Your dear, dear face. Oh Stanley, I've been so hungry!

They kiss. He breathes deep and sniffs her.

STANLEY

Ohh … you smell of beech nuts and broom flower.

He kisses her again and begins to fondle her.

HILDA

Stanley, can we?

STANLEY groans and buries his face in her bosom.

HILDA sighs deeply and holds him to her passionately.

EXT. CAKE SHOP AND STREET – COOKHAM – DAY.

VIEW THROUGH WINDOW: STANLEY and HILDA are at the
counter.

They come out of the shop with a bag of doughnuts and, laughing
together, walk down the street.

EXT. COOKHAM VILLAGE – DAY.

STANLEY and HILDA are walking down the street. The VICAR cycles past. He stops and nearly falls over with surprise.

> VICAR

Mrs Spencer!

HILDA gives him her hand cordially.

> HILDA

Vicar.

STANLEY is grinning. The VICAR looks from one to the other.

> VICAR

I'll say cheerio then!

He cycles off. STANLEY and HILDA smile happily.

EXT. CHURCHYARD – DAY.

STANLEY and HILDA are sitting near an old tombstone, eating doughnuts from the bag.

> HILDA

Mmmmmm!

> STANLEY

Manage another?

> HILDA

(Mouth full) Mmmmm.

She takes another doughnut.

EXT. CHURCHYARD – DUSK.

BIRD SONG.

STANLEY and HILDA are lying on the grass under a yew tree.

STANLEY looks around the churchyard, takes a small sketchbook out of his pocket, and starts sketching. HILDA leans over to see what he is doing. STANLEY gestures at the churchyard.

STANLEY

The holy suburb of heaven, Hilda.

She smiles at him, then sits up - her hands around her hunched knees.

STANLEY

What?

HILDA

Stan, do you think what we did last night was adultery?

STANLEY scratches his head and adjusts his glasses.

STANLEY

Well ... I don't see how it can be.

HILDA

It can. We're not married.

STANLEY

We are. In the eyes of God, we are.

She takes his hand and kisses his fingers.

HILDA

I don't care if it is adultery.

STANLEY

Good!

He jumps up, excited.

STANLEY

Good!

He capers round her.

> STANLEY

Whoopee!

HILDA laughs and throws a doughnut at him.

She stops suddenly.

> HILDA

Oh dear.

> STANLEY

What?

HILDA turns as he wipes the doughnut sugar from his face.

> HILDA

Patricia. How are we going to tell her? Oh Stanley,
how can we build happiness on someone else's
misery?

> STANLEY

No, that's all sorted out.

> HILDA

Sorted out?

INT. HALL – LINDWORTH HOUSE – NIGHT.

STANLEY and HILDA are coming into the house. HILDA closes the
front door.

> STANLEY

She says I'm an artist. Artists have needs, she says.

HILDA shakes her head. She doesn't understand. They walk down
the hall, STANLEY in front.

> STANLEY

I need you. So ...

They go through into the kitchen.

INT. KITCHEN – LINDWORTH HOUSE – NIGHT – CONTINUOUS.

STANLEY enters the kitchen, followed by HILDA.

> HILDA
>
> So, does this mean we're a family again? We can come
> back?

He opens the back door to the garden and goes out. HILDA follows.

EXT. GARDEN – LINDWORTH HOUSE – NIGHT.

STANLEY heads for the studio. HILDA follows.

> HILDA
>
> Stanley, I don't think I've got this straight. Could you
> explain it to me again?

> STANLEY
>
> Right. Patricia doesn't want to move in here. She
> wants to stay at the cottage with Dorothy.

He pushes into the studio.

INT. SPENCER STUDIO – LINDWORTH – NIGHT.

STANLEY turns on the lights. HILDA follows him in and closes
the door.

> HILDA
>
> Are you sleeping with her?

> STANLEY
>
> Who?

> HILDA
>
> Patricia! Are you sleeping with her?

STANLEY

Not as such.

HILDA follows him around, as he moves restlessly.

HILDA

Either you are, or you aren't.

STANLEY

To tell the truth, she can't manage it. There's
something wrong with her.

HILDA

You mean you haven't been to bed with her? Not at
all?

STANLEY

Not as such.

HILDA

Don't keep saying that!

STANLEY

So, the arrangement is ...

HILDA

Arrangement? Whose arrangement? What
arrangement?

STANLEY

That I can be married to both of you.

HILDA stares at him.

STANLEY

She says – Patricia – that when you and I are together
again, she'll ... she and I ...

HILDA sits down on a chair and watches him.

HILDA

What?

STANLEY

Well, she and I ... then we can do it. She and I can do
it too. I can have her as well. That's what I want Hilda.
It's what I need. She understands that. She's not
conventional. She's an upper- class woman.

HILDA

So, you're saying ... what you're saying is, after all
this dreadful misery. You throwing me off, saying
you never wanted to see me or your daughter again.
That you hated me. Now you're saying that you didn't
mean any of it? That you love me and want me here in
my own home again – back as I was before ... as your
mistress.

STANLEY holds a paintbrush in his hand, drops it and picks it up.

HILDA

Is that what you mean?

STANLEY

Put like that, yes.

HILDA rockets out of her chair and knocks over the side table
where STANLEY is putting back the painting brush. Everything
goes over with a crash.

HILDA

I don't know which one of you I want to kill first!

STANLEY comes towards her.

She hits him in the face. He grabs her hand. She pulls it free and
slams out.

EXT. THE GARDEN – AUGUSTUS JOHN'S HOUSE – DUSK.

AUGUSTUS and STANLEY are lying back in wicker chairs with cushions, watching TWO MALE GUESTS and FOUR BEAUTIFUL WOMEN, in outlandish gear, playing croquet on the lawn.

THREE BEAUTIFUL CHILDREN are running about barefoot, playing with a DOG.

> STANLEY

You know about women.

AUGUSTUS looks at him drily.

DORELIA comes into view. AUGUSTUS immediately gets to his feet and lumbers towards her.

She walks off, out of sight – with AUGUSTUS following her.

STANLEY, left alone, gets to his feet and sighs.

INT. STAIRWAY AND LANDING – AUGUSTUS'S HOUSE – NIGHT.

AUGUSTUS is going up the stairs, followed by STANLEY.

> STANLEY

I don't know if being divorced is colouring my outlook. Perhaps I'm becoming a libertine … ?

> AUGUSTUS

Ha ha ha!

> STANLEY

What I want to know is … Why must a man have only one woman? I mean, apart from the expense. Why all this possessive business?

They have reached the landing.

A PRETTY YOUNG WOMAN is waiting to come down the stairs.

AUGUSTUS

Oh, I don't stand for that. Pandora!

AUGUSTUS stops and gropes PANDORA. She smiles.

AUGUSTUS

(Over PANDORA'S shoulder) Spunky little turps -rag like you should be ranging the hills like a white-arsed collie.

STANLEY

(Touching AUGUSTUS on the shoulder) Really?

But AUGUSTUS is kissing PANDORA.

EXT. GARDEN – AUGUSTUS'S HOUSE – NIGHT.

There are fairy-lights in the trees. The effect is beautiful. A large table is set with food and drink. PEOPLE and CHILDREN are sitting and lying about.

AUGUSTUS

Don't worry about Hilda, my boy. Get around her.

STANLEY

(Miserable) How?

DORELIA, looking beautiful, comes into view and walks up to them. She's bearing a huge platter of fruit.

AUGUSTUS shakes his head. STANLEY timidly takes a banana.

She looks at him gravely and moves off. They watch her go.

AUGUSTUS

All you gotta do with a plain woman is say she's beautiful.

They watch DORELIA with the children.

AUGUSTUS

Tell her she's got the loveliest physog in Christendom.
Neck like a Delft jug. Bum like a Boucher.

A YOUNG MAN starts playing a pipe.

AUGUSTUS

(Raises his voice) Hilda de Milo. The Rokeby Hilda.
Hilda of Troy.

DORELIA and PANDORA start dancing together.

AUGUSTUS gets up to join the dance.

STANLEY watches.

AUGUSTUS

Tell a few lies!

EXT. CARLINE HOUSE – HAMPSTEAD – DAY.

STANLEY, in an old overcoat, rings the front doorbell.

INT. DRAWING ROOM – CARLINE HOUSE – DAY.

HILDA is sitting, her hands clasped. Her mother, MRS CARLINE,
eccentrically dressed in an artistic manner, comes into the room.

HILDA looks up, alarmed.

MRS CARLINE

I think I've upset him. I merely remarked that
whomsoever God hath joined together, let no man put
asunder.

STANLEY is suddenly in the doorway.

MRS CARLINE

Do come in, Stanley, if you're coming.

STANLEY

I didn't know you were going to be here. I thought it
was just going to be Hilda.

MRS CARLINE

I am here as the wakeful shepherd.

STANLEY looks at her.

MRS CARLINE

Someone has to protect Hilda.

STANLEY

Yes – me! There's no need for her to be unhappy. I'll
look after her.

MRS CARLINE

Splendid! Let every valley of sin, every mountain of
selfishness be brought low and the highway of God be
made plain. Sherry?

STANLEY

No. And I do wish you wouldn't keep bringing God
into it.

MRS CARLINE

What do you mean?

STANLEY

I'm not criticizing him. It's just that the ineffable
glory of him isn't always relevant. Can I talk to Hilda?

MRS CARLINE

Possibly. First – what is the position with the second
Mrs Spencer?

STANLEY

I love her and I want Hilda to love her.

BOTH WOMEN look at him, amazed.

EXT. SIDE OF CARLINE HOUSE – HAMPSTEAD – DAY.

STANLEY is looking up at the window where HILDA sits on the window-seat of her bedroom looking out of the window.

> STANLEY
>
> How can you leave me? You are me!

The GARDENER appears. He doesn't know whether to go or stay.

> STANLEY
>
> Please – can't you take me as I am? I need other
> women!

TWO SCULLERY MAIDS look out the kitchen window at STANLEY. HILDA looks down with an anguished look, then disappears.

> STANLEY
>
> I need experience. Then I'll be able to please you
> more. I'll know more.

MAISIE, holding the baby, now two years old, looks out of another window. MRS CARLINE opens the door, and approaches Stanley.

> STANLEY
>
> Patricia says I can have as many women as I want!

THE GARDENER stops in his tracks. MRS CARLINE retraces her steps. THE GARDENER beats a retreat.

> HILDA
>
> (Appearing at the window again.) Oh Stanley!

STANLEY steps forward, gazing at her.

> STANLEY
>
> I've never not wanted you. Never.

She looks down, her hair falling over the sill. Her gaze softens.

He moves closer to be nearer to her.

STANLEY

It's all right, Patricia says it's all right.

HILDA jerks back, infuriated. She bangs the window down.

STANLEY

(Calls up) She likes you!

He backs away, gazing up.

At the kitchen window, the SCULLERY MAIDS giggle.

INT. GWEN JOHN'S DINING ROOM – NIGHT.

GWEN JOHN is giving a dinner party.

The walls are covered with interesting post-impressionist paintings.

At the table, half-way through the main course, are: GWEN, HENRY LAMB, PANSY LAMB and DUDLEY TOOTH.

DUDLEY

What about Degas?

HENRY LAMB

Degas. He desire, mes amis, to peek through ze key 'ole ... to see women washing zemselves like leetle cats.

GWEN

Degas treated women as whores. Manet treated whores as women.

The MAID comes to the door.

MAID

It's Mister Spencer.

STANLEY, agitated, appears in the doorway. He looks dreadful in an old coat fastened with a safety pin.

GWEN

(Surprised) Stanley! Come in. Come and have ...

STANLEY

Gwen, will you talk to Hilda?

DUDLEY

Hello Stanley.

STANLEY

(To GWEN) Tell her she has to come back. She'll listen to you.

GWEN purses her lips, thinking.

GWEN

Sorry.

STANLEY

Why not?

GWEN

Can't do it.

STANLEY

You mean you won't.

GWEN

That's right.

STANLEY

Why not? You're all the bloody same, you lot!

He storms out.

DUDLEY

Poor Stanley. It must be hell to be in love with two women.

                    PANSY LAMB
Henry can barely manage one.

                    HENRY LAMB
Ha ha.

                    GWEN
(To DUDLEY) How's his work selling?

                    DUDLEY
Badly. People think it's pornographic.

                    HENRY LAMB
I saw the painting of him and Patricia.

                    GWEN
And?

                    HENRY
I wish I could afford to buy it.

INT. SITTING ROOM – MOOR THATCH COTTAGE – DAY.

A tea table is laid, with cups and saucers for two, sandwiches and a large cherry cake.

HILDA is sitting on the sofa in her hat and coat, clutching her handbag. DOROTHY is pouring the tea.

                    DOROTHY
It's very good of you.

                    HILDA
You asked me Dorothy, and I'm here.

                    DOROTHY
How are you?

                    HILDA
You've lost weight.

DOROTHY

Yes.

PATRICIA enters from the kitchen.

PATRICIA

Hilda, I do absolutely need a word with you.

HILDA, rises, aghast.

HILDA

Did Stanley do this? Ask you to be here?

DOROTHY

No, no.

PATRICIA

No, no, no, no, no! It was my idea.

HILDA waves away the cup of tea that DOROTHY is trying to offer her. PATRICIA takes it and drinks.

PATRICIA

Hilda. Won't you consider coming back to Cookham?
(She takes HILDA'S cup) It's your home after all. You
shouldn't have gone away so much. (She drinks.) I
did try to resist him you know. There's a dark side to
Stanley. He has urges.

HILDA

Of course he has. So have I.

PATRICIA

Oh. Dorothy.

She passes her cup to DOROTHY. DOROTHY refills it.

PATRICIA

(Leans in to HILDA) Hilda, we're on the same side.
Can't we solve this together?

HILDA sits down. *PATRICIA gestures imperiously.* DOROTHY hands her the cup of tea. PATRICIA sips, waiting.

> HILDA

(In a low voice) I will consider coming back to Cookham. If you will agree to leave Stanley.

> PATRICIA

Leave?

> HILDA

Divorce him.

> PATRICIA

Oh no, I couldn't do that.

> HILDA

Why not?

> PATRICIA

Apart from anything else, I should have to name you as co-respondent. I couldn't do that to you, Hilda. I have far too much respect for you.

> HILDA

You won't divorce him? Then will you agree to go away?

> PATRICIA

Go away?!

> HILDA

Give me back my house and leave Stanley alone.

> PATRICIA

May I remind you that you are speaking to his legal wife. There is no question of my conveying the house back to you.

> HILDA

Why not?

> PATRICIA

We've rented it out. We need the income.

> HILDA

But it isn't yours!

> PATRICIA

Of course it's mine!

> HILDA

(Confused) But . . . where's Stanley living?

> DOROTHY

In the studio.

HILDA is trying not to crack.

> HILDA

(Bravely) I should like my linen please. And the china.

> PATRICIA

I'm afraid it's all in use.

> HILDA

May I have my things please.

> PATRICIA

You were using double damask table napkins as paint rags! Nothing's worth anything. I can read The Times through the sheets, and as for the china . . . did you ever have a decent dinner service?

HILDA gets up and goes to the door.

> PATRICIA

Hilda! Please – won't you reconsider?

HILDA turns the doorknob. Her hand is shaking. She opens the door.

HILDA

(Tears in her eyes) You don't love Stanley. All he is to you is a means to pay your debts!

HILDA goes out.

EXT. MOOR THATCH COTTAGE – DAY – CONTINUOUS.

HILDA comes out of the front door and makes off down the path. PATRICIA, in the doorway, calls after her.

PATRICIA

Hilda! I'm having a horrible time. Nobody in the village will speak to me!

HILDA trudges away, head down.

DISSOLVE TO:

EXT. A PRIVATE MENTAL HOME – DAY.

In the garden, SEVERAL PATIENTS are sitting. There's a NURSE, and two ATTENDANTS.

DUDLEY walks up to the front of the building. He is carrying a bag of grapes.

INT. HILDA'S ROOM – MENTAL HOME – DAY.

HILDA, in her hat and coat, holding her handbag, is seated in an armchair by the window. To her left is a small desk.

DUDLEY puts the grapes into a bowl.

HILDA

He wrote me a letter. He wants to come and see me.

DUDLEY

Yes.

HILDA

No, don't let him. He hates illness. Anyway, he has to
make up his mind. He can't keep dithering between
me and Patricia.

HILDA turns and looks out of the window. DUDLEY, not knowing
what to do, sits. Pause. DUDLEY looks at his watch.

DUDLEY

Well, Hilda, I must dash. I'll bring you some books.

He stands up.

DUDLEY

Now, do try and rest. You must get well. For your
daughter. And for yourself, of course.

HILDA

I've written to Buckingham Palace.

DUDLEY

I beg your pardon?

HILDA

To complain. I mean, this can't go on, can it?

DUDLEY, trying to go, doesn't quite know what to do.

DUDLEY

I'll come again.

EXT. WOODS – DAY.

ON: Foxgloves.

>   STANLEY (V/O)
>
> The foxgloves are out ... I've got this little cottage
> now. Down the road from where we were. I put up the
> double bed ...

STANLEY is sitting at an easel, painting.

>   STANLEY
>
> Oh Hilda! You're the absolute essence of joy to me. I
> keep seeing you, your hands with the knuckles all
> knuckled – your hair hanging down like water – ohh!

INT. HILDA'S ROOM – MENTAL HOME – NIGHT.

HILDA is in bed. She looks up at the ceiling.

>   HILDA (V/O)
>
> I had such joy. Such ecstasy in you.

INT. STANLEY'S STUDIO – DAY.

STANLEY is working.

>   STANLEY (V/O)
>
> I miss you! It's using up all my energy!

He mixes paint and lifts the brush.

>   STANLEY (V/O)
>
> I dream you're there and I'm with you, and I'm with
> God, and it's all right, and ... then I wake up.

INT. HILDA'S ROOM – MENTAL HOME – NIGHT.

HILDA is seated in a nightdress, by the window, looking out.

>   HILDA (V/O)
>
> You know every line of me. Every cross-hatched
> surface. Every crevice. And I you. (Silence.) You were
> stolen from me.

INT. SPENCER STUDIO – LINDWORTH – NIGHT.

STANLEY is up on scaffolding, painting.

> STANLEY (V/O)
> I'm going to get a divorce from Patricia.

He throws paint at the canvas with rapid intensity.

INT. HILDA'S ROOM – MENTAL HOME – DAY.

HILDA is in bed. She looks ill. STANLEY sits next to her, holding her hand.

> STANLEY
> If I get a divorce, then everything will be as it was.
> You and me, man and wife, together in the eyes of
> God. You'd like that, wouldn't you?

> HILDA
> Let me get better, Stan – then I'll think straight. I
> must have my mind, you see, to be able to think.

He cuddles her.

> STANLEY
> Dear, darling Hilda. Oh, you're such a marvellous
> present to me. I want to paint and paint you. I haven't
> started to get you right.

He kisses her hand. She opens her arms and they embrace.

> NURSE
> Mr Spencer!

A NURSE is in the doorway. She taps her watch.

EXT. FRONT GARDEN – MOOR THATCH COTTAGE – DAY.

STANLEY and DOROTHY are standing outside the front door.

DOROTHY

She is worried about money. (A brief smile) That's
always been a problem, as we both know.

STANLEY

I should be well off by now. As it is, I'm deep in debt.

DOROTHY

That's what concerns her.

NEW ANGLE: Around the corner, PATRICIA leans against the wall,
listening, head down, tracing with her foot in the gravel.

STANLEY

What's she got to worry about? The courts would be
on her side. They were with Hilda.

DOROTHY

She isn't sure what her situation would be in the case
of an annulment.

STANLEY

I'd pay her anyway.

NEW ANGLE: PATRICIA lifts her head.

DOROTHY

Yes, I'm sure. But with two households, your
daughter, doctor's bills ... How is Hilda?

STANLEY

Oh, Hilda's fine. Absolutely her old self again. I'm
bringing her back home to Cookham.

DOROTHY

To your cottage? Oh, I didn't know. Is she installed?

NEW ANGLE: PATRICIA shows impatience.

STANLEY

Not as such. Look, try again. I'm not getting
anywhere.

DOROTHY

I honestly don't think there's any point. Not for an
annulment. If you were talking of divorce, well,
Patricia did mention the possibility of settling a sum
of money on her.

STANLEY

How much?

ANGLE ON: PATRICIA – intent.

DOROTHY

I couldn't say.

STANLEY

It's all the same in any case. I haven't got any.

PATRICIA dashes out from behind the corner of the house.

PATRICIA

You see? Well, you common little man, you'd better
take your hat and go because there are no favours for
you here!

STANLEY

I've done you all the favours.

PATRICIA

You? What have you done for me? Did you help me get
a show? No, it's all you, you, you!

STANLEY

If I didn't help, which is not true – it's because you
don't work. Dorothy works. When do you work? All

you do is spend money and crawl around after that
second-rate Bloomsbury lot.

PATRICIA

Who've been a damn sight more use to me than you
ever were!

STANLEY

So you suck up to them.

PATRICIA

How dare you insult my friends!

STANLEY

Friends? You don't know the meaning of the word.
And what you did to Hilda is enough to put me in
mind of murder.

PATRICIA

Dorothy, you're a witness to that threat.

STANLEY

You have the mouth of a pike, the beak of a cuttle fish
and the eyes of a conger eel!

PATRICIA

I suggest that you begin to take me seriously. You and
your hag can do and say what you want. There will
be no annulment. There will be no divorce. I am Mrs
Stanley Spencer. You will continue to support me. You
and your sad, ugly mistress will live with it, and like
it! In the meantime, here are the bills for my framing.
I'm having a show – thanks to my friends – to which
your presence will not be welcome!

She tries to give him the bills, but he ignores them.

So she thrusts them at DOROTHY, who looks at them briefly.

DOROTHY

Patricia, are you really asking Stanley ... ?

PATRICIA

Since I'm so hideous, I'll leave you two to see to it!

She marches into the house.

DOROTHY

I'm sorry.

Helplessly, she gives him the bills, and, as helplessly, he takes them.

STANLEY

You can't honestly be taking her side?

DOROTHY

Who else will?

STANLEY looks at her and goes.

INT. MOOR THATCH COTTAGE – DAY.

PATRICIA is on the sofa, weeping.

DOROTHY closes the front door.

DOROTHY sits next to her and puts an arm around her.

DOROTHY

Don't worry. Everything will be fine, darling.

PATRICIA looks at DOROTHY piteously.

PATRICIA

What's going to happen to me?

INT. HOSPITAL CORRIDOR – DAY.

STANLEY stands in the hospital corridor, his hat in his hand.

A DOCTOR and a NURSE hurry past.

A door opens – revealing NURSE #2 – who beckons to him.

INT. PRIVATE ROOM – HOSPITAL – DAY.

HILDA looks deathly ill. STANLEY is sitting by her bed.

> STANLEY

Well?

> HILDA

(*Weak*) They're going to take off my breast.

> STANLEY

Oh ducky, which one?

> HILDA

The left.

> STANLEY

Betsy. You'll still have Beatrice. You'll be an Amazon, dearest. One of a brave and noble race of women.

> HILDA

I hated telling you.

> STANLEY

It'll be all right. I'm here.

INT. PRIVATE ROOM – HOSPITAL – NIGHT.

STANLEY is seated by HILDA'S bed.

INT. PRIVATE ROOM – HOSPITAL – NIGHT – LATER.

STANLEY is seated by HILDA'S bed.

INT. PRIVATE ROOM – HOSPITAL – DAWN.

STANLEY, in a different position, is seated by HILDA'S bed. She turns her head slowly and smiles at him. Her head drops.

She dies.

INT. CORRIDOR – HOSPITAL – DAWN.

A long corridor. STANLEY looks small and alone. He holds his hat. His face is shocked.

DUDLEY and GWEN arrive. They are both weeping.

They take him gently away.

His legs almost buckle for a moment.

DISSOLVE TO:

EXT. COMMON – COOKHAM – DAY.

ON PUDDLE: The shadow is chased away and the puddle shimmers with sunlight.

As at the beginning of the film, STANLEY SPENCER (aged about 57) is painting, sitting on his low stool, his old pram, filled with paints, brushes, turps, paper and rags, parked next to him.

THE VICAR cycles by.

> VICAR
>
> Congratulations Stanley!

> STANLEY
>
> Thank you, Vicar!

EXT. HIGH STREET – COOKHAM – DAY.

PATRICIA and DOROTHY, with laden shopping baskets, come out of the greengrocer's shop. SUMMERS, a reporter, hurries after them.

SUMMERS

Lady Spencer? I do beg your pardon. I wondered if I
might have a few words?

During the following, traffic passes by on the street: THREE
MOTOR CARS, FOUR CYCLISTS (one of them a POLICEMAN), THE
HORSE-DRAWN RAG-AND-BONE CART, TWO UPPER-CLASS
WOMEN ON HORSEBACK and a BUS.

VARIOUS PEDESTRIANS pass on the pavements.

PATRICIA

Who are you?

SUMMERS

The Times. Congratulations on your elevation. Much
deserved, if I may say.

He walks along with them, in the gutter.

SUMMERS

Could I ask Sir Stanley's reaction?

They don't reply.

SUMMERS

I believe he's from quite an ordinary background. A
local boy. I mean, before he became so well- known.

PATRICIA

This is Miss Hepworth. Dorothy Hepworth. We are
both painters of repute. You might make a note of
that.

PATRICIA and DOROTHY cross the street. SUMMERS follows.

SUMMERS

I believe you and Sir Stanley no longer live together.

PATRICIA turns and glares at him.

DOROTHY

Sir Stanley needs a good deal of solitude for his work.

SUMMERS

I mean as man and wife.

PATRICIA

I don't think we need go any further with this.

PATRICIA marches off.

SUMMERS

Sorry! Didn't mean to intrude.

He follows them.

SUMMERS

If I could just have a few words about Sir Stanley's
work.

PATRICIA turns on him.

PATRICIA

Most of Stanley Spencer's work, in my estimation –
and I was trained at the Slade – is either vulgar or
deranged. Good day.

PATRICIA goes, leaving DOROTHY and SUMMERS standing by the
War Memorial. DOROTHY makes to follow PATRICIA, then pauses.

SUMMERS

Miss Hepworth?

DOROTHY

I . . . I'd like to say that Sir Stanley Spencer is rightly
acclaimed as one of England's greatest painters. I
believe him to be uniquely gifted. He has . . .

MONTAGE:

SHOTS OF Cookham, the countryside, trees, the church, churchyard and real people intercut with Stanley's paintings.

DOROTHY (V/O)

... how shall I say ... there is a sort of special human clumsiness about his work. It's deliberate of course. He paints people trapped, as it were, in their own flesh – pinned down to this earth, and yet they seem to soar. And he makes that seem so very possible. You'll have to look very hard to find a better draughtsman. And for invention he has no equal. Everything is celebrated and revered with a balance that speaks of the most tender, spiritual equality. He honours the smallest detail. I'd particularly draw your attention to Sir Stanley's colours. Without the shout of a colourist, they nonetheless show the most infinite variety and subtlety of tone.

SUMMERS

Thank you, Miss Hepworth.

EXT. COMMON – COOKHAM – DAY.

BIRDSONG.

STANLEY works.

A RETIRED COLONEL and his WIFE approach.

COLONEL

Morning.

STANLEY nods and smiles.

COLONEL

Congratulations Spencer.

COLONEL'S WIFE
Our very best wishes to you. You will come to dinner?

STANLEY, very much surprised, peers up at her.

STANLEY
Oh! Thank you.

He works. THE COLONEL watches. His WIFE seeks to move on.

COLONEL
Funny angle that.

STANLEY
It's the short perspective.

COLONEL
What?

STANLEY
I'm seeing things a bit from above, don't you know.
The way God would see them. Looking down – with
love.

COLONEL
Oh, ah, yes … I see.

THE COLONEL and his WIFE go.

STANLEY paints.

Alone, he works, humming a hymn to himself. He looks up from
time to time at the scene he is painting.

STANLEY (V/O)
Remember when I came down to Devon that time,
and we slept in a beach hut and you said the sea was
like opals? Oh, I wish I could smell you! I keep the
cupboard shut on your clothes so it won't go away. I
use your comb. I've even got your flannel. Oh, ducky,

I feel so close. It's wonderful being able to talk to you. I feel you understand everything now. It makes me feel closer to heaven with you there. I see this great picture of God and all His Angels sitting on all these beautiful clouds and on His left hand, Stanley! I'm only joking, of course. You'll love this when it's done. I'm doing Christ glorying in His gorgeousness. Lying down amongst buttercups and daisies. Rather far from the Holy Writ, but ... It's no good doing palm trees. I'm English.

ON: STANLEY.

STANLEY (V/O)

You know what, Hilda? I think the artist is a mediator between God and Man. Like the saint, he performs miracles. With God's help, of course. God's at his elbow, telling him what to rub out.

STANLEY stops work and sits still, his hands slack in his lap.

STANLEY (V/O)

You didn't look after yourself, you know. You should have done. For me and the baby. You should have thought about yourself more. Made sure you were happy. Then you wouldn't have been so ill. We wouldn't have to ...

He can't go on. There are tears on his face.

It takes a moment to recover.

STANLEY

I'm not lonely.

He looks up at the sky.

STANLEY

I loved being with you, but I enjoy it on my own. You're
here in my imagination. In some ways, it's better.
I make up the answers for you and sometimes ...
well ... sometimes they suit me better. I hope you
don't mind.

He looks round and sees PEOPLE in the distance.

STANLEY

I'm not lonely. I've had a great love. I've been blessed.
God blessed me with a talent, and a great love. Now
I'm alone to get on with the work.

STANLEY lifts his brush, dips and mixes paint.

STANLEY (V/O)

Sorrow and sadness is not me.

He stands and looks down at his canvas – pleased with what he
sees.

STANLEY

That's it.

PULL BACK SLOWLY as he packs up his things and puts them in
the pram.

He trudges off, away from us, across the Common.

Fade Out.

The End.

Other plays in print:

CAMILLE	(Bloomsbury)
DUSA, FISH, STAS and VI	(Bloomsbury)
MARLENE	(Bloomsbury)
MRS PAT	(Bloomsbury)
PIAF	(Bloomsbury)
QUEEN CHRISTINA	(Bloomsbury)
THE LADY FROM THE SEA	(Bloomsbury)
THE LITTLE MERMAID	(Bloomsbury)
THE SNOW PALACE	(Bloomsbury)
YERMA	(Bloomsbury)
STANLEY	(Nick Hern Books)
THE SEAGULL	(Nick Hern Books)
UNCLE VANYA	(Nick Hern Books)
THE CHERRY ORCHARD	(Cambridge University Press)

Bloomsbury
www.bloomsbury.com

Nick Hern Books
www.nickhernbooks.co.uk

Cambridge University Press
www.cambridge.org

Also from Quota Books . . .

PAM GEMS
PLAYS ONE

THE INCORRUPTIBLE
GARIBALDI, SI!
THE TREAT

*

PAM GEMS
PLAYS TWO

GO WEST YOUNG WOMAN
NELSON
NOT JOAN THE MUSICAL
KING LUDWIG OF BAVARIA

*

PAM GEMS
PLAYS THREE

BETTY'S WONDERFUL
CHRISTMAS
THE SOCIALISTS
GUINEVERE
ETHEL

*

PAM GEMS
PLAYS FOUR

FRANZ INTO APRIL
PASIONARIA
AUNT MARY
UP IN SWEDEN

*

PAM GEMS
PLAYS FIVE

THE BLUE ANGEL
LOVING WOMEN
NATALYA
LADYBIRD, LADYBIRD

*

PAM GEMS
PLAYS SIX

DEBORAH'S DAUGHTER
FINCHIE'S WAR
AT THE WINDOW
STELLA CAMPBELL

*

PAM GEMS
PLAYS SEVEN

THE ODD WOMEN
THE AMIABLE COURTSHIP
DARLING BOY
CEDRIC AND LOUISE
MY WARREN

*

PAM GEMS
PLAYS NINE

A DOLL'S HOUSE
GHOSTS
HEDDA GABLER
AFTER BIRTHDAY

Q

Available from: www.quotabooks.com

Q

website: www.quotabooks.com
email: info@quotabooks.com
Twitter: @Quotabooks

www.ingramcontent.com/pod-product-compliance
Lightning Source LLC
Chambersburg PA
CBHW071528030726
47598CB00001B/39